Bread Making

by Wendy Jo Peterson

Bread Making For Dummies®

Published by: **John Wiley & Sons, Inc.,** 111 River Street, Hoboken, NJ 07030-5774, www.wiley.com

Copyright © 2021 by John Wiley & Sons, Inc., Hoboken, New Jersey

Published simultaneously in Canada

No part of this publication may be reproduced, stored in a retrieval system or transmitted in any form or by any means, electronic, mechanical, photocopying, recording, scanning or otherwise, except as permitted under Sections 107 or 108 of the 1976 United States Copyright Act, without the prior written permission of the Publisher. Requests to the Publisher for permission should be addressed to the Permissions Department, John Wiley & Sons, Inc., 111 River Street, Hoboken, NJ 07030, (201) 748-6011, fax (201) 748-6008, or online at http://www.wiley.com/go/permissions.

Trademarks: Wiley, For Dummies, the Dummies Man logo, Dummies.com, Making Everything Easier, and related trade dress are trademarks or registered trademarks of John Wiley & Sons, Inc., and may not be used without written permission. Instant Pot is a registered trademark of Instant Brands, Inc. All other trademarks are the property of their respective owners. John Wiley & Sons, Inc., is not associated with any product or vendor mentioned in this book.

LIMIT OF LIABILITY/DISCLAIMER OF WARRANTY: WHILE THE PUBLISHER AND AUTHOR HAVE USED THEIR BEST EFFORTS IN PREPARING THIS BOOK, THEY MAKE NO REPRESENTATIONS OR WARRANTIES WITH RESPECT TO THE ACCURACY OR COMPLETENESS OF THE CONTENTS OF THIS BOOK AND SPECIFICALLY DISCLAIM ANY IMPLIED WARRANTIES OF MERCHANTABILITY OR FITNESS FOR A PARTICULAR PURPOSE. NO WARRANTY MAY BE CREATED OR EXTENDED BY SALES REPRESENTATIVES OR WRITTEN SALES MATERIALS. THE ADVISE AND STRATEGIES CONTAINED HEREIN MAY NOT BE SUITABLE FOR YOUR SITUATION. YOU SHOULD CONSULT WITH A PROFESSIONAL WHERE APPROPRIATE. NEITHER THE PUBLISHER NOR THE AUTHOR SHALL BE LIABLE FOR DAMAGES ARISING HEREFROM.

For general information on our other products and services, please contact our Customer Care Department within the U.S. at 877-762-2974, outside the U.S. at 317-572-3993, or fax 317-572-4002. For technical support, please visit https://hub.wiley.com/community/support/dummies.

Wiley publishes in a variety of print and electronic formats and by print-on-demand. Some material included with standard print versions of this book may not be included in e-books or in print-on-demand. If this book refers to media such as a CD or DVD that is not included in the version you purchased, you may download this material at http://booksupport.wiley.com. For more information about Wiley products, visit www.wiley.com.

Library of Congress Control Number: 2020945961

ISBN 978-1-119-75809-9 (pbk); ISBN 978-1-119-75810-5 (ebk); ISBN 978-1-119-75811-2 (ebk)

Manufactured in the United States of America

SKY10022687_111920

Contents at a Glance

Recipes at a Glance

Vegetarian

Breakfast

Dinner

Spreads, Sauces, and Dips

Table of Contents

Introduction

I f you've recently found yourself curious about bread making, you're not alone! The age-old ritual of mixing flour, water, and yeast to create a delicious loaf of bread is growing in popularity.

And it's not surprising. Bread is part of the soul. In fact, some scientists believe bread making has been around for 30,000 years. From flatbreads to loaves, bread can easily be considered the most widely consumed food on Earth. Every culture has some type of bread as a staple in their diet.

You no longer need to pound grains between rocks to yield flour, but bread making still requires a bit more effort than going to a store and simply buying a loaf. Bread making is a labor of love, and the smell of hot bread fresh from the oven is just one of the many rewards of making your own. With this book as your guide, you'll be reaping the rewards in no time!

About This Book

Think of this book as your own personal bread-making coach! You start by getting familiar with some of the science behind bread making. Don't worry, there won't be a quiz and you don't have to memorize any technical terms or formulas, but understanding how just a few ingredients combine to make a delicious loaf of bread is important. I explain which flours and types of yeast are used to make different kinds of bread, and I show you some bread-making techniques that will come in handy. Finally, I help you stock your kitchen for your bread-making adventure, before offering more than 85 recipes to choose from.

This book is a reference, which means you don't have to read it from beginning to end and you don't have to commit it to memory. Instead, you can dip into these pages over and over again to find the information you need. The Table of Contents and Index will point you in the right direction.

Sidebars (text in gray boxes) and anything marked with the Technical Stuff icon (more on that later) can be skipped without missing the main point of the subject at hand.

Here are a few suggestions for getting the most out of the recipes in this book:

» Read each recipe from top to bottom before you make your grocery list to ensure you have all the ingredients you need.

» In the ingredients list, *milk* means whole milk and butter means unsalted butter; *all-purpose flour* means white, unbleached, all-purpose flour; and *warm water* means water between 100 and 110 degrees (it should feel warm to the touch, but not hot).

» A "floured surface" is generally ½ cup of all-purpose flour on a flat surface. You can add more or less flour based on the stickiness of the dough. (If the dough is sticky, add a little more flour to the surface; if the dough is dryer, add a little less flour to the surface.)

» If your house is cool or drafty, consider allowing the dough to rise in a cold oven with the light on. Cover the dough bowl with a tea towel, place it in a cold oven, and turn on the oven light. (Be sure to leave a note on the oven, so no one accidentally heats the oven with the dough inside!)

» You can use either fresh or dried herbs. For easy substitution, just keep in mind that 1 teaspoon of dried is equivalent to 1 tablespoon of fresh.

» Pay special attention to the techniques called for, whether hand kneading or using a stand mixer with a dough hook. Technique affects the end result, so be sure to follow the recipe.

» If possible, use a scale to measure the ingredients instead of relying on measuring cups and spoons. Bread making is a science, and the more precise you can be with your measurements, the better.

» Any recipes that are vegetarian are marked with the tomato icon (🍅) in the Recipes in This Book and the Recipes in This Chapter lists. (Most of the recipes in this book are, not surprisingly, vegetarian!)

» The recipes in this book include information on how long you can store the bread. If you can't use the bread in the recommended timeframe, you can always place all or part of a loaf in a resealable plastic, freezer-safe bag and store it in the freezer for later use. To defrost, remove from the freezer and let the breads return to room temperature in the freezer bag, or place on a baking sheet and bake at 350 degrees for 10 minutes. Toasting bread is also a great way to defrost without the wait.

Within this book, you may note that some web addresses break across two lines of text. If you're reading this book in print an want to visit one of these web pages, simply key in the web address exactly as it's noted in the text, pretending as though the line break doesn't exist. If you're reading this as an e-book, you've got it easy — just click the web address to be taken directly to the web page.

Foolish Assumptions

In writing this book, I made a few assumptions about you, the reader:

>> You've tasted homemade or bakery-style bread and you know what you're aiming to achieve.

>> You have basic knowledge of cooking, baking, and measuring.

>> You're patient — bread making definitely is *not* a quick process!

Icons Used in This Book

Throughout the book, you'll icons in the margin. Here's what each icon means:

The Tip icon marks information that can save you time and money as you're planning recipes to make, shopping for ingredients, and making bread.

You don't have to commit this book to memory, but sometimes a piece of information is so important that I want you to remember it. When that happens, I flag it with the Remember icon.

Think of the Warning icon as a big orange traffic cone in the middle of the sidewalk, warning you about a hole you don't want to fall into.

Bread making is a science, and sometimes I wade into the weeds with technical information. When I do, I use the Technical Stuff icon. You can safely skip anything marked with this icon without missing anything essential about the topic at hand.

Beyond the Book

In addition to what you're reading right now, this product comes with a free access-anywhere Cheat Sheet that includes tips on how to form a round roll, the benefits of sourdough bread, and a bread baker's schedule you can follow if you like. To get this Cheat Sheet, go to www.dummies.com and type **Bread Making For Dummies Cheat Sheet** in the Search box.

Where to Go from Here

If you're brand-new to making breads, take your time and explore Part 1. If you've made bread before and you feel confident with the process, check out all the recipes in Part 2 — from savory to sweet to stuffed, you have more than 85 recipes to explore! If you're short on time, Part 3 offers ways to use up stale bread, my favorite sandwich ideas, and more.

I hope this book becomes your go-to bread-making guide, one that you flip through often when you crave freshly made bread. After all, everything is better with bread!

1
Getting Started with Bread Making

Chapter **1**

Understanding the Basics of Bread Making

B read is king, and bread making is equal parts art and science. In this chapter, you explore the science behind bread making and find out why a scale is so important for success.

If science wasn't your favorite subject in school, you may be tempted to flip ahead to the next chapter or just dive into a recipe, but especially if you're new to bread making, I urge you to give this chapter a read. It's only a few pages, and the information about how and why bread making works will not only help you understand what you're doing in the kitchen, but also give you the knowledge you'll need to figure out what went wrong if something does.

Donning Your Lab Coat: The Science of Bread

Science is *everything* in bread making. Each ingredient plays a specific role in the formation of bread. The good news is, this kind of science is fun! Plus, unlike in school, there won't be a test on Friday.

In this section, I fill you in on the main components of bread and the roles they play in making that delicious loaf you love.

Gluten

Gluten is the protein found in flour, and it's why the type of flour you use matters when you're baking, whether you're making cake or bread. (Turn to Chapter 2 for more on flour.) The forming of gluten is what gives rise, literally, to bread. Without gluten, your bread would feel like a brick.

When you add water to flour, it creates long, elastic strands from the gluten (known as the *gluten matrix*). Knead the flour strengthens those strands, which is important in giving your bread structure, so it can rise. (Chapter 3 explains the intricate details of kneading and stretching dough.)

Yeast

Yeast is another key ingredient of bread. Yeast is a living thing — it feeds off the carbohydrates in flour and expels carbon dioxide (a gas), which gets caught in the gluten matrix. That nifty matrix you formed while you were kneading holds the gas inside its chambers, and the dough rises. Magic!

Salt

Salt has an important role to play in bread making, and it's not just about flavor (although nothing is quite as tasty as a well-salted bread). Salt conditions the gluten, making it stronger and strengthening the elasticity of the strands. If you use too *little* salt, not only will your bread taste bland, but it will rise too quickly in an ill-formed matrix. If you use too *much* salt, it can kill the yeast.

REMEMBER

Bread making is all about balance, but don't fret! The recipes in this book have just the right balance of flour, yeast, and salt.

Heat

When you place your bread in the oven to bake, the gluten solidifies and holds its form. And when the baking is complete, the bread won't deflate. Instead, your well-formed gluten will hold its form as the bread cools and after it's sliced.

WARNING

Don't slice your bride too early! You'll probably be tempted to eat your bread straight out of the oven, but bread needs to fully cool before slicing or the texture will turn gummy and sticky.

Taking the Guesswork out of Baking Bread

Bread making is precise, and in order to have precision, you need a scale.

TIP

A food scale is one of the most important pieces of equipment when it comes to successful baking, and not just for breads. For around $12, you can purchase a decent food scale that measures in grams.

As a culinary teacher, I do an experiment where I ask each of my students to measure out 1 cup of flour and then have them weigh it. Some students measure out 128 grams; some, 142 grams; and others, closer to 200 grams (if they've packed the flour in the cup). The correct weight of 1 cup of all-purpose flour is 125 grams. Being a few grams off can make a *huge* difference in the outcome of your bread.

REMEMBER

Although the recipes in this book include both the metric measurements (grams) and U.S. imperial volume measurements (cups and teaspoons), I recommend using a scale and following the metric measurements.

Chapter **2**

Digging into the Ingredients

The most critical ingredient in bread making is flour. Flour is what gives the bread its structure, texture, and flavor. However, not all flours are created equally. In this chapter, I dive into the differences among various flours, so you can make any recipe, knowing how to swap flours in and out.

Although flours take center stage in bread making, additional ingredients make flour become bread. In this chapter, I walk you through all these other important ingredients — from yeast to salt to liquids and more.

Focusing on Flour

Flours come in all different varieties, from grains to protein. In this section, I look at the flours used most often in bread making. The following list just scratches the surface of flours used in bread making, though, so don't hesitate to branch out and try different kinds of flour to see which one you like best.

REMEMBER

The type of flour you use in baking matters. Cake flour yields the best cakes, but it's not what you want to use when making bread.

ALL YOU EVER WANTED TO KNOW ABOUT WHEAT

TECHNICAL STUFF

In the United States, wheat is grown in 42 of the 50 states. There are six wheat varieties: hard red winter, hard red spring, soft red winter, hard white, soft white, and durum. Technically, wheat is a member of the grass family (hence, the image of golden swaying wheat that may come to mind when you picture wheat).

Whole wheat is a whole grain, meaning it contains all the parts of the grain: the bran, germ, and endosperm. Whole wheat is naturally low in fat and a good source of fiber. It also has important nutrients, such as, selenium, potassium, and magnesium. In the 1990s, wheat products got a boost of nutrition with the enrichment of iron, folic acid, thiamin, riboflavin, and niacin. This came about as a means to combat birth defects and support nutrient deficiencies across the United States.

When the grass of wheat is dried and ground down, it becomes a whole-wheat flour. When the grass is stripped of everything except the endosperm, it becomes white flour. If you're looking for the most nutrient-dense flours, look for the words *stone ground* on the label — this old-world grinding technique is slower and helps retain more nutrition than the faster, more conventional techniques used today.

Bread tends to get a bad rap because it's often made with white and enriched flour instead of the whole-grain form. You can absolutely savor a great white bread, but just remember to balance your plate with whole grains. Also, branch out and try a variety of grains that boost nutrition and flavor in breads.

>> **All-purpose flour:** Many cookbooks use the term *flour* to mean "all-purpose flour." All-purpose flour contains 10 percent to 12 percent protein. Many manufacturers label their all-purpose flour with the percentage of protein so the consumer understands what they're using. You can find all-purpose flour bleached or unbleached; for bread making, choose an unbleached flour.

>> **Bread flour:** Bread flour typically ranges from 12 percent to 14 percent protein, which is an ideal range for forming gluten and creating the matrix (see Chapter 1).

>> **Cake flour:** Cake flour plays a role in certain breads, like Croissants (Chapter 9) and German Pretzels (Chapter 9). Cake flour is lower in protein (about 7 percent to 9 percent) than all-purpose flour and it's milled finer. These simple differences make a significant impact on texture. Although you

can swap out cake flour for all-purpose flour, the outcome won't result in as tender of a crumb.

» **Whole-wheat flour:** Whole-wheat flour contains the bran, germ, and endosperm of wheat and is around 14 percent protein. Whole-wheat flour produces a denser, often less airy or spongy bread. When you know how to work the grain, you can produce a great product with whole-wheat flour.

» **White whole-wheat flour:** A white whole-wheat flour has often been produced from a spring white wheat, so it's a whole-wheat product and can have a higher protein content (13 percent), but it has a milder flavor.

» **Winter red wheat flour:** Red refers to the color of the kernel of wheat grown. Winter red wheat flour produces a nuttier, more robust wheat flavor. Many artisan bread makers seek out a hard red wheat flour because of the flavor and higher protein (14 percent).

» **Einkorn:** *Einkorn* means "single grain" in German. Einkorn is the most primitive form of the wheat grain that you can find. Because it's an ancient grain, it produces a denser bread with a nuttier flavor than you may have tasted before. You can purchase einkorn as a berry, and then mill or sprout it to add it to breads, or you can purchase the flour and add it to your bread recipes. Einkorn has a protein content of 22 percent, but it's low in gluten.

TECHNICAL STUFF

Often, in recipes with ancient grains, you find a gluten product, whether in the form of flour or in vital wheat gluten added to the recipe to help form the matrix in bread.

» **Emmer:** Much like einkorn, emmer is an ancient grain that is high in protein (22 percent) and low in gluten.

» **Khorasan:** Khorasan is an ancient grain that has not been subjected to modern hybridization. At 15 percent protein, it can make a better bread than other ancient grains. It requires more liquid, though, because it absorbs more than other flours do. The grain produces a dense loaf of bread.

TECHNICAL STUFF

Some research studies have highlighted the cholesterol-lowering effects of eating more Khorasan grains.

» **Rye flour:** Rye is not a wheat at all, but a grass. Rye is a popular grain used throughout Europe and Russia. It has less gluten than wheat, producing a denser loaf of bread. You see rye flour used frequently in this book to provide a subtle flavor and increase the nutrition profile of the bread.

» **Semolina flour:** Semolina is a durum wheat and hard wheat, which is most commonly seen in pastas. However, when you use semolina in bread making, you get a pale yellow hue in the bread and subtle nutty undertones.

>> **Spelt flour:** Spelt is another fabulous ancient grain, and quite possibly my favorite whole grain to use when making bread. Spelt has a higher gluten content, making it a great substitute for whole-wheat flour in recipes with a range of 13 percent to 14 percent total protein.

>> **Sprouted-grain flour:** Sprouting wheat grains prior to milling or adding to dough improves digestibility. You can purchase sprouted whole-wheat flours, which typically has 13 percent to 14 percent protein content, and use it to make a great bread. You can also sprout your own grains (see the nearby sidebar), and add the sprouted grains to your bread mix.

>> **Rice flour:** You may consider rice flour an odd item on this list, but rice flour is actually an excellent flour to use with sourdough baking — not within the loaf, but in the *banneton* (a woven or braided basket that helps a loaf hold its shape and creates a desired design on the surface of the dough during its final proofing). Rice flour won't stick to the bread as it proofs, allowing the bread to easily release from the mold.

TIP

SPROUTING YOUR OWN GRAINS

Sprouting grains is easy! Just follow these steps:

1. **In a quart-size glass canning jar, place 1 cup of grains (like emmer, einkorn, or Khorasan).**

2. **Pour 12 ounces of filtered water over the grains.**

3. **Place a tea towel over the jar and place a rubber band over the tea towel to secure the towel as a lid for the jar.**

4. **Place the jar in a dark, cool cupboard and wait 24 hours; then drain and rinse the grains under cold, running water for 3 minutes.**

5. **Place the damp grains back in the jar; cover with the tea towel and use the rubber band to secure the tea towel.**

6. **Over the next two days, rinse the grains twice daily and return to the cupboard each time.**

7. **When you begin to see the grains sprout, transfer the grains to the refrigerator and use in salads, on sandwiches, or in baked goods.**

Looking At Everything Else

Flour is, not surprisingly, a major part of bread making. But you can't make bread with flour alone. Here are all the other ingredients that may go into your favorite bread:

>> **Yeast:** Yeast plays a major role in giving bread its rise (see Chapter 1 for more on how yeast works). For bread making, yeast comes in two main varieties:

- **Commercial yeasts:** The most common commercial yeast used in the United States is active dry yeast. This yeast is activated with warm water (100 to 110 degrees) and then fed a little sugar to begin bubbling and release carbon dioxide. You can find active dry yeast in individual packages or in a glass jar. Store the yeast in a cool, dark, dry space.

- **Wild yeasts:** When you move into sourdough breads and work with a starter, you'll discover wild yeasts. Wild yeasts are naturally occurring organisms in the fungus family that are floating around in the air, on our counters, on our skin, and in our flours. Wild yeasts are everywhere. By forming a starter, we are capturing and feeding the wild yeasts and creating a fermented yeast perfect for bread making.

WARNING

Be sure not to buy nutritional yeast! Nutritional yeast is deactivated, and it won't help your baked goods rise.

>> **Salt:** Salt has an important role to play in bread making, from adding flavor to tightening the structure of gluten, and it helps slow fermentation. You can play around with different salts, like sea salt or kosher salt. If you use fancier salts, be sure they don't have artificial coloring, or else they may cause discoloration in your dough.

>> **Liquid:** Liquids are responsible for rehydrating the flours and dissolving the yeast to help form the dough. Every bread recipe will have a liquid; however, varying liquids will create a different effect on the final product, from flavor to tenderness. Here are a couple liquids you may find:

- **Water:** Flour absorbs the water and helps to form the gluten. The steam released during baking helps the breads rise. You can use bottled, filtered, or tap water in the recipes in this book.

- **Milk:** Milk is a nutrient-dense liquid, with fats, sugar, and protein. The protein helps strengthen the dough, the fat helps tenderize it, and the sugars found naturally in milk feed the yeast. For the purposes of the recipes in this book, I used whole milk.

- **Non-dairy milk:** If you have a dairy allergy, you can play around with replacing cow's milk with nutty alternatives, from almond milk to coconut milk. Non-dairy milks will naturally add their flavors and won't provide the same protein strength, but they make for a decent substitute.

» **Eggs:** Eggs impart a golden color to dough, as well as provide structure, tenderness, and richness. Think about a rich brioche bun, and you'll understand the importance of eggs.

» **Fat:** Fats can help soften the dough and create a tender crumb. Not every recipe calls for fat, and some fats impart a distinct flavor in the dough. Here are a couple popular fats used in bread making:

- **Butter:** Everything's better with butter! Rich, cultured butter is my favorite, but because it's harder to find, I've tested all the recipes in this book with unsalted butter. Butter provides tenderness to breads and actually softens the gluten. Getting the right balance of butter is important to create soft, but not crumbly, breads.

- **Oils:** A touch of oil on the surface of dough helps prevent the dough from drying out. Mixed in, oil tenderizes the bread.

- **Bacon fat or lard:** These types of fats are often seen in older recipes where people creatively used up rendered fat they had on hand. Bacon fat and lard provide flavor and tenderness to bread.

» **Fruits, nuts, or seeds:** Not every bread recipe calls for fruits, nuts, or seeds, but they can give bread more nutrition and flavor. Fruits also provide sugars that feed the yeast. Nuts and seeds add in essential fats, crunch, and texture to the dough. Here's what each of these ingredients brings to the table:

- **Dried fruits:** Dried cherries, apricots, raisins, currants, blueberries, and dates are great additions to dough. They don't add to the structure, but these fun mix-ins do add texture. The sweetness of dried fruits also provides a *substrate* (food) for the yeasts to feed on and can create a sweeter-tasting bread.

- **Nuts:** The most commonly used nuts are walnuts, pecans, hazelnuts, and almonds. Nuts are better protected from high heat when mixed into the dough, instead of being sprinkled on the surface where they may burn at high heat. Nuts add great texture and a dose of nutrition in breads.

- **Seeds:** Flax, chia, sesame, and sunflower seeds are regularly enjoyed around the globe in breads. They add in nutrition and texture. Seeds can often handle higher heat than nuts. They may be best suited mixed into the dough and not just sprinkled on the surface. Seeds are nutrition powerhouses, packed with healthy fats and antioxidants. If you travel to Europe you'll frequently see seeds and nuts added to breads.

TIP

Store dried fruit, nuts, and seeds in an airtight container placed in a cool, dark pantry to extend their shelf life.

» **Honey, molasses, sugar, or dates:** Whether you opt for honey, molasses, sugar, or pureed dates, you'll get added sweetness, food for the yeast, and a touch of color through caramelization. If you opt to reduce or cut out sugar in a recipe, the crust may suffer in color. As a dietitian, I recognize that not everyone should have added sugars in their diet. So, if you prefer to substitute sugar, consider using a date puree, which provides fiber and essential nutrients like vitamins and minerals.

IN THIS CHAPTER

Chapter **3**

Mastering Basic Bread-Making Techniques

Whether you're using your hands or a stand mixer, making bread requires patience, strength, and skill. Many people assume that making bread is as simple as tossing together flour, water, yeast, and salt — and in some breads, it *is* that easy. But most yeast breads require more.

In this chapter, I explore the finite details of making a great bread. I also fill you in on how to store your bread so you can enjoy it for days (or even weeks!) to come.

Note: If you're only interested in sourdough bread, turn to the next chapter for all the information you need.

Following Six Steps to Making Great Bread

Before you break out the bread pan to bake your first loaf, you need to understand the steps required to reach a great loaf of bread. Bread doesn't lie: If you rush through or drag out these steps, your bread will show it.

REMEMBER

Bread baking isn't magic, but it is a science. And when you stick to the steps, you can master the chemical reactions, too.

Step 1: Measuring your ingredients

Accuracy is key in bread making, and the plain truth is that weighing ingredients on a kitchen scale is more accurate than measuring volume with cups and spoons (see Chapter 1 for more on this subject). In the recipes in this book, I list ingredients in in grams first, followed by the measurements in volume, like this:

125 grams (1 cup) all-purpose flour

TIP

Because of variances in humidity, flour mills, and temperature, you may need to adjust how much flour you use. Experience will teach you when to use more or less flour and water. The more you make bread, the better you'll be at making these adjustments on your own, but especially if you're just getting started with bread, stick to the recipe your first time through.

Step 2: Mixing the dough

Two key mixing methods are used in bread making:

>> **Straight dough method:** In the straight dough method, you combine and mix all the ingredients. Then you knead the dough until it is smooth and can be stretched without breaking.

>> **Sponge method:** The sponge method has two stages. First, you mix together the yeast, the liquid, and part of the flour and allow it to rise. When the dough has doubled in size, you add the remaining flour and ingredients and knead the dough.

TIP

The sponge method is often used with denser flours that absorb more water, such as whole-wheat flour. The sponge method allows the flour to hydrate before it's mixed more, allowing for a lighter, airier product in the end.

TIP

If you're new to kneading, check out the nearby sidebar for step-by-step instructions.

Step 3: Letting it rise

You're starting to smell the flavors of your bread taking shape. But don't get impatient and pop the dough into the oven too soon! You need to let the dough fully rise and ferment first.

HOW TO KNEAD DOUGH

Most of the recipes in the book specify an exact time to use a stand mixer with the dough hook attachment and at what level. But it's still important to know how to knead dough by hand. Follow these steps to knead dough:

1. **Form the dough into a ball.**

2. **Pat the dough into a flatter ball.**

3. **Lift the part of the dough that is closest to you, and fold it over the top.**

   Use the heal or palm of your hand to push the dough down into the rounded dough (see the nearby figure).

4. **Turn the dough a quarter turn to the left, and repeat Step 3.**

   Keep repeating until the dough is smooth and has elasticity. If the dough is sticky, coat your hands and dust the dough with a little flour before continuing to knead.

Generally, when you use a stand mixer with the dough hook attachment, you can knead dough in 5 to 10 minutes. By hand, the same process can take 10 to 15 minutes — but kneading is a great form of exercise!

As the yeast feeds on the sugars in the bread, they release gas. The gas is captured in the gluten matrix (see Chapter 1), and the dough rises. Fermentation, or rising, is complete when the dough has doubled in size. The length of time it takes varies based on the type of flour, the amount of yeast, and the temperature.

While the dough is rising, keep it in a warm, draft-free place. To help the dough not dry out, place a dampened tea towel over the bowl. The towel will keep the dough from drying out and add humidity to the air as the dough rises.

Step 4: Punching and shaping the dough

When the dough has doubled in size, it's time to use a dough scraper and place the dough onto a floured surface. You don't *literally* need to punch the dough — instead, you gently fold it down to redistribute the gas throughout the dough. If you do this too many times, you may end up with a flat baked product, so be gentle to your dough. Folding over one or two times should be enough.

After the dough has been folded over, it's time to shape the dough. Whether you're making rolls, baguettes, or loaves, there's technique involved. The recipes in this book describe the shaping in detail so you'll end up with the best results.

If the dough seems difficult to shape or too wet to work with, cover the dough and place it into the refrigerator and let it chill for an hour and see if it's easier to shape. Some doughs, like sweet breads, require at least 6 to 12 hours of chilling for best results.

Shaping can take time. Measuring out equal pieces of dough is a process. If you're rolling the dough into knots or pretzels, it can take a couple tries to stretch and shape the long pieces, allowing the gluten to relax and stretch.

Step 5: Proofing the dough

After you've shaped the dough, it's time for a final rising, referred to as *proofing*. Some ovens are equipped with a bread proofing setting, which is a slightly warmer temperature than a standard home (usually between 80 and 115 degrees). For each recipe, the length of proofing required is different, but usually it's anywhere from 15 minutes to an hour.

Step 6: Baking

Now you've come to the fun part! Depending on the recipe, you may brush the bread with an egg wash for a golden glaze or top the dough with seeds. Some recipes even have you *score* the dough, or mark it with a serrated knife or *bread lame* (a scoring knife that looks similar to a box cutter or razor). Regardless of what the recipe calls for, just be gentle and make sure not to deflate your gorgeous creation before baking.

When you place the dough into a hot oven, you'll see a quick, initial rise, often referred to as *oven spring*. This is when the gases from the yeast get trapped in the matrix of gluten, allowing the bread to rise and hold its form.

WARNING

Avoid opening the oven — when you open the oven, you allow cool air to enter and disrupt the baking process.

When is your bread done? Instead of thumping the loaf and playing a guessing game, use an instant-read thermometer. For a typical loaf of white or wheat bread, the goal is 190 to 210 degrees. For a bread that's rich in fat or egg based, like challah, aim for 180 to 190 degrees.

BEYOND THE OVEN

Not every bread is baked. Some breads are steamed, cooked in a skillet, or even boiled. Here's a guide to each of these techniques and when and why they're used:

- **Steaming:** A crispy bread crust is often the result of moisture inside the oven while baking. To achieve this effect, some recipes have you place a cast-iron or oven-safe pan at the bottom of your oven or on the bottom rack while the oven is heating up. Then, to create steam, after the oven has completely heated, you place your bread pan on the middle rack of the oven and pour 1 to 2 cups of water into the empty pan you heated at the bottom of the oven or on the bottom rack. When you close the oven door, the water will create a steam bath for the bread as it begins to bake.

  Another steaming method is to mist the bread loaf with water before placing the pan into the oven and then misting again several times during baking. However, this approach isn't without risk: The temperature may drop every time the oven door is opened, which could negatively impact your bake.

- **Skillet cooking:** English muffins aren't actually baked in an oven. Instead, they're cooked in a skillet. Another yeast bread that can be cooked on the stovetop is flatbread.

- **Boiling:** Bagels are the only breads in this book that get a prebake dip in boiling water. This boiling technique gives the bagel its signature chewy crust, and because you add honey to the mix, it helps give bagels their golden crust, too. Yum!

TIP

To take the temperature, wait until the bread is near its baking time. Then pull the bread out of the oven with potholders and shut the oven door to keep the heat inside in case you need to continue baking. Insert the thermometer in the center of the dough, making sure not to touch the thermometer to the sides of the pan. If the temperature is lower than the desired doneness, place the bread back into the oven for a couple minutes, approximately 5 minutes for every 5 to 10 degrees the temperature is off.

Storing Bread

Before you place another loaf of bread in the refrigerator, hear me out. The quickest way to stale bread is through the refrigerator. The breads you bake at home won't have preservatives, so the bread will turn stale more quickly. Most freshly baked breads only last one to five days at room temperature; the higher the fat content, the longer the shelf life.

WARNING

Don't slice bread before it has cooled completely. Yes, you may be tempted to slice bread fresh from the oven, but that can result in a gummy bread. Some loaves, like a rye sourdough bread, actually need up to two *days* to form a crust! But for most breads, one to three hours of cooling is best before slicing.

When the bread is cooled, place it in a brown paper bag or wrap it in a tea towel. A bread with a softer crust should be stored in an airtight, sealed container. (Every recipe this book provides instructions for storing.)

TIP

If you know you won't be able to enjoy the bread before it becomes stale, wrap the bread tightly in plastic wrap or bee's wax paper and place it in a freezer-friendly resealable bag. You can store it in the freezer this way for up to a month. You can even freeze sliced bread for quicker toast in the morning — just grab a slice and place it in your toaster. The heat from your toaster will be ample to defrost and toast your bread. You may need to toast it twice to get the perfect crust. If you're reheating a frozen loaf of bread, spritz or rub the surface with water and then bake at 350 degrees for 15 to 20 minutes.

Chapter **4**

Uncovering the Secrets of Sourdough

Sourdough bread baking has recently grown in popularity in the United States — partly due to a pandemic creating a shortage of yeast and partly due to interest in the health benefits of fermented bread. This chapter helps you grow your own starter and walks you through the steps of making your first great loaf of sourdough bread.

REMEMBER

If your dear Aunt May gave you a starter with different directions than the ones I offer here, don't fret! There are many different approaches to growing, feeding, and baking sourdough. The techniques I share in this book are ones that have worked for me (and my friends, family, and clients all around the globe), but my way isn't the only way!

THE SCIENCE OF FERMENTED BREADS

TECHNICAL STUFF

Sourdough starters are living, breathing globs of vinegar-smelling goo. In that gooey mix are thriving bacteria and yeasts that create some of the most delicious breads you've ever tasted. But, are there really healthy benefits to sourdough? Many people believe the answer to be a resounding "Yes!"

I'm an avid sourdough baker, and my love of sourdough may make me look more positively at the science. But my background in nutrition also keeps my beliefs in check. The science supports many health claims around sourdough, but not all that you read on the Internet is true. (I know, shocker!) In this section, I take a closer look at some of the science-supported claims.

Digestibility, the process of sourdough, and the longer fermentation done in the dough allows for the bacteria *Lactobacillus* to do its work on breaking down the gluten and sugars in the bread. With that said, some studies show that white bread is white bread, and it will still affect your blood sugar the same, sourdough or not. The bacteria are killed in baking, so sourdough bread doesn't contribute to improved *gut flora* (the bacteria in the intestines). But the bacteria do their work *before* the bread is baked, breaking apart chemical compounds during the long and slow fermenting process, leading to a bread that is easier to digest and exposing beneficial vitamins, minerals, and compounds that improve the overall bread quality.

But white bread — sourdough included — is still void of fiber and lacking essential vitamins and minerals found in whole grains. The greatest benefits seen in sourdough are when the bread is made from whole grains, such as rye, whole wheat, or spelt. Compounds inside the breads are broken down with beneficial compounds becoming more readily available.

If your curiosity is getting the best of you, head over to the website of the National Library of Medicine (https://pubmed.ncbi.nlm.nih.gov). Here, you can search for "sourdough" and read all about the current research being done on the subject.

Growing a Starter

To grow your own fermented goo, you need the following:

>> Two 16-ounce glass jars (like Mason jars)

>> Unbleached all-purpose flour

>> Water

>> A scale that measures in grams

>> A rubber band

When you've gathered all these items, you're ready to begin growing a starter. (Figure 4-1 summarizes the process.)

Day 1

Let the journey begin! To begin, follow these steps:

1. Place a clean glass jar on the scale and tare the scale to 0.

2. Place 50 grams of flour into the glass jar.

3. Tare the scale to 0 again and add 50 grams of water.

4. Using a spoon, give the mixture a stir.

5. Screw the lid *loosely* onto the jar.

TIP

If you tighten the lid too tightly it will hinder the release of gas from the jar. As the bacteria and yeast grow, they'll eat and release carbon dioxide, so be sure to keep the lid *loosely* fitted.

6. Place the jar in a dark, cool spot (like a pantry or cupboard), and let it rest for 24 hours.

Day 2

On the second day, follow these steps:

1. Place the second clean glass jar on the scale and tare the scale to 0.

2. Transfer from the first jar 50 grams of the starter.

3. Discard the remaining starter.

Don't use or save the discarded starter. Throw it in the trash or compost it.

4. Tare the scale to 0 and add 50 grams of flour.

5. Tare the scale to 0 again and add 50 grams of water.

This is a 1:1:1 ratio (starter:flour:water).

6. Using a spoon, give the mixture a stir.

7. Screw the lid *loosely* onto the jar.

8. Place the jar in a dark, cool spot (like a pantry or cupboard), and let it rest for 24 hours.

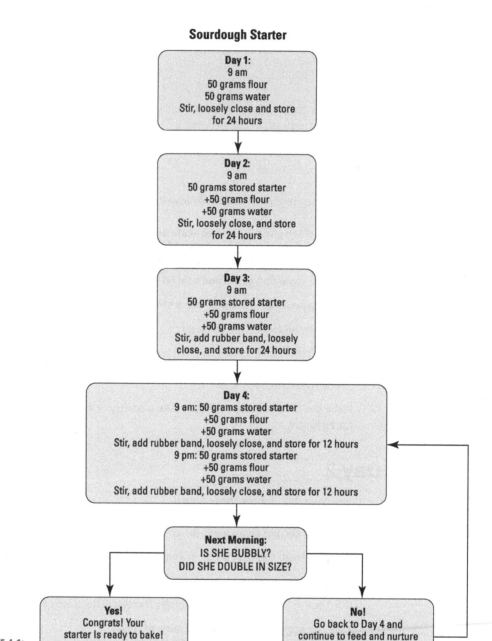

Sourdough Starter

Day 1:
9 am
50 grams flour
50 grams water
Stir, loosely close and store
for 24 hours

Day 2:
9 am
50 grams stored starter
+50 grams flour
+50 grams water
Stir, loosely close, and store
for 24 hours

Day 3:
9 am
50 grams stored starter
+50 grams flour
+50 grams water
Stir, add rubber band, loosely
close, and store for 24 hours

Day 4:
9 am: 50 grams stored starter
+50 grams flour
+50 grams water
Stir, add rubber band, loosely close, and store for 12 hours
9 pm: 50 grams stored starter
+50 grams flour
+50 grams water
Stir, add rubber band, loosely close, and store for 12 hours

Next Morning:
IS SHE BUBBLY?
DID SHE DOUBLE IN SIZE?

Yes!
Congrats! Your
starter Is ready to bake!
Follow a recipe to make
great bread!

No!
Go back to Day 4 and
continue to feed and nurture
your starter. Some starters
take 10 days to get active!

FIGURE 4-1:
A sourdough
starter flow chart.

WHAT TO DO WITH YOUR DISCARD

You may be screaming about tossing out so much flour and feeling a shameful sense of waste. But saving and storing starter day after day can become overwhelming. I've seen too many new bakers fret about using their starter, only to get frustrated and quit baking sourdough or put it in their fridge to try again later. I pride myself on being green, but even *I* dump my starter into my trash bin or compost. It's okay to dump your discard! Just be sure to do so in the trash or compost — don't pour it down your sink! Sourdough starter or dough placed down your sink drain can wreak havoc on your pipes! Hot water and dough can create a cement-like mixture.

If you want to store your discard, you can keep a separate (labeled) jar in your refrigerator where you place all your discard. Then, when the mood strikes, you can whip up one of the recipes in Chapter 13, which is full of sourdough discard recipes. Sourdough discard is a great yogurt, egg, or buttermilk substitute. The tartness is mild, and the starter discard can give the product a light, airy texture.

Day 3

On the third day, follow these steps:

1. **Place a clean glass jar on the scale and tare the scale to 0.**

2. **Transfer from the other jar 50 grams of the starter.**

3. **Discard the remaining starter.**

    Don't use or save the discarded starter. Throw it in the trash or compost it.

4. **Tare the scale to 0 and add 50 grams of flour.**

5. **Tare the scale to 0 again and add 50 grams of water.**

    This is a 1:1:1 ratio (starter:flour:water).

6. **Using a spoon, give the mixture a stir.**

7. **Screw the lid *loosely* onto the jar.**

8. **Place a rubber band around the jar at the line where the starter is now.**

    The rubber band will serve as a marker showing you how much the starter is growing each day.

9. **Place the jar in a dark, cool spot (like a pantry or cupboard), and let it rest for 24 hours.**

Days 4 through 11

Now you're ready to increase your feedings to twice daily, 12 hours apart. Follow these steps every day from days 4 through 10:

1. **Place a clean glass jar on the scale and tare the scale to 0.**

2. **Transfer from the other jar 50 grams of the starter.**

3. **Discard the remaining starter.**

   Don't use or save the discarded starter. Throw it in the trash or compost it.

4. **Tare the scale to 0 and add 50 grams of flour.**

5. **Tare the scale again and add 50 grams of water.**

   This is a 1:1:1 ratio (starter:flour:water).

6. **Using a spoon, give the mixture a stir.**

7. **Screw the lid *loosely* onto the jar.**

8. **Place the rubber band around the jar at the line where the starter is now.**

   The rubber band will serve as a marker showing you how much the starter is growing each day.

9. **Place the jar in a dark, cool spot (like a pantry or cupboard), and let it rest for 12 hours.**

10. **Repeat Steps 1 through 9.**

KNOWING WHEN YOUR STARTER IS READY

How do you know when your starter is ready to use?

Some folks swear by the float test. This is where you take a spoonful of your starter and put it into a glass of water. If it floats, it's assumed to be ready. For the most part, this is a reliable test with a sourdough starter.

But using a rubber band to mark where your starter begins really gives you an idea of the vitality of your starter. When it doubles in size, it's ready to use. Look for large and small bubbles throughout the starter.

Every time you feed the starter, look to see how much the starter has grown. Is it bubbly? Has it doubled in size? If you answer "Yes" to both of these questions, it's time to bake your first loaf of bread. If you answer "No," continue to feed your starter twice daily until you have a vibrant, bubbly starter.

TIP

If you want to expedite this process, purchase rye flour. Rye flour naturally has more wild yeasts and bacteria in the grain, so the starter will grow faster. You can use 25 grams of rye flour and 25 grams of unbleached all-purpose flour for the flour mixture.

Caring for a Starter

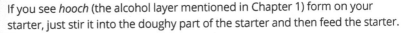

To keep your starter alive, you can store it on the counter or in the refrigerator or freezer:

TIP

>> **If you plan to bake daily:** Keep your starter on the counter and feed it twice daily, 12 hours apart.

>> **If you plan to bake anywhere from once a week to once a month:** Keep your starter in the refrigerator and feed it once a week. In the refrigerator your starter goes dormant, slowing down its need to be fed.

   If you see *hooch* (the alcohol layer mentioned in Chapter 1) form on your starter, just stir it into the doughy part of the starter and then feed the starter.

>> **If you don't plan to bake for more than a month:** Keep your starter in the freezer. Freezing temperatures won't kill all your yeasts or *Lactobacillus* mix. The freezer can be a great place to store a starter if you get burned out on baking or you're traveling for an extended period of time.

If you're storing your starter on the counter, you can use it whenever you're ready to make a loaf of bread. If you're storing it in the refrigerator or freezer, you'll need to revitalize your starter before baking.

When you want to bake a loaf of bread, you need to take your starter out of the refrigerator 12 hours prior to baking. Leave the jar at room temperature (65 to 80 degrees). Let your starter rise, about 2 to 4 hours. Then feed your starter. In 8 to 10 hours, your starter will be ready to use again.

TIP

If you're storing your starter in the freezer, you'll need to feed the starter for at least three to five days before it'll be ready to use. Freezing is best when you'll have a long lull in baking. You can store your starter in the freezer for six months to a year.

Then follow these steps:

1. **Place a clean glass jar on the scale and tare the scale to 0.**

2. **Add 50 grams of the starter in the jar.**

3. **Tare the scale to 0 and add 50 grams of flour.**

4. **Tare the scale to 0 again and add 50 grams of water.**

5. **Using a spoon, give the mixture a stir.**

6. **Screw the lid *loosely* onto the jar.**

7. **Place a rubber band around the jar at the line where the starter is now.**

   The rubber band will serve as a marker showing you how much the starter is growing each day.

8. **Place the jar in a warm spot in your kitchen.**

   Many people like to use their oven (turned off) with the light on.

   After about six to eight hours, your starter should be bubbly and ready to use to bake bread.

To bake bread, you'll use however much starter you need in a recipe (usually around 50 to 100 grams), and then create another jar to keep your starter going, and discard the remaining amount. To break this down for you more simply:

>> You have a jar with starter (say, about 150 grams of starter in total in this jar).

>> You take 50 grams out to bake bread.

>> You take 50 grams out to put in another jar and continue the starter jar, which you feed as described earlier.

>> The remaining 50 grams you dispose of in the trash or compost. (Or check out the recipes in Chapter 13 using sourdough discard.)

COPING WITH COMMON STARTER WOES

Yes, your starter can have troubles. Generally speaking, most starter troubles start with a mistake a person makes. For example, cross contamination, from not using clean jars, utensils, or hands while dealing with a starter, can invite unfriendly foes into your jar. If you see a dark brown or pink streak in your starter, it's time to start again. Molds and unfriendly yeasts can take over, so it's important to always use clean tools and clean hands.

I bake a lot, and I'm not immune from starter woes. In fact, I have a funny story about my own starter getting overheated: I had placed my starter on the center of my stovetop. It's a warm spot and it had always kept my starter happy . . . until the fateful day I turned on my oven and forgot to move Elvira (yes, that was her name). The heat from the oven went up the backside of my stovetop and baked poor Elvira. She was toast, and I had to start again.

Now when I'm keeping my starter warm in the oven or on top, I place a sticky note on the oven to remind myself not to bake my poor starter. Also, I keep an extra batch of starter on hand, either in my freezer, in my refrigerator, or dried. You can never be too careful — sourdough starter is like gold!

TIP

This may be a great time to name your starter! Go ahead, give it a fun name. Naming your starter may help ensure that you always keep your starter growing!

Before returning your jar to the refrigerator be sure to feed the starter using the same 1:1:1 ratio. Refrigerate until ready to use again.

The more you bake, the more vivacious your starter will be. Some bakers who have a healthy, well-used starter can leave theirs unfed (in the refrigerator) for a month between feedings. But with a brand-new starter, it's important to feed weekly and keep your starter healthy.

DRYING YOUR STARTER

Most bakers enjoy sharing their starters across the globe, and to do so, they send it off in its dried form. To dry your starter, follow these steps:

1. **Feed it as you normally would.**

2. **Place a piece of parchment paper on the counter.**

3. **Pour a thin layer of sourdough starter on the parchment paper.**

4. **Let the starter dry for three to five days, until completely dry.**

5. **Break the starter into pieces and store the pieces in an airtight container or glass jar.**

Dried starter can keep for a year safely in your pantry. To use the dried starter, follow these steps:

1. **Place a clean glass jar on a scale and tare the scale to 0.**

2. **Add 30 grams of dried starter to the jar.**

3. **Tare the jar to 0 again and add 30 grams of warm water.**

4. **Stir the mixture and let it bubble for 4 to 8 hours.**

5. **Feed your starter as you normally would (1:1:1 ratio) until it becomes active, doubling in size.**

I recommend fully waking up your starter by feeding it twice a day for two to three days before baking.

Forming Your Dough

Finally, what you've been waiting for: making your first loaf of sourdough bread! In this section, I break down the exact process to making sourdough bread. There are variances as you advance your skills in sourdough bread making, but the basics will get you started and moving in the right direction. When your starter is ready to bake, these are the general steps you take in baking a bread loaf. Chapter 7 has all the sourdough bread recipes you need to get started.

TIP

Making sourdough bread can be tricky, so keep in mind the following tips:

>> **Watch videos if you struggle with shaping, folding, or stretching.** Sourdough is a constant learning process. You never stop learning — that's the fun of it!

- **Pay attention to how the seasons affect your bread.** Adjust your sails when it's summer or winter. If it's very warm, use less starter or bulk-rise for less time. If it's cold, you may want to increase your starter or bulk-rise longer.

- **Feed your starter and keep it well loved and viable.** Neglected starters don't thrive.

- **Start with the Rustic Sourdough recipe (Chapter 7) and make it two or three times per week for a whole month.** Get the feel for it. Learn from this one loaf and perfect it. Then advance to other recipes.

- **Don't give up.** Keep practicing!

- **Realize that appearance is not as important as flavor and texture.** If it tastes good, great! That's what matters most.

- **When you have the sourdough process down, share a loaf and starter with a friend!** Spread the love. Oh, and don't forget to give them a copy of this book, too!

Step 1: Autolyzing

You'll start by pulling out a large, glass mixing bowl. In this bowl, you'll gently mix together your flour, water, and starter in the recipe you're following. The dough will look like a shaggy mess. Don't worry, it'll get there! Allow the mixture to *autolyze* (hydrate the flour, allowing the enzymes to be activated). This process can take anywhere from ten minutes to an hour.

TECHNICAL STUFF

Some bakers wait to add the starter, but after testing numerous loaves, I haven't seen a difference based on when I added the starter, and think this technique cleans up the process for beginners.

Step 2: Adding salt

Next, you'll fold in the salt. Sprinkle the salt over the dough and lift the bottom edge of the dough and fold into the center. If your hands are feeling sticky, dip them in water and continue. Give the bowl a quarter turn, lift up the bottom edge and gently stretch the dough up and fold it over the center. Repeat this twice more. This process is called *stretching and folding* (see Figure 4-2), and it's very different from kneading dough. Cover the bowl with a warm, damp towel and begin the bulk rise.

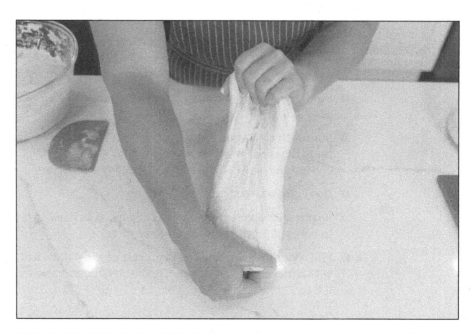

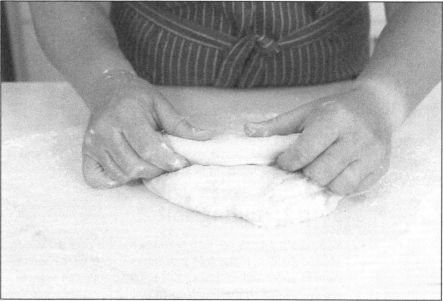

FIGURE 4-2:
Stretching,
folding, and
shaping
sourdough.

Step 3: Bulk fermenting

How long you bulk ferment depends greatly on the amount of starter used in the recipe and the temperature of your home. If you're making a basic white sourdough, you can simply cover the dough and let it rest and ferment for eight to ten hours. If you're making a whole-grain variety, you'll want to help the gluten formation by folding the dough (as described in Step 2, with four quarter turns and folds) every 30 to 60 minutes twice more.

Production could look like this:

>> 8 p.m.: Autolyze the dough and feed the starter.

>> 8:30 p.m.: Add in the salt and fold.

>> 9:30 p.m.: Perform four stretch and folds.

>> 10:30 p.m.: Perform four stretch and folds and rest the dough for eight to ten hours.

Step 4: Shaping

By now your dough has probably doubled in size, and you'll see bubbles just under the surface of the dough. Sprinkle flour onto a counter or workspace. Use a dough scraper and scrape out the dough onto a floured surface. Sprinkle the dough lightly with flour and flour your hands. Using the same stretch-and-fold technique described earlier, stretch and fold the dough to tighten the tension in the dough. Let the dough rest for ten minutes to relax the gluten.

After resting, stretch and fold the bottom piece of dough over to the center. Next, stretch and fold the top piece of dough over to the center. Using two hands, gently pull the dough toward you, tucking and tightening the shape of the dough. If you're forming a round, you'll tuck in the sides and form a tightened ball.

Step 5: Cold proofing or second rise

If you're using a *banneton* (a woven or braided basket that helps a loaf hold its shape and creates a desired design on the surface of the dough during its final proofing), add rice flour to the banneton, filling in the crevices, and place the tightened dough shape into your preform banneton (see Figure 4-3). Cover with a damp tea towel.

If you're using a Dutch oven, place the parchment paper into the Dutch oven and place the dough onto the parchment paper. Cover with the lid.

If you want a more sour-flavored dough, place the dough in the refrigerator for 4 to 24 hours (even longer in some recipes). If you prefer a less pronounced sour flavor, let the dough rest at room temperature for an hour.

FIGURE 4-3:
Tightened
and shaped
sourdough
being placed
into a prepared
banneton.

After cold proofing your dough, spread out a piece of parchment paper and gently turn the banneton over onto the parchment paper. Place the parchment paper into a Dutch oven.

Step 6: Scoring

This is when the artists among us get happy! Sourdough can be scored into beautiful designs. Artistry is not my forte, however, so I prefer to be simple with either a long slice into the dough, about ⅛ inch to ¼ inch deep or an *X* across the top (see Figure 4-4).

TECHNICAL STUFF

Scoring sourdough isn't just decorative — it has a purpose. The skin is taut and tight after shaping, and when the dough gets placed into a very hot oven, it wants to rise and push on the surface. Scoring with a lame or serrated knife allows for gasses to release at those score marks, creating a picturesque loaf of baked bread.

Step 7: Baking

Some like it hot, and sourdough bread likes it hotter! Make sure your oven rack is in the center of your oven and allows enough space for your Dutch oven to fit into the oven. Then crank your oven to 450 or 500 degrees. After you heat the oven, secure the lid on your Dutch oven and place the dough into the hot oven. Quickly close the oven door and set the timer for 30 minutes. After 30 minutes, carefully remove the lid and bake for another 20 to 30 minutes, or until the dough is golden in color and has reached an internal temperature of 200 to 210 degrees.

FIGURE 4-4:
Scoring a
sourdough boule.

Step 8: Cooling

This part may break your heart, but hear me out. You really must let the dough rest and cool for at least one to three hours prior to slicing. If you don't wait, your dough can turn into a gummy mess. Some loaves, like rye breads, deserve a good 24 to 48 hours of cooling before slicing! But, a basic white loaf can be sliced after a few hours outside the oven.

REMEMBER

Artisan breads take time and patience. The wait is worth the rewards!

A TYPICAL BAKER'S SCHEDULE

To help you get a better picture of a baking timeline and structure of sourdough planning, here's my typical baker's schedule:

6 a.m.: Place the starter on the counter and let it bubble up throughout the day.

6 p.m.: Check the starter. If it doesn't seem bubbly or viable, do a day of feedings. If it seems bubbly and viable, begin the recipe. After prepping the recipe, feed the starter and either return it to your refrigerator or leave it on the counter to bake again tomorrow.

7 p.m.: Stretch and fold the dough.

8 p.m.: Stretch and fold the dough. Cover for the night.

6 a.m.: Shape and tighten the dough. Place the dough into a rice-floured banneton. Place in the refrigerator to bake at a later time (that night or the next night) or cover and leave on the counter to rise 1 to 2 hours before baking.

7 a.m.: If the bread was left out to rise, begin heating the oven 1 hour prior to baking. If you're slow to put the bread into the oven, heat the oven to 500 degrees and then reduce to 450 degrees when the Dutch oven is inside and the door is closed.

8 a.m.: Line a Dutch oven with parchment paper and flip the dough into the Dutch oven. Next, score the dough with an X or one single line. Place the lid onto the Dutch oven and put into the oven. Close the door. Set a timer for 30 minutes.

8:30 a.m.: Remove the lid. Reset the timer to 20 to 30 minutes (depending on the loaf and how dark you'd like the crust).

9 a.m.: Remove from the oven. Hold the parchment paper and remove the dough to a cooling rack. Let the dough cool for at least 3 hours or up to 12 hours for rye bread. Then slice and serve.

Chapter **5**

Stocking Your Kitchen

Whether you're making sourdough bread or a classic yeast bread, you need specific tools to make a successful loaf. Modern conveniences, like stand mixers and digital scales, are helpful for beginning bread makers and experienced bread makers alike. In this chapter, I let you know which tools I think are absolutely necessary and which tools are fun to have as you advance in your bread-making skill. I also fill you in on which ingredients you should have on hand so that you can start baking a loaf of bread whenever the mood strikes!

Loading Up on the Tools of the Trade

As fun as it is to have a gourmet kitchen, full of kitchen toys, most cooks don't need it. In this section, I let you know which tools are absolutely necessary for success and which are nice to have. Great bread has been made for centuries without these tools, but you may be more apt to make bread regularly when you have these items on hand.

Must-have tools

If you're going to make bread, you need, at a minimum, the following:

>> **Oven:** In order to bake bread, your kitchen must have an oven. Some breads (like English muffins and flatbreads) can be made on the stovetop, but most breads need an oven that heats to at least 500 degrees.

>> **Dutch oven:** A Dutch oven is a round, deep pan that's safe at high temperatures. Look for a 6- to 8-quarter Dutch oven that doesn't have plastic handles or a plastic knob on the lid. A cast-iron Dutch oven, like one from Lodge (www.lodgemfg.com/product/dutch-oven), is cost-friendly and easy to use.

To clean a cast-iron pan, use salt and oil and only rinse with water, not soapy water.

REMEMBER

>> **Metric scale:** A digital scale that can measure small, metric amounts, such as grams, is a foolproof way to succeed in bread making. Although volume is often used in baking (with cups, teaspoons, and tablespoons), a scale is not expensive (less than $15) and worth the investment.

>> **Parchment paper:** Parchment paper can handle the high heat and will help your dough not stick to the surface of your baking pan. Parchment is a cellulose paper that is nonstick and perfect for baking your favorite loaf of bread.

>> **Bread pan:** You can find stoneware, metal, or glass bread pans, but stoneware and glass may create a softer bottom crust. For the purpose of the recipes in this book, I recommend that you use a metal bread pan. For most recipes, the standard size bread pan is 8½ x 4½ x 2½ inches, and if you only have one pan, this is the size you want to buy.

Here's a reference guide on sizes:

- 5¾ x 3¼ x 2 inches (mini) = 2 cups

- 7⅜ x 3⅝ x 2 inches = 3 cups

- 8 x 4 x 2½ inches = 4 cups

- 8½ x 4½ x 2½ inches = 6 cups

- 9¼ x 5¼ x 2½ inches = 8 cups

>> **Stand mixer with dough hook attachment:** When necessary, the recipes in this book have been made using a KitchenAid stand mixer with a dough hook. You can knead by hand, but it takes longer. A good stand mixer will save you time and energy.

>> **Instant-read thermometer:** Instant-read thermometers are probe thermometers that tell you the temperature within seconds of being inserted into the bread. You can purchase a good instant-read thermometer for less than $20.

>> **Large stock pot:** Stock pots are used for boiling water for bagels and can double as a baking vessel when you want to make two round loaves. Choose a stock pot that has a top diameter of at least 10 inches and a height of at least 8 inches, with a minimum capacity of 12 quarts. Look for a stainless-steel pot that's oven-safe to 500 degrees, with a metal lid. (Most glass lids are only oven-safe up to 350 degrees.)

>> **Glass mixing bowl:** You can use a stainless-steel bowl with most yeast breads, but when you're working with sourdough breads, you should use glass or nonreactive surfaces. Plastic bowls are lightweight but often retain the smells of foods, which can transfer to breads.

>> **Heavy baking sheet:** A multifunctional jelly roll pan, with raised edges, can save on space. A standard baking sheet is 15 x 13 inches and made of aluminum. You want a pan that can withstand high heat and heavy use. Nordic Ware (www.nordicware.com/bakeware/baking-sheets) is a well-rated brand for bakeware.

>> **Serrated bread knife:** Whether you're slicing roast beef, cutting a tender cake, or slicing off thick slices of crusty bread, you need a serrated bread knife. An 8- or 10-inch bread serrated knife can also be used to score the tops of breads before baking. Expect to pay $30 to $50 for a decent bread knife.

>> **Dry measuring cups and spoons:** If you use a scale, you don't need dry measuring cups, but recipes outside of this book may use volumetric measurements, so it's a good idea to have them on hand.

>> **Liquid measuring cups and spoons:** If you use a scale, you don't need liquid measuring cups, but recipes outside of this book may use volumetric measurements, so it's a good idea to have them on hand. A Pyrex 4-cup liquid measuring cup can help with heating milk and melting chocolate in the microwave.

Optional tools

As you progress and get more confident in your bread-making skills you may want to buy some more tools. The following tools aren't necessary, but they can enhance your enjoyment of artisan bread making:

>> **Bench scraper:** A bench scraper is a flat, stainless-steel blade (not sharp) that is used to cut dough or scrape a workspace clean. You can use a chef's knife for this purpose if you don't have a bench scraper on hand.

>> **Dough scraper:** When you make a lot of bread, you find yourself wanting to scrape out every little piece of dough possible from the dough bowl. Dough scrapes are often plastic and somewhat flexible.

>> **Banneton:** If you've always wondered how people get those cool, floured lines on bread, now you know! A banneton is a preformed shape, whether oval or round, that bread bakers use to proof loaves in the final proofing stage. Make sure you dust your banneton with rice flour to prevent the dough from sticking to (and deflating) your proofed dough.

>> **Lame or scoring tools:** If you're an artist at heart, a good lame or scoring tool may feed your heart. For creative types, adding a decorative touch to the surface of the dough can set a loaf apart from everyone else's. A serrated knife can serve this same purpose, just not as intricately. If you prefer the simple X or slices across the top, you can skip this tool.

>> **Silicone baking sheet:** You use silicone baking sheets to line metal baking sheets. They're nonstick and incredibly versatile. One popular brand is Silpat. Silicone baking sheets cost around $16 and last for about two years.

>> **Pastry brush:** When you need to brush on an egg wash, a pastry brush can come in handy. Hands can work, too, but the brush marks won't be as uniform across the top if you use your hands.

Stocking Your Kitchen

When your kitchen is stocked with the right ingredients, you can make bread any day of the week.

Dry goods

Dry goods are foods that can be safely stored in a pantry, mostly for extended periods of time.

>> Flour

- All-purpose unbleached white flour

- Bread flour

- Rye flour

- Semolina flour

- Whole spelt flour
- Whole-wheat flour

» Active dry yeast

» Oils
- Avocado oil
- Extra-virgin olive oil

» Herbs (dried or fresh)
- Parsley
- Rosemary
- Thyme

» Spices
- Cardamom
- Cumin
- Garlic powder
- Kosher salt
- Onion powder
- Sea salt

» Nuts
- Almonds
- Pecans
- Walnuts

» Seeds
- Chia seeds
- Flax seeds
- Pumpkin seeds
- Sesame seeds

» Sundried tomatoes

- » Canned fruit
  - Cherries
  - Peaches
  - Pineapple
- » Dried fruit
  - Apricots
  - Blueberries
  - Cherries
  - Raisins
- » Dark chocolate (60 percent cacao or higher)
- » Cocoa powder
- » Honey
- » Maple syrup
- » Molasses
- » Vanilla extract
- » Fruit jam
- » Oatmeal

TIP

Spices and dried herbs should be used within a year or two, so if you've had spices lingering in your cabinets for an extended stay, it's time to add them to the compost and start fresh. Stick with small jars to start with, and only buy larger jars if you use the ingredient frequently.

Refrigerated items

Most refrigerated items only can be stored for a week or two, so you'll buy them based on the recipes you're planning to make soon. My approach is to avoid food waste as much as possible, so the following recommendations are based on common ingredients used in this book. When you plan what you're going to make, you can decide what items to buy for the week ahead.

- » Milk
- » Eggs
- » Cheese

- Cheddar
- Cottage cheese
- Cream cheese
- Gouda
- Mozzarella
- Parmesan

>> Bacon

>> Sausage

>> Pepperoni

Fresh produce

Fresh produce items have a varying shelf-life. Store potatoes, onions, and fresh garlic in a cool, dark place in your pantry so they don't sprout roots. Items like apples, beets, lemons, and oranges require refrigeration; although they can keep for an extended period (weeks to months in a cool refrigerator), check their freshness when you have a menu planned for the week ahead.

I recommend keeping the following items on hand for the recipes in this book:

>> Apples

>> Beets

>> Chives

>> Lemons

>> Oranges

>> Spinach

2

Baking Scrumptious Breads

IN THIS PART . . .

Create the perfect sandwich and toasting breads.

Discover old-world sourdough recipes.

Create savory breads, perfect for dinner

Play with dough through fun shaping techniques.

Explore the world with unique European, Middle Eastern, and Asian breads.

Satisfy a sweet tooth with decadent treats or breakfast-inspired breads.

Make hearty stuffed breads to fill your family up.

Use your leftover sourdough starter in creative ways.

Make zesty spreads and dips to pair with your favorite bread.

Chapter **6**

Bread Basics

C lose your eyes and imagine fresh-baked bread, hot out of the oven, the aroma dancing through the hall and onto the street. There really is nothing quite like fresh baked bread.

This chapter is a great place to start your journey with making bread. They're perfect for slicing, toasting, and making into sandwiches (see Chapter 17 for ideas).

REMEMBER

Cutting into a warm loaf of bread is tempting, but let your breads cool completely before taking that first slice (see Chapter 3).

TIP

Many of the recipe in this book call for a standard loaf pan lined with parchment paper, as shown in Figure 6-1. Most of the doughs in this chapter are gently patted into a square (see Figure 6-2), and then rolled up. As you roll the squared bread dough, you slightly tuck in the ends (see Figure 6-3). After rolling, you can pinch the seam closed before being placed into the parchment-lined loaf pan for baking.

FIGURE 6-1:
Lining a loaf pan with parchment paper.

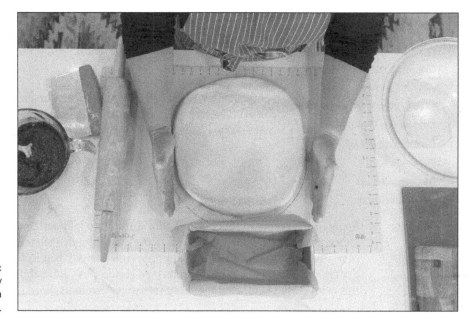

FIGURE 6-2:
Dough gently patted into a square.

FIGURE 6-3:
Rolling a bread
log for a loaf pan.

Crusty Overnight Bread

PREP TIME: 10 MIN PLUS 8 HR FOR RISING	BAKE TIME: 30 MIN	YIELD: 8 SERVINGS

INGREDIENTS

300 grams (2 cups plus
1 tablespoon) all-purpose flour

225 grams (¾ cup plus
3 tablespoons) warm water

9 grams (1½ teaspoons)
kosher salt

5 grams (1¾ teaspoons) active
dry yeast

1½ cups water for steaming

DIRECTIONS

1 In a medium bowl, place the all-purpose flour, warm water, salt, and yeast.

2 Stir together. The dough will be shaggy and sticky.

3 Cover the surface of the bowl with a damp tea towel and place the bowl into the refrigerator for at least 8 hours or up to 48 hours.

4 Take the dough out of the refrigerator and place it on a floured surface.

5 Pat the dough into an 8-x-8-inch square.

6 Roll the dough into a log.

7 Spray a bread pan with cooking spray.

8 Line a bread pan with parchment paper.

9 Place the log-rolled dough into the bread pan and allow the bread to rest for 30 to 60 minutes.

10 Place a shallow cast-iron or oven-safe pan on the lowest rack of the oven.

11 Preheat the oven to 450 degrees.

12 After the oven has preheated, slice down the center of the dough with a serrated knife or bread lame about ½ inch deep.

13 Place the bread pan on the center rack of the oven.

14 Pour the water for steaming into the cast-iron or oven-safe pan on the lowest rack of the oven.

15 Close the oven door quickly as the steam releases.

16 Bake for 25 to 30 minutes or until the bread reaches an internal temperature of 190 degrees and has a deep golden crust.

17 Remove the bread from the bread pan by lifting the parchment paper.

18 Allow the bread to cool at least 1 hour before slicing and serving.

PER SERVING: *Calories 138 (From Fat 4); Fat 0g (Saturated 0g); Cholesterol 0mg; Sodium 437mg; Carbohydrate 29g (Dietary Fiber 1g); Protein 4g.*

TIP: After cooling, wrap in plastic wrap and store up to 2 days at room temperature.

NOTE: The water used for steaming doesn't need to be weighed in grams, because that level of accuracy isn't necessary.

Grandma's White Bread

PREP TIME: 30 MIN PLUS 2 HR FOR RISING	BAKE TIME: 35 MIN	YIELD: 10 SERVINGS

INGREDIENTS

300 grams (1¼ cups plus 1 teaspoon) warm water

7 grams (1 packet or 2¼ teaspoons) active dry yeast

20 grams (5 teaspoons) granulated sugar

500 grams (4 cups) bread flour

28 grams (2 tablespoons) butter, softened or at room temperature

9 grams (1½ teaspoons) kosher salt

DIRECTIONS

1 In the bowl of a stand mixer with a dough hook attached, place the water, yeast, and sugar.

2 Stir to mix on low speed (level 1).

3 Allow the mixture to rest for 10 minutes to see that yeast is active and bubbly.

4 Add the flour.

5 Turn the stand mixer onto low speed (level 2) and knead the dough for 3 minutes.

6 Add the butter and salt to the mixing bowl, and turn the stand mixer onto medium-low speed (level 2 to 3).

7 Knead the dough for 5 minutes, scraping down the sides as needed at the beginning.

8 Remove the dough hook.

9 Cover the bowl with a damp tea towel, and place in a warm, draft-free spot in your kitchen.

10 After 1½ hours, check to see if the dough has doubled in size. If it hasn't, cover the bowl and allow the dough to rise for another 30 minutes. If it has doubled in size, take the dough out of the bowl and place it on a floured surface.

11 Gently press and flatten the dough to release the excess air bubbles.

12 Form the dough into a 8-x-8-inch square.

13 Roll up the dough into a log, tucking in the ends as you roll the dough.

14 Spray a bread pan with cooking spray.

15 Place a piece of parchment paper into the bread pan.

16 Place the dough, seam side down, into the bread pan.

17 Cover and allow the dough to rise for 30 minutes.

18 Preheat the oven to 350 degrees.

19 Bake the bread for 30 to 35 minutes or until it reaches an internal temperature of 180 to 190 degrees.

20 Remove the bread from the bread pan by lifting the parchment paper.

21 Allow the bread to cool at least 1 hour before slicing and serving.

PER SERVING: *Calories 211 (From Fat 28); Fat 3g (Saturated 2g); Cholesterol 6mg; Sodium 351mg; Carbohydrate 39g (Dietary Fiber 1g); Protein 6g.*

TIP: After cooling, wrap in a tea towel and store up to 2 days in a bread box or brown paper bag at room temperature.

Wheat Sandwich Bread

PREP TIME: 30 MIN PLUS 2 HR FOR RISING	BAKE TIME: 30 MIN	YIELD: 10 SERVINGS

INGREDIENTS

245 grams (1 cup) milk

28 grams (2 tablespoons) cold butter

170 grams (1½ cups) whole-wheat flour

12 grams (1 tablespoon) sugar

40 grams (2 tablespoons) molasses

7 grams (1 packet or 2¼ teaspoons) active-dry yeast

42 grams (½ cup) wheat germ

120 grams (1 cup) all-purpose flour

9 grams (1½ teaspoons) kosher salt

DIRECTIONS

1   In a small saucepan, heat the milk over medium heat, stirring constantly, until small bubbles begin to form, about 5 minutes.

2   Remove the pan from the heat and add the butter to cool the mixture.

3   In the bowl of a stand mixer with a dough hook attached, add the whole-wheat flour, sugar, and molasses.

4   Pour in the warm milk and turn the mixer on low speed (level 1). Mix for 1 minute.

5   Add in the yeast and mix for 1 more minute.

6   Let the mixture rest for 10 minutes.

7   In a separate bowl, mix together the wheat germ, all-purpose flour, and salt.

8   Add the dry ingredients to the stand mixer bowl.

9   Knead on medium-low speed (level 2) for 5 minutes, scraping down the sides as needed.

10   Cover the bowl with a damp tea towel and allow to rise for 1 hour or until it has doubled in size.

11   Place the dough onto a floured surface.

12   Gently press and flatten the dough to release excess air bubbles.

13   Form the dough into a 8-x-8-inch square.

14 Roll up the dough into a log, tucking in the ends as you roll the dough.

15 Spray a bread pan with cooking spray and line the pan with parchment paper.

16 Place the dough, seam side down, into the bread pan.

17 Cover and allow the dough to rise for 1 hour.

18 Preheat the oven to 400 degrees.

19 Bake the bread for 25 to 30 minutes or until it reaches an internal temperature of 180 to 190 degrees.

20 Remove the bread from the bread pan by lifting the parchment paper.

21 Allow the bread to cool at least 1 hour before slicing and serving.

PER SERVING: *Calories 174 (From Fat 36); Fat 4g (Saturated 2g); Cholesterol 9mg; Sodium 363mg; Carbohydrate 30g (Dietary Fiber 3g); Protein 6g.*

TIP: After cooling, wrap in a tea towel and store up to 3 to 5 days in a bread box or brown paper bag at room temperature.

VARY IT! If you have bacon fat drippings, you can replace the butter with bacon fat. It adds a subtle, smoky flavor to the bread and is a great way to use up rendered fat.

Hearty Whole-Wheat Bread

PREP TIME: 20 MIN PLUS 2½ HR FOR RISING	BAKE TIME: 35 MIN	YIELD: 8 SERVINGS

INGREDIENTS

340 grams (3 cups) whole-wheat flour

42 grams (2 tablespoons) honey

294 grams (1¼ cups) warm water

7 grams (1 packet or 2¼ teaspoons) active dry yeast

26 grams (2 tablespoons) sunflower or canola oil

9 grams (1½ teaspoons) kosher salt

DIRECTIONS

1 In the bowl of a stand mixer with a dough hook attached, place the whole-wheat flour, honey, water, and yeast.

2 Mix for 1 minute on medium-low speed (level 2).

3 Let the mixture rest for 10 minutes.

4 Add the oil and salt to the bowl, and knead on medium-low speed (level 2) for 6 minutes.

5 Cover the bowl with a damp tea towel and allow to rise for 1½ hours or until it has doubled in size.

6 Place the dough onto a floured surface.

7 Gently press and flatten the dough to release excess air bubbles.

8 Form the dough into an 8-x-8-inch square.

9 Roll up the dough into a log, tucking in the ends as you roll the dough.

10 Spray a bread pan with cooking spray and line the pan with parchment paper.

11 Place the dough, seam side down, into the bread pan.

12 Cover and allow the dough to rise for 1 hour.

13 Preheat the oven to 350 degrees.

14 Bake for 30 to 35 minutes or until the bread reaches an internal temperature of 180 to 190 degrees.

15 Remove the bread from the bread pan by lifting the parchment paper.

16 Allow the bread to cool at least 1 hour before slicing and serving.

PER SERVING: *Calories 194 (From Fat 39); Fat 4g (Saturated 0g); Cholesterol 0mg; Sodium 439mg; Carbohydrate 36g (Dietary Fiber 5g); Protein 6g.*

TIP: After cooling, wrap in a tea towel and store up to 1 or 2 days in a bread box or brown paper bag at room temperature.

Golden Egg Bread

PREP TIME: 20 MIN PLUS 2 HR FOR RISING	BAKE TIME: 35 MIN	YIELD: 8 SERVINGS

INGREDIENTS

8 grams (2½ teaspoons) active dry yeast

59 grams (¼ cup) warm water

227 grams (⅔ cup) warm milk

37.5 grams (3 tablespoons) sugar

113 grams (½ cup) butter, melted and cooled

2 eggs

390 grams (3¼ cup) all-purpose flour

8 grams (1¼ teaspoons) kosher salt

DIRECTIONS

1 In the bowl of a stand mixer with a dough hook attached, place the yeast, water, milk, and sugar.

2 Mix for 30 seconds on medium-low speed (level 2).

3 Add the butter and eggs, and mix on low speed (level 1) for 1 minute.

4 Add the flour and salt, and mix on medium-low speed (level 2) for 7 minutes.

5 Cover the bowl with a damp tea towel and allow the dough to rise for 1 hour or until it has doubled in size.

6 Place the dough onto a floured surface.

7 Gently press and flatten the dough to release excess air bubbles.

8 Form the dough into a 8-x-8-inch square.

9 Roll up the dough into a log, tucking in the ends as you roll the dough.

10 Spray a bread pan with cooking spray and line the pan with parchment paper.

11 Place the dough, seam side down, into the bread pan.

12 Cover and allow the dough to rise for 1 hour.

13 Preheat the oven to 375 degrees.

14 Bake for 30 to 35 minutes or until the bread reaches an internal temperature of 195 to 200 degrees.

15 Remove the bread from the bread pan by lifting the parchment paper.

16 Allow the bread to cool at least 1 hour before slicing and serving.

PER SERVING: Calories 335 (From Fat 128); Fat 14g (Saturated 8g); Cholesterol 86mg; Sodium 420mg; Carbohydrate 44g (Dietary Fiber 2g); Protein 8g.

TIP: After cooling, wrap in a tea towel and store up to 3 to 5 days in a bread box or brown paper bag at room temperature.

VARY IT! Craving a slightly sweet, breakfast bread? You can roll up this dough with ¼ cup of a cinnamon-sugar mixture and bake for a slightly sweet taste.

Farmhouse Bread

PREP TIME: 20 MIN PLUS 2 HR FOR RISING	BAKE TIME: 35 MIN	YIELD: 10 SERVINGS

INGREDIENTS

500 grams (4 cups) bread flour

7 grams (1 packet or 2½ teaspoons) active dry yeast

235 grams (1 cup) warm water

9 grams (1½ teaspoons) kosher salt

50 grams (¼ cup) bacon fat or lard

2 cups water for steaming

DIRECTIONS

1 In the bowl of a stand mixer with a dough hook attached, place the flour, yeast, warm water, salt, and bacon fat.

2 Stir together on low speed (level 1). The dough will be shaggy and slightly sticky.

3 Allow the dough to rest for 10 minutes.

4 Knead the dough on medium-low (level 2) for 6 minutes.

5 Cover the bowl with a damp tea towel and allow the dough to rise for 1 hour or until it has doubled in size.

6 Place the dough onto a floured surface.

7 Gently press and flatten the dough to release excess air bubbles.

8 Form the dough into an 8-x-8-inch square.

9 Roll up the dough into a log, tucking in the ends as you roll the dough.

10 Spray a bread pan with cooking spray and line the pan with parchment paper.

11 Place the dough, seam side down, into the bread pan.

12 Cover and allow the dough to rise for 1 hour.

13 Place a cast-iron or oven-safe pan on the lowest rack of the oven.

14 Preheat the oven to 425 degrees.

15 Slice the surface of the bread down the center about ½ inch deep.

16 Place the bread pan into the oven and pour the water for steaming into the cast-iron or oven-safe pan to create steam.

17 Quickly shut the oven door and bake for 10 minutes.

18 Reduce the temperature to 375 degrees and continue baking for 20 to 25 minutes or until the bread reaches an internal temperature of 180 to 190 degrees.

19 Remove the bread from the bread pan by lifting the parchment paper.

20 Allow the bread to cool at least 1 hour before slicing and serving.

PER SERVING: *Calories 229 (From Fat 54); Fat 6g (Saturated 2g); Cholesterol 5mg; Sodium 350mg; Carbohydrate 37g (Dietary Fiber 1g); Protein 6g.*

TIP: After cooling, wrap in a tea towel and store up to 2 days in a bread box or brown paper bag at room temperature.

TIP: This bread makes for a great grilled-cheese sandwich, even if it's beginning to turn stale.

Potato Bread

INGREDIENTS

400 grams russet potatoes (about 2 large potatoes), cut into large cubes

60 grams (¼ cup) water from cooking the potatoes

4 grams (1¼ teaspoons) active dry yeast

330 grams (2¾ cups cups) bread flour

12 grams (2½ teaspoons) kosher salt

2 cups water for steaming

DIRECTIONS

1 In a 6-quart saucepan, place the potatoes and cover with water.

2 Bring to a boil and then reduce to a simmer for 15 minutes, uncovered.

3 Drain the potatoes and reserve 60 grams (¼ cup) of the cooking water.

4 Return the potatoes to the saucepan and heat for an additional 2 to 3 minutes while mashing the potatoes with a potato masher, or until the potatoes begin to dry out.

5 Cool for 15 minutes before continuing.

6 In the bowl of a stand mixer with a dough hook attached, stir together the potatoes, potato water, and yeast on low speed (level 1) for 2 minutes.

7 Add in the bread flour and salt, and knead the dough on medium-low speed (level 2) for 10 minutes.

8 Cover the bowl with a damp tea towel and allow the dough to rise for 45 minutes or until it has doubled in size.

9 Place the dough onto a floured surface.

10 Gently press and flatten the dough to release excess air bubbles.

11 Form the dough into an 8-x-8-inch square.

12 Roll up the dough into a log, tucking in the ends as you roll the dough.

13 Spray a bread pan with cooking spray and line the pan with parchment paper.

14 Place the dough, seam side down, into the bread pan.

15 Cover and allow the dough to rise for 30 minutes.

16 Place a cast-iron or oven-safe pan on the lowest rack of the oven.

17 Preheat the oven to 450 degrees.

18 Place the bread pan into the oven and pour the water for steaming into the cast-iron or oven-safe pan to create steam.

19 Quickly shut the oven door and bake the bread for 10 minutes.

20 Reduce the temperature to 425 degrees and continue baking for 35 to 40 minutes or until the bread reaches an internal temperature of 180 to 190 degrees.

21 Remove the bread from the bread pan by lifting the parchment paper.

22 Allow the bread to cool at least 2 hours before slicing and serving.

PER SERVING: *Calories 159 (From Fat 6); Fat 1g (Saturated 0g); Cholesterol 0mg; Sodium 472mg; Carbohydrate 33g (Dietary Fiber 2g); Protein 5g.*

TIP: After cooling, wrap in a tea towel and store up to 3 or 4 days in a bread box or brown paper bag at room temperature.

NOTE: Potato bread is a German-style bread that pairs well with mustard and bratwurst (German sausages) or salami.

Dark Rye Bread

PREP TIME: 20 MIN PLUS 1 HR 15 MIN FOR RISING	BAKE TIME: 35 MIN	YIELD: 10 SLICES

INGREDIENTS

7 grams (2½ teaspoons) active dry yeast

207 grams (¾ cup plus 2 tablespoons) warm water

240 grams (2 cups) all-purpose flour

103 grams (1 cup) dark rye flour

11.4 grams (5 teaspoons) caraway seeds, divided

9 grams (1½ teaspoons) kosher salt

30 grams (2 tablespoons plus 1 teaspoon) canola oil or bacon fat drippings, divided

1 egg, whisked

DIRECTIONS

1   In the bowl of a stand mixer with a dough hook attached, place the yeast, water, all-purpose flour, rye flour, and 8 grams (4 teaspoons) of the caraway seeds.

2   Stir together on low speed (level 1) for 1 minute.

3   Allow the dough to rest for 10 minutes.

4   Add the salt and 28 grams (2 tablespoons) oil and knead on medium-low speed (level 2) for 5 minutes.

5   Rub the surface of the dough with the remaining 5 grams (1 teaspoon) of oil.

6   Cover the bowl with a damp tea towel and let the dough rise for 45 minutes or until it has doubled in size.

7   Place the dough onto a floured surface.

8   Gently press and flatten the dough to release excess air bubbles.

9   Form the dough into an 8-x-8-inch square.

10   Roll up the dough into a log, tucking in the ends as you roll the dough.

11 Spray a bread pan with cooking spray and line the pan with parchment paper.

12 Place the dough, seam side down, into the bread pan.

13 Cover and allow the dough to rise for 30 minutes.

14 Preheat the oven to 400 degrees.

15 Brush the top of the bread dough with the whisked egg and sprinkle with the remaining 2 grams (1 teaspoon) of caraway seeds.

16 Bake for 30 to 35 minutes or until the bread reaches an internal temperature of 180 to 190 degrees.

17 Remove the bread from the bread pan by lifting the parchment paper.

18 Allow the bread to cool at least 1 hour before slicing and serving.

PER SERVING: *Calories 164 (From Fat 39); Fat 4g (Saturated 0g); Cholesterol 21mg; Sodium 357mg; Carbohydrate 27g (Dietary Fiber 2g); Protein 5g.*

TIP: After cooling, wrap in a tea towel and store up to 2 or 3 days in a bread box or brown paper bag at room temperature.

VARY IT! Add a teaspoon of dried dill for a vibrant twist in flavors.

Oatmeal Bread

PREP TIME: 20 MIN PLUS 17½ HR FOR RISING	BAKE TIME: 35 MIN	YIELD: 10 SERVINGS

INGREDIENTS

130 grams (1½ cups) old-fashioned oats

220 grams (¾ cup) boiling water

9 grams (1½ teaspoons) kosher salt

15 grams (2 teaspoons) honey

3 grams (1 teaspoon) active dry yeast

118 grams (½ cup) warm water

370 grams (3 cups) all-purpose flour

57 grams (¼ cup) butter, softened or at room temperature

DIRECTIONS

1 In a medium, heat-safe bowl, place the old-fashioned oats, boiling water, and salt.

2 Mix together. Allow the mixture to rest for 10 minutes.

3 In a separate bowl, place the honey, yeast, and warm water.

4 Mix together. Allow the mixture to rest for 5 minutes.

5 In the bowl of a stand mixer with a dough hook attached, stir together all the ingredients (the oat mixture, the yeast mixture, the flour, and the butter) on medium-low speed (level 2) for 2 minutes or until combined.

6 Cover the bowl with a damp tea towel and allow the dough to rest for 5 hours.

7 Using the stand mixer, knead the mixture for 5 minutes.

8 Cover the bowl with a damp tea towel and allow the dough to rest for 12 hours or overnight.

9 Place the dough onto a floured surface.

10 Gently press and flatten the dough to release excess air bubbles.

11 Form the dough into an 8-x-8-inch square.

12 Roll the dough into a log, tucking in the ends as you roll the dough.

13 Spray a bread pan with cooking spray and line the pan with parchment paper.

14 Place the dough, seam side down, into the bread pan.

15 Cover and allow the dough to rise for 30 minutes.

16 Preheat the oven to 450 degrees.

17 Place the bread into the oven and bake for 5 minutes.

18 Reduce the temperature to 400 degrees and bake for another 30 minutes.

19 Remove the bread from the bread pan by lifting the parchment paper.

20 Allow the bread to cool at least 1 hour before slicing and serving.

PER SERVING: *Calories 233 (From Fat 53); Fat 6g (Saturated 3g); Cholesterol 12mg; Sodium 351mg; Carbohydrate 39g (Dietary Fiber 2g); Protein 6g.*

TIP: After cooling, wrap in a tea towel and store up to 3 days in a bread box or brown paper bag at room temperature.

VARY IT! Sunflower seeds can be kneaded into this dough for added nutrition and texture.

Chapter **7**

Sourdough Breads

Sourdough is magical! Cultivating your own yeast, stretching and folding the dough to form beautiful airholes . . . and you can't deny the winning flavor. Sourdough starters can be passed down from generation to generation, forming a bond through the decades. Sourdough is also an important gateway bread in the world of breadmaking.

You may be hesitant to embark on this chapter, but let me assure you, many of the best artisan breads are made from long ferment times and a sourdough starter. This reason alone is why I decided to introduce sourdough breads early on in this part. Sourdough breads *do* take longer, but the results are worth the wait.

TIP

Before making any of the recipes in this chapter, review Chapter 5. Take note of the techniques and terminology, and have a sourdough starter on hand. If you don't have the time to patiently wait for a starter to grow, ask a neighbor to share his, or buy one online through King Arthur Flour (https://shop.kingarthurbaking.com).

TIP

The more you bake sourdough, the better the sourdough starter will perform and the more familiar you'll become with the technique, texture, and performance of the dough. I recommend making the simple Rustic Sourdough recipe one to three times per week for a month before advancing to other recipes in this chapter.

REMEMBER

Every time you use your starter in a recipe, take time to replenish and feed the starter. Refer to Chapter 5 for help.

Rustic Sourdough

PREP TIME: 20 MIN PLUS 11 HR FOR RISING	BAKE TIME: 55 MIN	YIELD: 10 SERVINGS

INGREDIENTS

50 grams (¼ cup) sourdough starter

350 grams (1½ cups) room-temperature water

500 grams (4 cups) bread flour

12 grams (2½ teaspoons) kosher salt

DIRECTIONS

1 In a large glass bowl, mix together the sourdough starter and water, stirring to dissolve the starter.

2 Add in the flour and stir to combine until it's a shaggy dough.

3 Let rest for 30 minutes.

4 Sprinkle the salt over the surface of the dough.

5 Stretch and fold the dough 4 times (see Chapter 5 for details).

6 Cover the dough bowl with a damp tea towel and set aside to rise in a warm, draft-free spot for 8 to 10 hours or overnight.

7 Dust a flat surface with flour.

8 Transfer the risen dough to the floured surface.

9 Flip the dough over to lightly coat both sides with flour and coat your hands in flour.

10 Fold the dough in toward the center on all sides.

11 Gently roll the dough toward your body, turn, and roll. Repeat 4 times, until a rounded boule is formed.

12 Place a piece of parchment paper in a Dutch oven.

13 Place the rounded boule dough onto the parchment paper and place the lid over the surface.

14 Let the dough rest for 1 hour.

15 Set the oven rack to the middle position in the oven and preheat the oven to 500 degrees.

16 After the oven is preheated, score the top of the dough with an X ½-inch deep, to allow steam to escape.

17 Put the lid back on the Dutch oven and place the Dutch oven in the oven.

18 Reduce the temperature to 450 degrees and bake for 30 minutes.

19 Remove the lid from the Dutch oven and bake for an additional 20 to 25 minutes or until the bread reaches an internal temperature of 180 to 190 degrees and the crust is golden in color.

20 Remove the bread from the Dutch oven by lifting the parch-ment paper.

21 Allow the bread to cool on a wire rack for 1 to 3 hours before slicing.

PER SERVING: *Calories 190 (From Fat 8); Fat 1g (Saturated 0g); Cholesterol 0mg; Sodium 466mg; Carbohydrate 38g (Dietary Fiber 1g); Protein 6g.*

TIP: After cooling, wrap in a tea towel and store up to 2 days in a bread box or brown paper bag at room temperature.

VARY IT! Add 40 grams (¼ cup) of chopped nuts, seeds, or grain berries to the dough for added nutrition.

Golden Honey Wheat Sourdough

PREP TIME: 35 MIN PLUS 11 HR 30 MIN FOR RISING	BAKE TIME: 55 MIN	YIELD: 10 SERVINGS

INGREDIENTS

50 grams (¼ cup) sourdough starter

25 grams (1 tablespoon plus ½ teaspoon) honey

365 grams (1½ cups) room-temperature water

200 grams (1⅔ cups) bread flour

260 grams (2⅓ cups) whole-wheat flour

12 grams (2½ teaspoons) kosher salt

DIRECTIONS

1. In a large glass bowl, mix together the sourdough starter, honey, and water, stirring to dissolve the starter.

2. Add in the bread flour and whole-wheat flour, and stir to combine until it's a shaggy dough.

3. Let rest for 30 minutes.

4. Sprinkle the salt over the surface of the dough.

5. Stretch and fold the dough 4 times (see Chapter 5 for details).

6. Cover the dough bowl with a damp tea towel and set aside to rise in a warm, draft-free spot for 30 minutes.

7. Stretch and fold the dough 4 times.

8. Cover the dough bowl with a damp tea towel and set aside to rise in a warm, draft-free spot for 30 minutes.

9. Stretch and fold the dough 4 times.

10. Cover the dough bowl with a damp tea towel and set aside to rise in a warm, draft-free spot for 30 minutes.

11. Stretch and fold the dough 4 times.

12. Cover the dough bowl with a damp tea towel and set aside to rise in a warm, draft-free spot for an additional 6 to 8 hours, or until the dough has doubled in size.

13. Dust a flat surface with flour.

14. Transfer the risen dough to the floured surface.

15. Flip the dough over to lightly coat both sides with flour and coat your hands in flour.

16 Fold the dough in toward the center on all sides.

17 Gently roll the dough toward your body, turn, and roll. Repeat 4 times, until a rounded boule is formed.

18 Place a piece of parchment paper in a Dutch oven.

19 Place the rounded boule dough on the parchment paper and place the lid over the surface.

20 Let the dough rest for 1½ hours.

21 Set the oven rack to the middle position in the oven, and preheat the oven to 500 degrees.

22 After the oven is preheated, score the top of the dough with an X about ½-inch deep, to allow steam to escape.

23 Return the lid to the Dutch oven and place the Dutch oven in the hot oven.

24 Reduce the temperature to 440 degrees and bake for 30 minutes.

25 Remove the lid and bake for an additional 20 to 25 minutes or until the bread reaches an internal temperature of 180 to 190 degrees and the crust is golden in color.

26 Remove the bread from the Dutch oven by lifting the parchment paper.

27 Allow the bread to cool on a wire rack for 1 to 3 hours before slicing.

PER SERVING: *Calories 178 (From Fat 8); Fat 1g (Saturated 0g); Cholesterol 0mg; Sodium 467mg; Carbohydrate 37g (Dietary Fiber 4g); Protein 6g.*

TIP: After cooling, wrap in a tea towel and store up to 2 days in a bread box or brown paper bag at room temperature.

NOTE: Stretching and folding whole-wheat dough helps form the gluten, but if you forget don't panic. Your dough will still be tasty — it just may not rise perfectly.

NOTE: With sourdough breads, you don't want to press out all the bubbles, so be sure to *gently* roll versus pressing down and deflating.

VARY IT! Add 40 grams (¼ cup) chopped nuts, seeds, or grain berries to the dough for added nutrition.

Ciabatta

PREP TIME: 45 MIN PLUS 6 HR 30 MIN FOR RISING	BAKE TIME: 30 MIN	YIELD: 9 SERVINGS

INGREDIENTS

150 grams (⅔ cup) sourdough starter

400 grams (1¾ cups) warm water

350 grams (3 cups) bread flour

50 grams (½ cup) whole-wheat flour

100 grams (¾ cup) all-purpose flour

14 grams (1 tablespoon) sea salt

14 grams (1 tablespoon) extra-virgin olive oil

2 cups water, for steaming

DIRECTIONS

1 In a stand mixer bowl, mix together the sourdough starter and warm water, stirring to dissolve the starter.

2 Add in the bread flour, whole-wheat flour, and all-purpose flour, and stir to combine until it's a shaggy dough.

3 Let rest for 30 minutes.

4 Sprinkle the salt over the surface of the dough.

5 Knead the dough on level 2 of a stand mixer for 12 minutes.

6 Pour the extra-virgin olive oil into a large glass bowl and rub the oil up the sides of the bowl.

7 Place the dough into the glass bowl.

8 With damp hands, stretch and fold the dough 4 times (see Chapter 5 for details).

9 Cover the dough bowl with a damp tea towel and set aside to rise in a warm, draft-free spot for 30 minutes.

10 With damp hands, stretch and fold the dough 4 times.

11 Cover the dough bowl with a damp tea towel and set aside to rise in a warm, draft-free spot for 30 minutes.

12 With damp hands, stretch and fold the dough 4 times.

13 Cover the dough bowl with a damp tea towel and set aside to rise in a warm, draft-free spot for 30 minutes.

14 With damp hands, stretch and fold the dough 4 times.

15 Cover the dough a final time and rest for 4 to 6 hours, for a total of 6 to 8 hours during the bulk rise.

16   Line a heavy baking sheet with parchment paper and dust with flour.

17   Dust a work surface with flour.

18   Divide the dough (inside the bowl) into 3 pieces using a bench scraper or wet hands.

19   Pull out and work with 1 piece of dough at a time.

20   Place the piece of dough onto the floured surface and shape into an oblong loaf.

21   Gently use your fingers to create indentations on the surface of the dough.

22   Place this piece of dough onto the baking sheet upside-down (with the dimpled surface on the baking sheet).

23   Repeat with the remaining pieces of dough.

24   Let the loaves rest for 30 minutes.

25   Place the oven rack in the center of the oven, place a cast-iron or oven-safe pan on the bottom of the oven, and pre-heat the oven to 500 degrees.

26   Place the baking sheet in the oven, pour the water (for steaming) into the bottom cast-iron pan, and quickly close the oven door.

27   Bake for 25 to 30 minutes.

28   Cool the bread for 1 hour before slicing.

PER SERVING: *Calories 246 (From Fat 23); Fat 3g (Saturated 0g); Cholesterol 0mg; Sodium 605mg; Carbohydrate 48g (Dietary Fiber 3g); Protein 8g.*

TIP: After cooling, wrap in a tea towel and store up to 2 days in a bread box or brown paper bag at room temperature.

NOTE: Ciabatta bread is perfect for paninis (hot pressed sandwiches). See Chapter 18 for ideas!

Spelt Baguettes

| PREP TIME: 20 MIN PLUS 11 HR FOR RISING | BAKE TIME: 30 MIN | YIELD: 9 SERVINGS |

INGREDIENTS

50 grams (¼ cup) sourdough starter

360 grams (1½ cups) room-temperature water

400 grams (4 cups) whole spelt flour

50 grams (⅓ cup) bread flour

12 grams (2½ teaspoons) fine sea salt

DIRECTIONS

1   In a large glass bowl, mix together the sourdough starter and water, stirring to dissolve the starter. Add in the whole spelt flour and bread flour, and stir to combine until it's a shaggy dough. Let rest for 15 minutes.

2   Sprinkle the salt over the surface of the dough. Stretch and fold the dough 4 times (see Chapter 5 for details). Cover the dough bowl with a damp tea towel and set aside to rise in a warm, draft-free spot for 30 minutes.

3   Stretch and fold the dough 4 times. Cover the dough bowl with a damp tea towel and set aside to rise in a warm, draft-free spot for 30 minutes.

4   Stretch and fold the dough 4 times. Cover the dough bowl with a damp tea towel and set aside to rise in a warm, draft-free spot for 30 minutes.

5   Stretch and fold the dough 4 times. Allow the covered dough to rest an additional 6 to 8 hours or until doubled in size.

6   Dust a flat surface with flour. Transfer the risen dough to the floured surface. Divide the dough into 3 equal pieces, setting aside 2 pieces.

7   Keep in mind the elongated shape of a baguette while shaping the dough: With the first piece, flatten it gently and then focus on lengthening the dough. Fold the side closest to you over the center and press down. Turn the dough 180 degrees and repeat, folding the dough over the center and flattening with your hand (see Figure 7-1). Using two hands and starting at the left side, fold with your right hand in toward the center and press with your left palm to stick the dough. Coat your hands with flour, as needed. Turn the dough 180 degrees and repeat on the other side. Turn the elongated piece of dough over with the seam side down on the flat surface. Pinch the seam closed. Starting from the center, use your fingers to rock the dough back and forth from the center to the ends, elongating the dough as you go. This is a gentle process to roll the dough out to create a long baguette shape, about 15 to 20 inches in length.

8 Set the baguette aside and repeat with the remaining 2 pieces of dough.

9 Place a piece of parchment paper on a heavy baking sheet and place the baguettes about 4 inches apart on the baking sheet. Let rest for 30 minutes.

10 Set the oven rack to the middle position of the oven, and preheat the oven to 500 degrees.

11 After the oven is preheated, score the top of each baguette with 3 angled slices, about ½-inch deep, to allow steam to escape.

12 Place the baguettes into the oven and reduce the temperature to 425 degrees. Bake for 25 to 30 minutes or until the bread reaches an internal temperature of 180 to 190 degrees and the crust is golden in color.

13 Allow the bread to cool on a wire rack for 30 to 60 minutes before slicing.

PER SERVING: *Calories 184 (From Fat 11); Fat 1g (Saturated 0g); Cholesterol 0mg; Sodium 521mg; Carbohydrate 38g (Dietary Fiber 5g); Protein 8g.*

TIP: After cooling, wrap in a tea towel and store up to 2 days in a bread box or brown paper bag at room temperature.

VARY IT! If you can't find spelt flour, you can use bread flour instead.

FIGURE 7-1: Flip the dough 180 degrees and fold and press with the heel of your hand to seal the side closest to you.

Seedy Sourdough

| PREP TIME: 20 MIN PLUS 16 HR FOR RISING | BAKE TIME: 50 MIN | YIELD: 10 SERVINGS |

INGREDIENTS

150 grams (⅔ cup) hot water

50 grams (⅓ cup) flaxseeds

50 grams (⅓ cup) sunflower seeds

25 grams (3 tablespoons plus 1 teaspoon) pumpkin seeds

50 grams (¼ cup) sourdough starter

360 grams (1½ cups) room-temperature water

120 grams (1¼ cups) rye flour

350 grams (3 cups) bread flour

50 grams (⅓ cup) chia seeds

14 grams (1 tablespoon) fine sea salt

DIRECTIONS

1 In a small glass bowl, mix together the hot water, flaxseeds, sunflower seeds, and pumpkin seeds; set aside.

2 In a large glass bowl, mix together the sourdough starter and room-temperature water, stirring to dissolve the starter. Add in the rye flour and bread flour; stir to combine until it's a shaggy dough. Let rest for 15 minutes.

3 Drain the water from the seeds. Sprinkle the seeds, chia seeds, and salt over the surface of the dough.

4 Stretch and fold the dough 4 times (see Chapter 5 for details). Cover the dough bowl with a damp tea towel and set aside to rise in a warm, draft-free spot for 30 minutes.

5 Stretch and fold the dough 4 times. Cover the dough bowl with a damp tea towel and set aside to rise in a warm, draft-free spot for 30 minutes.

6 Stretch and fold the dough 4 times. Cover the dough bowl with a damp tea towel and set aside to rise in a warm, draft-free spot for 30 minutes.

7 Stretch and fold the dough 4 times. Allow the dough to rest an additional 6 hours or until doubled in size.

8 Dust a flat surface with flour. Transfer the risen dough to the floured surface. Flip the dough over to lightly coat both sides with flour and coat your hands in flour.

9 Fold the dough in toward the center on all sides. Gently roll the dough toward your body, turn, and roll. Repeat 4 times, until a rounded boule is formed.

10 Working with a banneton coated with rice flour or a Dutch oven with parchment paper, cover the dough with a towel and place the dough in a cold proof vessel in the refrigerator for 8 to 12 hours.

11 Set the oven rack to the middle position of the oven, and preheat the oven to 500 degrees.

12 After the oven is preheated, remove the dough from the refrigerator.

13 Place the dough into a parchment-lined Dutch oven and score the top of the dough with one deep cut, about 1 inch deep. Place the lid on the Dutch oven and place the Dutch oven in the oven. Reduce the temperature to 440 degrees and bake for 30 minutes.

14 After 30 minutes, remove the lid from the Dutch oven and bake for an additional 20 to 25 minutes or until an internal temperature of 180 to 190 degrees is reached and the crust is golden in color.

15 Allow the bread to cool on a wire rack for at least 5 to 8 hours before slicing.

PER SERVING: *Calories 272 (From Fat 74); Fat 8g (Saturated 1g); Cholesterol 0mg; Sodium 546mg; Carbohydrate 42g (Dietary Fiber 6g); Protein 9g.*

TIP: After cooling, wrap in a tea towel and store up to 3 days in a bread box or brown paper bag at room temperature.

NOTE: Rye breads can sit for 24 hours before slicing, and some bread enthusiasts believe they should cool for 2 full days before being sliced!

NOTE: Rye flour is fun to experiment with, but it doesn't have much gluten, so the dough will need multiple stretches and folds to help give the bread structure.

NOTE: This bread really develops a unique flavor with a cold proof. If you don't want to wait, you can shape, rest for an hour, and bake after the initial proofing time. But if you favor a good sour and rye flavor, don't skip the longer cold proof time.

VARY IT! Try swapping out any of the seeds with sesame seeds, walnuts, pecans, or hazelnuts. Adding in dried fruit makes this a tasty breakfast bread.

Semolina Pizza Dough

PREP TIME: 25 MIN PLUS 4 HR FOR RISING	BAKE TIME: 12 MIN	YIELD: 4 SERVINGS

INGREDIENTS

200 grams (1 cup) sourdough starter

300 grams (1¼ cups) room-temperature water

350 grams (2¾ cups) bread flour

120 grams (¾ cup) semolina flour

14 grams (1 tablespoon) sea salt

15 grams (1 tablespoon) extra-virgin olive oil

Pizza toppings of your choice

DIRECTIONS

1   In a large glass bowl, mix together the sourdough starter and water, stirring to dissolve the starter.

2   Add in the bread flour and semolina flour, and stir to combine until it's a shaggy dough.

3   Let rest for 15 minutes.

4   Add the salt over the surface of the dough.

5   Stretch and fold the dough 4 times (see Chapter 5 for details).

6   Cover the dough bowl with a damp tea towel and set aside to rise in a warm, draft-free spot for 4 to 6 hours.

7   Dust a flat surface with flour.

8   Dump the risen dough onto the floured surface.

9   Flip the dough over to lightly coat both sides with flour and coat your hands in flour.

10   Divide the dough into 4 equal parts.

11   Roll out each piece of dough to an 8-inch circle.

12   Cover and let the dough rest for 10 minutes.

13   Working with 1 piece at a time, roll out each piece of dough into the desired shape (based on your baking sheet or pizza stone), to ½-inch thickness.

14 Line a baking sheet with parchment paper and liberally sprinkle with semolina flour.

15 Place 1 pizza dough onto the surface.

16 Top with desired pizza toppings (see Chapter 14 for ideas).

17 Set the oven rack to the middle position of the oven, and preheat the oven to 550 degrees. If you're working with a pizza stone, place the stone into the oven while it's heating.

18 When you're ready to bake, place the parchment paper onto the baking stone or place the baking sheet into the hot oven.

19 Bake until the pizza is bubbled and browned on top, about 8 to 12 minutes depending on the thickness of toppings.

PER SERVING (DOUGH ONLY): *Calories 554 (From Fat 55); Fat 6g (Saturated 1g); Cholesterol 0mg; Sodium 1,360mg; Carbohydrate 106g (Dietary Fiber 5g); Protein 17g.*

TIP: Store cooked pizza in the refrigerator up to 2 days. To freeze, place rolled dough onto a parchment-lined baking sheet; freeze for 2 hours and then wrap in plastic wrap for storage. Dough can be frozen for up to 1 month.

NOTE: Pizza dough can be rolled and frozen for nights you crave frozen pizza! Simply top and bake in a 450-degree oven for 20 to 25 minutes.

NOTE: This is a great swap for a commercial yeast dough, and the semolina flour gives this bread a nutty and crunchy texture.

NOTE: Pizza dough does not need to be perfectly shaped into a circle. If it's easier to fit onto a baking sheet as oblong or oval pizzas, feel free to roll out in that form. One large square loaf can also be formed and baked.

VARY IT! Try a layer of pesto and goat cheese or a simple Margherita pizza for a fun appetizer!

Sourdough Spelt and Sesame Bagels

PREP TIME: 40 MIN PLUS 8 HR 45 MIN FOR RISING	BAKE TIME: 22 MIN	YIELD: 10 SERVINGS

INGREDIENTS

165 grams (¾ cup) sourdough starter

250 grams (1 cup) warm water

15 grams (1 tablespoon) granulated sugar

350 grams (3 cups) bread flour

130 grams (1⅓ cups) whole spelt flour

12 grams (2½ teaspoons) sea salt

30 grams (1 tablespoon plus 1 teaspoon) honey (for boiling)

20 grams (2 tablespoons plus ½ teaspoon) sesame seeds

DIRECTIONS

1 In a stand mixer bowl, mix together the sourdough starter, water, and sugar, stirring to dissolve the starter.

2 Add in the bread flour and whole spelt flour, and stir to combine until it's a shaggy dough.

3 Let rest for 30 minutes.

4 Sprinkle salt over the surface of the dough.

5 Knead the dough on level 2 of a stand mixer for 6 minutes.

6 Cover the dough with a damp tea towel and allow the dough to rest an additional 8 to 10 hours or until it has doubled in size.

7 Place a piece of parchment paper onto a heavy baking sheet.

8 Lightly flour a work surface for shaping bagels.

9 Transfer the risen dough to the lightly floured surface and divide the dough into 10 equal pieces (aim for 100 to 105 grams each).

10 Roll each piece into a ball between the palms of your hands.

11 Flatten the balls.

12 Using wet hands, poke your finger into the center of the dough and gently stretch the center hole to about 1 inch circumference.

13 Place the bagel shapes onto the parchment paper.

14 Cover the dough with a damp tea towel and let rest for 15 minutes.

15 Fill a large stock pot with water and the honey.

16 Over high heat, bring to a boil.

17 Preheat the oven to 450 degrees.

18 Using wet hands and working with 2 to 3 bagels at a time, immerse the bagels into the boiling water and let them rise to the surface, about 1 minute.

19 Scoop the bagels out of the water and place back onto the parchment-lined baking sheet.

20 Repeat with the remaining bagels.

21 Sprinkle the bagels with sesame seeds.

22 Place the baking sheet into the oven.

23 Reduce the temperature to 425 degrees, and bake for 22 minutes or until golden brown and an internal temperature of 180 to 190 degrees has been reached.

24 Allow the bagels to cool for at least 30 minutes prior to slicing.

PER SERVING: *Calories 229 (From Fat 18); Fat 2g (Saturated 0g); Cholesterol 0mg; Sodium 468mg; Carbohydrate 46g (Dietary Fiber 3g); Protein 8g.*

TIP: After cooling, place in an airtight container and store at room temperature up to 3 days or in the freeze up to 3 months.

NOTE: When working with wet hands, imagine your hands are misted with water, not drenched in a bathtub. They only need to be lightly wet to work with this sticky dough. If the dough is frustrating you, stick the dough into the refrigerator for 30 minutes prior to working with the dough. Cold dough holds its shape better.

VARY IT! Steak seasoning, poppy seeds, dried onions, or cinnamon-and-sugar mixtures can all make for fun toppings. Pick your favorites and give them a try! Just skip salt toppings — the salt will result in a bagel with a moist surface and the bagels won't keep as long.

Chapter **8**

Savory Breads

The breads in this chapter are made with commercial yeast. These breads are quicker to make than sourdough and could be a great complement to an evening dinner or brunch. Typically, these breads only need to rise an hour or two.

Feel free to experiment a little with these recipes. If you're missing an ingredient, don't feel like you have to stick to some of the flavor additions. Take a peek at the suggestions at the end of each recipe to get some ideas on ways to swap out ingredients.

Some of my personal favorite breads use fresh, seasonal ingredients, like beets or cilantro. Next time you're at a farmer's market, pick up ingredients that you like. If these ingredients intimidate you, don't fret — this recipe includes the standard flavor fusions like rosemary, garlic, olive, and onion breads, too.

Finally, you don't have to make all these breads into loaves, although loaves are the easiest to form. You can also try your hand at rolls, baguettes, and twists. In the next chapter, I break down the shaped breads in details, so if you want to venture into shaping the breads in this chapter, take a peek at Chapter 9. You may feel inspired to add a twist or knot along the way!

Garlic and Herbed Bread

PREP TIME: 1 HR 15 MIN PLUS 1 HR 30 MIN FOR RISING	BAKE TIME: 30 MIN	YIELD: 12 SERVINGS

INGREDIENTS

1 head of garlic

53 grams (¼ cup) extra-virgin olive oil, divided

12.6 grams (1½ tablespoons) active dry, instant yeast

294 grams (1¼ cups) warm water

12.5 grams (1 tablespoon) sugar

540 grams (4½ cups) bread flour

100 grams (⅔ cup) chopped walnuts

40 grams (⅓ cup) powdered milk

60 grams (1 cup) chopped fresh parsley

28 grams (2 tablespoons) chopped fresh thyme

1 egg, beaten

DIRECTIONS

1 Preheat the oven to 400 degrees.

2 Remove the outer skin of the garlic head.

3 Using a sharp knife, slice of the top of the garlic head to expose the top part of the cloves.

4 Place a small piece of foil on a flat surface.

5 Place the garlic head on the foil, cut side up and drizzle with 1 tablespoon of the extra-virgin olive oil.

6 Wrap the foil around the garlic head.

7 Place the foil-wrapped garlic into the oven and roast for 35 to 40 minutes or until easy to squeeze.

8 Remove the garlic from the foil and allow to cool for 30 minutes or until easy to handle.

9 Squeeze out the inner cloves from the skin lining of the garlic head.

10 Reserve the olive oil for brushing the bread prior to baking.

11 In the bowl of a stand mixer with a dough hook attachment, mix together the yeast, water, and sugar. Let the mixture rest and bubble for 5 minutes.

12 Add the bread flour, walnuts, powdered milk, parsley, thyme, egg, and roasted garlic to the yeast mixture, and knead with the dough hook on speed 2 for 5 minutes.

13 Pour the remaining extra-virgin olive oil into a glass bowl.

14 Place the kneaded dough in the glass bowl, and flip it over to coat it on all sides. Cover with a damp tea towel and let the dough rise for 1 hour.

15 Line a baking sheet with parchment paper.

16 Press out the air from the dough and divide the dough into two equal pieces.

17 Shape the dough into oblong-shaped loaves or round boules.

18 Place the dough onto the parchment paper. Cover with a damp tea towel and let the dough rise for 30 minutes.

19 Preheat the oven to 350 degrees.

20 Score the top of the breads with a long slice about ½ inch deep.

21 Brush the bread dough surface with the remaining olive oil from the garlic.

22 Bake for 30 to 35 minutes or until the loaves reach an internal temperature of 180 to 190 degrees.

23 Allow the breads to cool for 1 hour prior to slicing.

PER SERVING: *CALORIES 292 (From Fat 110); Fat 12g (Saturated 2g); Cholesterol 21mg; Sodium 21mg; Carbohydrate 38g (Dietary Fiber 2g); Protein 9g.*

TIP: After cooling, store in an airtight container at room temperature for up to 3 days. To freeze, wrap tightly in plastic wrap and place in a freezer-safe resealable bag for up to 1 month.

VARY IT! You can use Marcona almonds or sunflower seeds in place of walnuts.

Cottage Cheese and Dill Bread

PREP TIME: 25 MIN PLUS 1 HR 15 MIN FOR RISING	BAKE TIME: 30 MIN	YIELD: 16 SERVINGS

INGREDIENTS

14 grams (1 tablespoon plus 2 teaspoons) active dry yeast

118 grams (½ cup) warm water

12 grams (1 tablespoon) sugar

450 grams (2 cups) cottage cheese (4 percent milk fat)

38 grams (¼ cup) chopped green onions

6 grams (2 tablespoons) dried dill

9 grams (1½ teaspoons) kosher salt

2 eggs, beaten

540 grams (4½ cups) all-purpose flour

57 grams (¼ cup) salted butter, melted

DIRECTIONS

1 In the bowl of a stand mixer with a dough hook attachment, mix together the yeast, water, sugar, and cottage cheese. Let the mixture rest and bubble for 10 minutes.

2 Add the onions, dill, salt, eggs, and flour to the yeast mixture and knead with the dough hook on speed 2 for 7 minutes.

3 Spray a glass bowl with cooking spray and place the kneaded dough into the glass bowl.

4 Cover the bowl with a damp tea towel and let the dough rise for 45 minutes to 1 hour or until doubled in size.

5 Spray two bread pans with cooking spray and place parchment paper into the bread pans.

6 Gently press down on the dough and divide the dough in half.

7 Place the 2 pieces of doughs on a floured surface.

8 Pat each piece of dough into an 8-x-8-inch square and roll up, tucking the ends in as you roll the dough.

9 Place each piece of dough into a bread pan.

10 Cover the bread pans with a damp tea towel and let the doughs rise for 30 minutes.

11 Preheat the oven to 350 degrees.

12 Bake the breads for 30 to 35 minutes or until they reach an internal temperature of 200 degrees.

13 When the breads come out of the oven, immediately brush the surface with melted butter.

14 Serve warm or let cool for 1 hour before slicing.

PER SERVING: *Calories 193 (From Fat 47); Fat 5g (Saturated 3g); Cholesterol 38mg; Sodium 363mg; Carbohydrate 28g (Dietary Fiber 1g); Protein 8g.*

TIP: After cooling, store in an airtight container at room temperature for up to 3 days. To freeze, wrap tightly in plastic wrap and place in a freezer-safe resealable bag for up to 1 month.

NOTE: The cottage cheese and eggs give a richness to this dough, making it a perfect addition to a brunch menu or served alongside dinner.

TIP: If you want to make these into rolls, divide the dough into 16 balls and bake in standard muffin pans coated with cooking spray. Bake rolls for 20 to 25 minutes.

NOTE: If the cottage cheese is very liquidy, strain off the excess liquid or add in flour (as needed) to help balance the moisture.

VARY IT! If you're out of dill, use can use thyme, parsley, or basil instead. If you have fresh herbs on hand, use about ¼ cup of fresh herbs in place of the dried. You can also use 1 teaspoon onion powder in place of the chopped green onions. Ricotta cheese can be substituted for the cottage cheese, too.

Jalapeño Bread

PREP TIME: 20 MIN PLUS 1 HR FOR RISING	BAKE TIME: 30 MIN	YIELD: 16 SERVINGS

INGREDIENTS

17 grams (2 tablespoons) active dry yeast

117 grams (½ cup) warm water

4 grams (1 teaspoon) sugar

200 grams (2 cups) shredded cheddar cheese

28 grams (2 tablespoons) unsalted butter, melted

35 grams (⅓ cup) chopped pickled jalapeño peppers, drained

5 grams (1 teaspoon) salt

2 eggs

480 grams (4 cups) all-purpose flour

103 grams (1 cup) rye flour

DIRECTIONS

1 In the bowl of a stand mixer with a dough hook attached, mix together the yeast, water, and sugar. Let the mixture rest for 5 minutes.

2 Add in the shredded cheese, butter, jalapeños, salt, and eggs.

3 Mix for 1 minute on speed 2.

4 Add in the all-purpose flour and rye flour, and continue kneading the dough on speed 2 for 5 minutes.

5 Cover the bowl with a damp tea towel and allow the mixture to rise for 45 minutes to 1 hour in a warm, draft-free spot.

6 Lightly dust a flat surface with flour.

7 Put the dough onto the floured surface and divide the dough in half.

8 Flatten each piece of dough into an 8-x-8-inch square and roll up the dough into a log, tucking in the ends as you roll.

9 Spray 2 bread loaf pans with cooking spray and line with parchment paper.

10 Place each piece of dough into a bread pan.

11 Place the oven rack in the center position and preheat the oven to 400 degrees.

12 When the oven has heated, place the bread pans onto the center rack, close the oven door, and reduce the heat to 350 degrees.

13 Bake for 30 minutes or until golden brown and an internal temperature of 200 degrees is reached.

14 Remove the bread from the bread pans and allow to cool for at least 1 hour prior to slicing.

PER SERVING: *Calories 209 (From Fat 60); Fat 7g (Saturated 4g); Cholesterol 43mg; Sodium 227mg; Carbohydrate 29g (Dietary Fiber 2g); Protein 8g.*

TIP: After cooling, store in an airtight container at room temperature for up to 3 days. To freeze, wrap tightly in plastic wrap and place in a freezer-safe resealable bag for up to 1 month.

TIP: You can make these breads into individual rolls or bake in a muffin pan. Equally divide the dough into 16 pieces, roll into a ball, and place into a greased or sprayed oven tin. Bake for 25 minutes or until done.

VARY IT! Go bold with pepper jack cheese or mellow with colby. Swap out the jalapeños with black olives or black beans for a fun twist!

Onion Bread

PREP TIME: 25 MIN PLUS 2 HR FOR RISING	BAKE TIME: 25 MIN	YIELD: 10 SERVINGS

INGREDIENTS

13 grams (1 tablespoon) extra-virgin olive oil

1 medium onion, chopped

4 grams (1 teaspoon) sugar

5 grams (1 teaspoon) balsamic vinegar

245 grams (1 cup) warm milk

59 grams (¼ cup) warm water

8 grams (2 teaspoons) sugar

8 grams (1 tablespoon) active dry yeast

390 grams (3¼ cup) bread flour

9 grams (1½ teaspoons) kosher salt

1 egg

28 grams (2 tablespoons) unsalted butter, softened or at room temperature

30 grams (2 tablespoons) water, for brushing

DIRECTIONS

1   In a medium skillet, heat the olive oil over medium-high heat.

2   Add in the chopped onion and sauté for 5 minutes, stirring frequently.

3   Sprinkle in the sugar and balsamic vinegar and stir for 1 minute.

4   Remove the onion mixture from the heat and allow to cool for 10 minutes.

5   Meanwhile, in the bowl of a stand mixer with a dough hook attached, mix together the milk, water, sugar, and yeast. Let the mixture rest for 5 minutes.

6   Add the bread flour, salt, egg, and onion mixture to the bowl of the stand mixer.

7   Knead the dough on speed 2 for 6 minutes.

8   Coat the dough with butter.

9   Cover the bowl with a damp tea towel and let the dough rise for 1 hour or until doubled in size.

10   Lightly dust a flat surface with flour.

11   Put the dough onto the floured surface and press the dough gently.

12 Roll the dough into an oblong baguette shape.

13 Place a piece of parchment paper onto a heavy baking sheet and place the dough onto the parchment paper.

14 Cover and let the dough rise for 1 hour.

15 Preheat the oven to 400 degrees.

16 Using a serrated knife or bread lame, slice 3 diagonal slices across the surface of the dough, about ½-inch deep.

17 Brush the surface of the dough with water.

18 Place the dough into the oven and bake for 10 minutes.

19 Quickly brush or spritz the dough again with water and continue baking for 15 minutes or until an internal temperature of 180 to 190 degrees is reached.

PER SERVING: *Calories 214 (From Fat 51); Fat 6g (Saturated 2g); Cholesterol 30mg; Sodium 371mg; Carbohydrate 34g (Dietary Fiber 1g); Protein 7g.*

NOTE: After cooling, store in an airtight container at room temperature for up to 3 days. To freeze, wrap tightly in plastic wrap and place in a freezer-safe resealable bag for up to 1 month.

TIP: You can use a spray bottle to spray the surface gently with water to create steam while baking.

TIP: Prefer rolls? Divide the dough into 10 equal pieces and roll into rounds. Slice the surface of the dough before baking.

VARY IT! Add in ¼ cup grated Parmesan cheese or chopped salami for a savory addition.

Pumpkin Seed Bread

PREP TIME: 15 MIN PLUS 1 HR 30 MIN FOR RISING	BAKE TIME: 20 MIN	YIELD: 12 SERVINGS

INGREDIENTS

13 grams (1½ tablespoons) active dry yeast

294 grams (1¼ cup) warm water

12 grams (1 tablespoon) sugar

480 grams (4 cups) bread flour

60 grams (½ cup) pumpkin seeds (green, husked seeds)

23 grams (⅓ cup) powdered nonfat instant dry milk

9 grams (1½ teaspoons) kosher salt

1 egg

28 grams (2 tablespoons) sunflower oil or extra-virgin olive oil

DIRECTIONS

1 In the bowl of a stand mixer with a dough hook attached, mix together the yeast, water, and sugar. Let the mixture rest for 5 minutes.

2 Add in the flour, pumpkin seeds, milk, salt, egg, and oil.

3 Mix on speed 2 for 7 minutes.

4 Cover the bowl with a damp tea towel and allow the mixture to rise for 45 minutes to 1 hour in a warm, draft-free spot.

5 Lightly dust a flat surface with flour.

6 Put the dough onto the floured surface and divide in half.

7 Form the two doughs into a rustic formed, oblong-shaped baguette by flattening gently to about 12 inches in length and rolling slightly.

8 Place a piece of parchment paper onto a heavy baking sheet.

9 Place the free-formed baguettes onto the parchment paper, cover, and let rise for 45 minutes.

10 Place the oven rack in the center position and preheat the oven to 400 degrees.

11 When the oven has heated, place the baking sheet onto the center rack, close the oven door, and reduce the heat to 350 degrees.

12 Bake for 20 to 25 minutes or until golden brown and an internal temperature of 190 degrees is reached.

13 Allow the bread to cool for at least 1 hour prior to slicing.

PER SERVING: *Calories 200 (From Fat 643); Fat 5g (Saturated 1g); Cholesterol 18mg; Sodium 179mg; Carbohydrate 32g (Dietary Fiber 1g); Protein 7g.*

TIP: After cooling, store in an airtight container at room temperature for up to 2 days. To freeze, wrap tightly in plastic wrap and place in a freezer-safe resealable bag for up to 1 month.

NOTE: This bread makes for a perfect breakfast bread. Serve with scrambled eggs or cheese and meats for a European-style breakfast.

NOTE: This bread can also be baked into rolls. Divide the dough into 12 to 16 rolls and bake for 15 to 20 minutes.

VARY IT! Swap out any nut or seed for the green pumpkin seeds.

Rosemary Bread

PREP TIME: 15 MIN PLUS 1 HR 15 MIN FOR RISING	BAKE TIME: 45 MIN	YIELD: 12 SERVINGS

INGREDIENTS

13 grams (1½ tablespoons) active dry yeast

294 grams (1¼ cup) warm water

12 grams (1 tablespoon) sugar

480 grams (4 cups) bread flour

62 grams (½ cup) chopped walnuts

3 grams(1 tablespoon) chopped, dried rosemary

23 grams (⅓ cup) powdered nonfat instant dry milk

28 grams (2 tablespoons) extra-virgin olive oil

6 grams (1 teaspoon) kosher salt

1 egg

DIRECTIONS

1 In the bowl of a stand mixer with a dough hook attached, mix together the yeast, water, and sugar. Let the mixture rest for 5 minutes.

2 Add in the remaining ingredients and mix on speed 2 for 6 minutes.

3 Cover the bowl with a damp tea towel and allow the mixture to rise for 45 minutes to 1 hour in a warm, draft-free spot.

4 Lightly dust a flat surface with flour.

5 Form the dough into a round boule.

6 Place a piece of parchment paper onto a heavy baking sheet.

7 Place the boule onto the parchment paper, cover, and let rise for 30 minutes.

8   Place the oven rack in the center position and preheat the oven to 400 degrees.

9   When the oven has heated, place the baking sheet onto the center rack, close the oven door, and reduce the heat to 350 degrees.

10 Bake the boule for 45 to 50 minutes or until golden brown and an internal temperature of 190 degrees is reached.

11 Allow the bread to cool for at least 1 hour prior to slicing.

PER SERVING: *Calories 216 (From Fat 59); Fat 7g (Saturated 1g); Cholesterol 18mg; Sodium 179mg; Carbohydrate 32g (Dietary Fiber 2g); Protein 7g.*

TIP: After cooling, store in an airtight container at room temperature for up to 5 days or in the refrigerator for up to 1 week. To freeze, wrap tightly in plastic wrap and place in a freezer-safe resealable bag for up to 3 months.

NOTE: This bread can be baked as two smaller boules or as 12 to 16 rolls.

TIP: Serve this savory bread with stews or roasts.

VARY IT! Add in chopped garlic, grated Parmesan, or olives for zesty additions.

Southwestern Cilantro Bread

PREP TIME: 15 MIN PLUS 1 HR 30 MIN FOR RISING	BAKE TIME: 30 MIN	YIELD: 16 SERVINGS

INGREDIENTS

16 grams (2 tablespoons) active dry yeast

117 grams (½ cup) warm water

450 grams (2 cups) cottage cheese (4 percent milk fat)

24 grams (2 tablespoons) sugar

480 grams (4 cups) all-purpose flour

103 grams (1 cup) rye flour

2 green onions, finely chopped

13 grams (¼ cup) chopped cilantro

12 grams (2 teaspoons) salt

2 eggs

DIRECTIONS

1 In the bowl of a stand mixer with a dough hook attached, mix together the yeast, water, cottage cheese, and sugar. Let the mixture rest for 5 minutes.

2 Add in the all-purpose flour, rye flour, onions, cilantro, salt, and eggs.

3 Knead the dough on speed 2 for 5 minutes.

4 If your dough is still sticky, add in ¼ cup more all-purpose flour at a time, until it pulls from the edge of the bowl while kneading.

5 Cover the bowl with a damp tea towel and let the dough rise for 1 hour or until doubled in size.

6 Spray 2 bread pans with cooking spray and place parchment paper into the bread pans.

7 Place the dough onto a lightly floured surface.

8 Gently press down on the dough and divide the dough in half.

9 Pat each piece of dough into an 8-x-8-inch square and roll up, tucking in the ends as you roll the dough.

10 Place the dough into the bread pans.

11 Cover the bread pans with a damp tea towel and let the doughs rise for 30 minutes.

12 Preheat the oven to 400 degrees.

13 Place the dough into the oven and bake for 5 minutes.

14 Reduce the heat to 350 degrees and continue baking for 25 minutes or until an internal temperature of 180 to 190 degrees is reached.

15 Allow the breads to cool for 1 hour prior to slicing.

PER SERVING: *Calories 179 (From Fat 21); Fat 2g (Saturated 1g); Cholesterol 31mg; Sodium 245mg; Carbohydrate 31g (Dietary Fiber 2g); Protein 9g.*

TIP: After cooling, store in an airtight container at room temperature for up to 5 days or in the refrigerator for up to 1 week. To freeze, wrap tightly in plastic wrap and place in a freezer-safe resealable bag for up to 1 month.

NOTE: The cottage cheese and eggs give a richness to this dough, making it a perfect addition to a brunch menu or served alongside dinner.

TIP: If you want to make these into rolls, divide the dough into 16 balls and bake in standard muffin pans coated with cooking spray. Bake rolls for 20 to 25 minutes.

NOTE: If the cottage cheese is very liquidy, strain off the excess liquid or add in flour (as needed) to help balance the moisture.

NOTE: Rye is a whole-grain flour that doesn't have much gluten, so the rise may not be as significant with this loaf when baking. The rye also provides a unique flavor. You can use whole-wheat or spelt flour in place of the rye flour if you like.

Sun-Dried Tomato and Olive Bread

PREP TIME: 35 MIN PLUS 2 HR 30 MIN FOR RISING	BAKE TIME: 45 MIN	YIELD: 16 SERVINGS

INGREDIENTS

7 grams (1 package) active dry yeast

235 grams (1 cup) warm water

245 grams (1 cup) warm milk

25 grams (2 tablespoons) sugar

81.5 grams (½ cup) semolina flour

55 grams (½ cup) chopped sun-dried tomatoes

64 grams (½ cup) pitted black olives

9 grams (1½ teaspoons) salt

3 grams (1½ teaspoons) coarsely ground black pepper

226 grams (2 cups) whole-wheat flour

360 grams (3 cups) all-purpose flour

28 grams (2 tablespoons) extra-virgin olive oil

DIRECTIONS

1 In the bowl of a stand mixer with a dough hook attachment, mix together the yeast, water, milk, and sugar. Let the mixture rest and bubble for 5 minutes.

2 Add the semolina flour, tomatoes, olives, salt, and pepper to the yeast mixture and mix for 1 minute on speed 2.

3 Add the whole-wheat flour and all-purpose flour and knead on speed 2 for 4 minutes. Let the dough rest for 15 minutes.

4 Knead on speed 2 for 7 minutes.

5 If the dough still seems sticky, sprinkle in ¼ cup all-purpose flour and continue to knead for an additional minute.

6 Coat the dough with extra-virgin olive oil.

7 Cover the bowl with a damp tea towel and let the dough rise for 1½ hours or until doubled in size.

8 Gently press down on the dough and divide it in half.

9 Place the 2 pieces of dough on a floured surface.

10 Form the 2 pieces of dough into round boules.

11 Place a piece of parchment paper onto a heavy baking sheet.

12 Place the boules onto the parchment paper and over the bread pans and let the doughs rise for 1 hour.

13 Preheat the oven to 350 degrees.

14 Bake the breads for 45 to 50 minutes or until they reach an internal temperature of 180 degrees.

15 Allow the breads to cool at least 1 hour prior to slicing.

PER SERVING: *Calories 166 (From Fat 29); Fat 3g (Saturated 1g); Cholesterol 2mg; Sodium 294mg; Carbohydrate 30g (Dietary Fiber 3g); Protein 5g.*

TIP: After cooling, store the bread tightly wrapped at room temperature for up to 3 days. To freeze, wrap tightly in plastic wrap and place in a freezer-safe resealable bag for up to 3 months.

TIP: This is a hearty, rustic style bread which pairs perfectly with stews or summer salads. Serve with creamy goat cheese or cream cheese.

Swiss Gruyère Bread

PREP TIME: 25 MIN PLUS 1 HR 45 MIN FOR RISING	BAKE TIME: 30 MIN	YIELD: 10 SERVINGS

INGREDIENTS

4 slices bacon

8 grams (1 tablespoon) active dry yeast

12 grams (1 tablespoon) sugar

352 grams (1½ cups) warm water

420 grams (3½ cups) bread flour

5 grams (1 teaspoon) apple cider vinegar

6 grams (1 teaspoon) salt

100 grams (1 cup) grated Gruyère (Swiss) cheese

13 grams (1 tablespoon) extra-virgin olive oil

DIRECTIONS

1 In a large, heavy skillet, cook the bacon over medium heat for 8 minutes, flipping as needed to cook both sides.

2 Remove the bacon onto a cutting board.

3 Cool and reserve the bacon drippings.

4 In the bowl of a stand mixer with a dough hook attachment, mix together the yeast, water, and sugar. Let the mixture rest and bubble for 5 minutes.

5 Chop the cooled bacon.

6 Add the flour, vinegar, bacon, salt, and cheese to the yeast mixture and mix for 1 minute on speed 2.

7 Add in the bacon drippings and knead the dough on speed 2 for 5 minutes.

8 Coat the dough with extra-virgin olive oil.

9 Cover the bowl with a damp tea towel and let the dough rise for 45 minutes or until doubled in size.

10 Gently press down on the dough and divide it in half.

11 Place the 2 pieces of dough on a floured surface.

12 Form each piece of dough into a round snakelike baguette shape (see the Spelt Baguettes recipe in Chapter 7 for details).

13 Place a piece of parchment paper onto a heavy baking sheet.

14 Place the baguettes onto the parchment paper.

15 Cover with a towel and let rise for 1 hour.

16 Place the baking rack in the center of the oven and preheat the oven to 450 degrees.

17 Place the breads into the oven and immediately drop the temperature to 400 degrees.

18 Bake for 30 to 40 minutes or until the breads reach an internal temperature of 180 to 190 degrees.

19 Allow the breads to cool at least 1 hour prior to slicing.

PER SERVING: *Calories 241 (From Fat 72); Fat 8g (Saturated 3g); Cholesterol 17mg; Sodium 302mg; Carbohydrate 32g (Dietary Fiber 1g); Protein 9g.*

TIP: After cooling, store the bread tightly wrapped at room temperature for up to 3 days. To freeze, wrap tightly in plastic wrap and place in a freezer-safe resealable bag for up to 1 month.

TIP: Craving a warm bowl of soup? This bread is perfect to dip into your favorite tomato, bean, or potato soup!

VARY IT! You can use cheddar or pepper jack instead of Gruyère for a quick twist of flavors.

Summary Beet Bread

PREP TIME: 15 MIN PLUS 1 HR 30 MIN FOR RISING	BAKE TIME: 30 MIN	YIELD: 16 SERVINGS

INGREDIENTS

225 grams (1½ cups) boiled golden beetroot, skin removed

7 grams (1 packet) active dry yeast

50 grams (¼ cup) warm water

400 grams (3⅓ cups) all-purpose flour

1 egg

8 grams (1½ teaspoons) salt

85 grams (⅔ cup) chopped walnuts

26 grams (2 tablespoons) extra-virgin olive oil

DIRECTIONS

1 In a bowl, mash the cooked beets with a potato masher or ricer.

2 In the bowl of a stand mixer with a dough hook attached, mix together the yeast, water, and mashed beets. Let the mixture rest for 5 minutes.

3 Add in the flour, egg, salt, and chopped walnuts.

4 Knead the dough on speed 2 for 2 minutes.

5 Add in the extra-virgin olive oil and continue to mix on speed 2 for 8 minutes.

6 Cover the bowl with a damp tea towel and let the dough rise for 45 minutes or until doubled in size.

7 Place the dough onto a lightly floured surface.

8 Gently press down on the dough and divide the dough in 3 equal pieces.

9 Roll out each piece into a long, snakelike shape, about 1 inch thick and 10 inches in length.

10 Braid the 3 strands of dough (see Figure 8-1).

11 Place a piece of parchment paper onto a heavy baking sheet.

12 Place the braided bread onto the parchment paper, cover, and let the dough rest for 45 minutes.

13 Preheat the oven to 400 degrees.

14 Place the dough into the oven, turn the heat down to 350 degrees, and bake for 30 minutes or until an internal temperature of 180 to 190 degrees is reached.

15 Allow the bread to cool for 1 hour prior to slicing.

PER SERVING: *Calories 152 (From Fat 51); Fat 6g (Saturated 1g); Cholesterol 13mg; Sodium 210mg; Carbohydrate 21g (Dietary Fiber 1g); Protein 4g.*

TIP: After cooling, store the bread tightly wrapped at room temperature for up to 3 days. To freeze, wrap tightly in plastic wrap and place in a freezer-safe resealable bag for up to 1 month.

TIP: This bread is pure summer and perfect to serve with your favorite charcuterie board. Serve with goat cheese and chopped walnuts or a drizzle of honey.

VARY IT! You can use red or purple beets, but your dough will gray slightly while baking. Pumpkin seeds or sunflower seeds can be swapped in for walnuts.

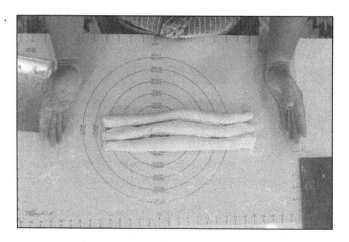

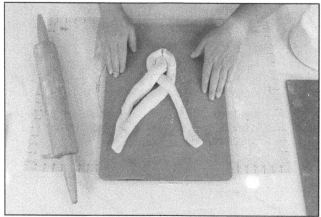

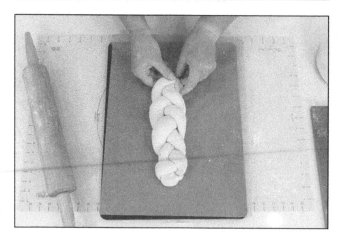

FIGURE 8-1:
Braiding bread.

Chapter **9**

Shaped Breads

n this chapter, you explore shaped breads — from rolls to knots to pretzels. Some of these recipes require a bit more time and patience than the recipes in other chapters, but the extra work pays off.

TIP

Read through the ingredients and instructions prior to starting these breads. You may be surprised the length of time required to make them.

Buttery Dinner Rolls

PREP TIME: 20 MIN PLUS 4 HR FOR RISING	BAKE TIME: 15 MIN	YIELD: 16 SERVINGS

INGREDIENTS

7 grams (2 teaspoons) active dry yeast

59 grams (¼ cup) warm water

25 grams (2 tablespoons) sugar

245 grams (1 cup) warm milk

6 grams (1 teaspoon) salt

113 grams (½ cup) unsalted butter, divided

390 grams (3¼ cups) all-purpose flour

1 egg

14 grams (1 tablespoon) safflower oil

DIRECTIONS

1 In the bowl of a stand mixer with a dough hook attachment, mix together the yeast, water, and sugar. Let the mixture rest for 5 minutes.

2 Add in the warm milk, salt, and 57 grams (¼ cup) of the butter. Mix on speed 2 for 1 minute. Add in 195 grams (1½ cup plus 2 tablespoons) of the flour. Mix on speed 2 for 2 minutes. Add in the egg and the remaining flour. Mix on speed 2 for 4 minutes. Cover the bowl with a damp tea towel and allow the mixture to rise for 1 hour in a warm, draft-free spot.

3 Slightly press down on the dough to release the air. Rub the dough with oil, cover the bowl with plastic wrap, and refrigerate for at least 2 hours or up to 24 hours. Letting the dough refrigerate for at least 8 hours will help develop the flavors.

4 Lightly dust a flat surface with flour. Divide the dough in half to make it easier to roll.

5 Roll 1 piece of the dough into a large rectangular shape (about 8 x 12 inches). Using a pastry brush, brush the top of the square with melted butter. Fold in half on the long edge. Using a pizza cutter or dough blade, cut the dough into 8 equal rectangles. Repeat with the remaining piece of dough. Brush the tops with the remaining butter, cover with a towel, and set aside.

6 Liberally coat a 16 rounds in a muffin pan with butter. Place a buttery piece of dough into each spot of the tin to open like a butterfly (see Figure 9-1). Allow the rolls need to rest 1 hour before baking.

7 Preheat the oven to 350 degrees.

8 Bake the rolls for 15 to 20 minutes or until golden brown and an internal temperature of 190 to 200 degrees is reached. Serve the rolls hot out of the oven or allow to cool before serving.

PER SERVING: *Calories 169 (From Fat 70); Fat 8g (Saturated 4g); Cholesterol 30mg; Sodium 182mg; Carbohydrate 21g (Dietary Fiber 1g); Protein 4g.*

TIP: Store at room temperature in an airtight container up to 3 days.

TIP: You will need two 12-muffin pans for this recipe. In each of the unused muffin spaces, add 1 tablespoon of water; this helps your pan stay in good shape and keeps it from warping. If you don't have two pans, you can shape and bake on a baking sheet, but they'll spread more than they will in pans.

TIP: If you like working with exact pieces, know that the average weight of a roll is about 45 to 50 grams, so weigh each piece out as you work with the dough to get approximately the same size in each roll.

VARY IT! You can add in chopped garlic or fresh herbs like rosemary or thyme, or sprinkle with Parmesan cheese if you like.

FIGURE 9-1:
Placing the dough in the muffin tin.

Crusty Sourdough Rolls

PREP TIME: 30 MIN
PLUS 7 HR FOR RISING

BAKE TIME: 25 MIN

YIELD: 16 SERVINGS

INGREDIENTS

220 grams (1 cup) hot water (for soaking)

25 grams (¼ cup) whole-kernel Khorasan, einkorn, or spelt grains

50 grams (¼ cup) starter

385 grams (1⅔ cups) warm water

500 grams (4 cups) bread flour

30 grams (¼ cup) sunflower seeds

14 grams (1 tablespoon) kosher salt

DIRECTIONS

1   In a small bowl, place the hot water and whole kernels of Khorasan, einkorn, or spelt grains. Let this mixture soak for 30 minutes or until Step 3.

2   In a large glass bowl, mix together the starter and warm water. Add in the bread flour and sunflower seeds until it looks like a shaggy mess. Cover with a damp tea towel and let the dough rest for 30 minutes.

3   Drain the kernels from the water.

4   Place the kernels and salt onto the dough mixture.

5   Stretch and fold the dough 6 times to incorporate the grains.

6   Cover with a towel and rest for 30 minutes.

7   Stretch and fold the dough another time.

8   Cover with a towel and rest for 6 to 8 hours.

9   Lightly flour a flat surface.

10   Place the dough onto the floured surface, flipping to coat each side of the dough.

11   Working with floured hands, divide the dough into 16 equal pieces (weighing about 60 grams each). Cover the dough while working with each piece.

12 To roll the dough, pinch the dough to the center and rotate a quarter turn, repeating until a round roll begins to take shape.

13 Place the rounded roll onto a well-floured surface and coat with flour.

14 Place the roll, pinched side up, onto a parchment-lined baking sheet.

15 Repeat with the remaining pieces of dough.

16 Cover and let the rolls rest for 1 hour.

17 With the oven rack set to the center, preheat the oven to 450 degrees.

18 When the oven has heated, place the baking sheet onto the center rack, close the oven door, and reduce the heat to 400 degrees.

19 Bake for 25 minutes or until golden brown and an internal temperature of 180 degrees is reached.

20 Serve hot or at room temperature.

PER SERVING: *Calories 135 (From Fat 14); Fat 2g (Saturated 0g); Cholesterol 0mg; Sodium 340mg; Carbohydrate 25g (Dietary Fiber 1g); Protein 5g.*

NOTE: Store in a bread box or wrapped in an airtight container for 2 days. Freeze in an airtight container for up to 1 month.

TIP: This roll makes for a perfect addition to a breakfast or dinner! Serve this with your favorite soup, salad, or boiled eggs.

VARY IT! If you can't find these old-world grains, try quinoa, flaxseeds, or millet instead.

Hot Dog Buns

PREP TIME: 20 MIN PLUS 1 HOUR 45 MIN FOR RISING	BAKE TIME: 15 MIN	YIELD: 10 SERVINGS

INGREDIENTS

245 grams (1 cup) whole milk

113 grams (½ cup) unsalted butter

25 grams (2 tablespoons) sugar

7 grams (2 teaspoons) active dry yeast

480 grams (4 cups) all-purpose flour

2 eggs

12 grams (2 teaspoons) kosher salt

DIRECTIONS

1   Place the milk in a heat-safe bowl and microwave on high for 1 minute and 30 seconds.

2   Pour the hot milk into the bowl of a stand mixer with a dough hook attached.

3   Add in the butter and stir until the butter has melted and the milk has cooled.

4   Add in the sugar and yeast.

5   Let the mixture rest for 5 minutes.

6   Add in the flour, eggs, and salt and mix on speed 2 for 8 minutes.

7   Cover the bowl with a damp tea towel and allow the mixture to rise for 1 hour in a warm, draft-free spot.

8   Place a piece of parchment paper on a heavy baking sheet.

9   Lightly dust a flat surface with flour.

10   Place the dough on the floured surface and roll out the dough in a 20-x-20-inch square.

11   Cut the dough into 10 equal squares.

12   Working with 1 piece at a time, roll out the square into a 6-x-4-inch rectangle.

13   Roll up the rectangle from the long side, tucking the ends as you roll.

14   Pinch the seam between your fingers to seal the seam.

15   Place the hot dog roll, seam-side down, onto the parchment paper.

16 Repeat Steps 11–14 with the remaining pieces of dough.

17 Cover the shaped buns with a towel and allow the breads to rise for 45 minutes.

18 Preheat the oven to 350 degrees.

19 Bake the buns for 15 to 20 minutes or until golden brown and an internal temperature of 200 degrees is reached.

20 Allow the buns to cool for at least 30 minutes prior to slicing.

PER SERVING: *CALORIES 295 (From Fat 104); Fat 12g (Saturated 7g); Cholesterol 69mg; Sodium 453mg; Carbohydrate 40g (Dietary Fiber 1g); Protein 7g.*

TIP:STORE in an airtight container at room temperature or in a bread box for 3 days or in the freezer for up to 1 month.

VARY IT!Prefer a seeded bun? Brush the surface of the buns with an egg wash (1 egg plus 1 tablespoon of water, whisked), and sprinkle the tops with sesame seeds, onion flakes, or poppy seeds.

VARY IT!If you'd like to add in more whole grains, replace 1 cup of all-purpose flour with 1 cup of whole-wheat flour.

TIP: To make hamburger buns, check out the nearby sidebar.

MAKING HAMBURGER BUNS

To make hamburger buns, when you get to Steps 9 through 15 in the Hot Dog Buns recipe, do the following instead:

1. **Divide the dough into 8 portions for regular hamburger buns.**

2. **Working with 1 piece of dough at a time, form the dough into a ball shape.**

3. **Gently pull a piece up toward the center, and then rotate the dough one-quarter turn, repeating until the dough shape tightens.**

4. **Pinch the seam at the top, and rock the ball in a circular motion on the flat surface to smooth out the ball shape.**

5. **Flatten the dough into a 4-inch round.**

6. **Place the round onto the parchment paper and repeat with remaining pieces of dough.**

Bakery Sandwich Rolls

PREP TIME: 20 MIN PLUS 1 HR 30 MIN FOR RISING	BAKE TIME: 20 MIN	YIELD: 12 SERVINGS

INGREDIENTS

8 grams (1 tablespoon) active dry yeast

294 grams (1¼ cups) warm water

28 grams (2 tablespoons) safflower or canola oil

68 grams (⅓ cup) sugar

1 egg

420 grams (3½ cups) bread flour

9 grams (1½ teaspoons) kosher salt

DIRECTIONS

1 In the bowl of a stand mixer with a dough hook attached, mix together the yeast, water, oil, and sugar. Let the mixture rest for 5 minutes.

2 Add in the egg, flour, and salt. Mix on speed 2 for 6 minutes.

3 Cover the bowl with a damp tea towel and allow the mixture to rise for 45 minutes in a warm, draft-free spot.

4 Lightly dust a flat surface with flour.

5 Place the dough onto the floured surface and divide into 12 parts. These are a rustic formed, oblong sandwich-style baguette.

6 Form the dough by flattening each piece gently to about 6 inches in length and rolling slightly to form a baguette.

7 Place the parchment paper onto 2 heavy baking sheets.

8 Place the free-formed baguettes onto the parchment paper (about 6 per baking sheet), cover, and let rise for 45 minutes.

9 Place 2 oven racks equally spaced apart from the bottom and top of the oven and preheat the oven to 400 degrees.

10 When the oven has heated, score the tops of the rustic sandwich baguettes with a single slit down the center of the top, about ½-inch deep.

11 Place the baking sheets onto the racks, close the oven door, and reduce the heat to 350 degrees.

12 Bake for 20 to 25 minutes or until golden brown and an internal temperature of 180 to 190 degrees is reached.

13 Allow the bread to cool for at least 30 minutes prior to slicing.

PER SERVING: *Calories 176 (From Fat 30); Fat 3g (Saturated 0g); Cholesterol 18mg; Sodium 298mg; Carbohydrate 31g (Dietary Fiber 1g); Protein 5g.*

TIP: Store in an airtight container at room temperature or a bread box for up to 3 days.

TIP: Serve these breads with your favorite sandwich toppings! These are my go-to submarine-style sandwiches for picnics and family outings. They're also great in French dip sandwiches!

Croissants

PREP TIME: 5 HR PLUS 2 HR 45 MIN FOR RISING	BAKE TIME: 15 MIN	YIELD: 14 SERVINGS

INGREDIENTS

8 grams (2½ teaspoons) active dry yeast

310 grams (1⅓ cups) warm water

40 grams (¼ cup) sugar

500 grams (3½ cups) pastry or cake flour

8 grams (1¼ teaspoons) salt

200 grams (1 cup) cold, unsalted butter

1 egg yolk

46 grams (3 tablespoons) whole milk

DIRECTIONS

1 In the bowl of a stand mixer with a dough hook attached, mix together the yeast, water, and sugar. Let the mixture rest for 5 minutes. Add in the pastry flour and salt. Knead for 5 minutes. Cover and let rise in the refrigerator for about 30 minutes.

2 Meanwhile, to prepare the butter, fold a piece of parchment paper to form an 8-x-8-inch square. Open the paper and place the butter in the middle. Refold the paper and use a rolling pin to press the butter until flat. Roll out the butter with a rolling pin until it reaches the folded edges. The butter should be equal in thickness throughout. Place the butter form in the refrigerator for 20 minutes.

3 Take the dough and butter out of the refrigerator. Roll out the dough on a floured work surface into a rectangular shape. The dough should be three times the width of the butter form. Place the butter form in the center of the dough and fold over both sides of dough onto the butter to create the layers. Press the ends together so that the butter stays in place. Carefully roll out the dough widthwise. Starting from the middle, roll to both sides.

4 Carefully dust flour on the surface of the dough. Again, looking at the dough as though it is divided into thirds, fold the left third onto the middle third and press carefully. Brush off the excess flour, place the right third on top and press firmly. Wrap the dough in parchment paper and place in the refrigerator for 30 to 45 minutes.

5 Repeat this process 3 more times (roll out, brush off flour, fold, refrigerate). This results in a total of 81 layers of butter in the dough. Be sure to fully chill the dough between rollings. After the final folding, roll the dough out to about 8 x 24 inches.

6 Cut the dough into triangles: Make marks on the upper edges every 4 inches. On the bottom edge, make the first mark at

2 inches and then mark at 4-inch intervals. Cut the dough with a pizza cutter. For each triangle, make a 1-inch slit at the wide part of the triangle. Brush off any excess flour.

7   Roll the wider end toward the tip (see Figure 9-2). Bend the ends slightly inward to form a croissant shape, and place the croissant on a baking sheet covered with parchment paper. Repeat until all croissants are formed. Cover and let rise at room temperature for approximately 45 minutes.

8   Preheat the oven to 375 degrees.

9   In a small bowl, mix the egg and milk. Brush the croissants with the egg mixture.

10   Bake for 15 to 17 minutes or until they have a deep, golden color.

PER SERVING: *Calories 250 (From Fat 111); Fat 12g (Saturated 8g); Cholesterol 46mg; Sodium 226mg; Carbohydrate 31g (Dietary Fiber 1g); Protein 4g.*

TIP: Store in an airtight container at room temperature for up to 3 days. Croissants freeze well, either baked or unbaked. Frozen croissants can be stored for up to 3 months. To bake, defrost unbaked, frozen croissants overnight, covered on a parchment-lined baking sheet, and bake in the morning as in the recipe.

FIGURE 9-2:
Roll the croissant.

Sharon's Challah Bread

PREP TIME: 25 MIN PLUS 3 HR FOR RISING	BAKE TIME: 45 MIN	YIELD: 16 SERVINGS

INGREDIENTS

235 grams (1 cup) warm water

8 grams (1 tablespoon) active dry yeast

50 grams (¼ cup) sugar

3 eggs, divided

72 grams (⅓ cup) canola or safflower oil

480 grams (4 cups) all-purpose flour, divided

12 grams (2 teaspoons) Kosher salt

Sesame seeds (optional)

Poppy seeds (optional)

Sea salt (optional

DIRECTIONS

1 In the bowl of a stand mixer with a dough hook attachment, mix the water, yeast, and sugar. Let the mixture rest for 5 minutes.

2 Add in 2 of the eggs and the oil, and mix at speed 1 for 1 minute.

3 Add in 360 grams (3 cups) of the flour and the salt. Knead for 5 minutes.

4 If the dough seems wet and sticky, add in the remaining flour a little at a time until the dough is not sticky to the touch. Then knead for an additional 5 minutes. The dough should be smooth and only slightly sticky.

5 Place the dough into an oiled bowl

6 Cover and let rest in a warm spot for 2 hours. You can punch down gently once after about 1 hour and then let it continue to rise.

7 Ready a flat surface with flour.

8 Place the dough onto the floured surface and knead to release the air and get the dough smooth, about 2 minutes.

9 Divide the dough into 2 equal pieces. Divide each of the dough pieces into 3 equal pieces. Working with a scale can help ensure equal pieces.

10 Cover the dough with a towel when you aren't working with the dough.

11 Working with 1 piece at a time, roll out into 12-inch, snake-like pieces.

12 Cover and continue until you have 6 pieces.

13 Braid 2 loaves, with each loaf having 3 strands. (Refer to Figure 9-2 for a visual guide to braiding.)

14 Place parchment paper onto 2 baking sheets.

15 Place the braided loaves onto the baking sheets and cover the loaves.

16 Allow the loaves to rise for 1 hour.

17 Preheat the oven to 400 degrees.

18 In a small bowl, beat the remaining egg with a fork, until combined.

19 Using a pastry brush, brush the loaves, making sure to get into the crevices of the braids. Sprinkle the loaves with desired toppings or leave plain.

20 Bake for 7 minutes at 400 degrees and then lower the heat to 375 degrees for 25 to 30 minutes, or until an internal temperature of 180 to 190 is reached.

21 Slide the parchment paper onto a cooling rack to cool. Do not leave the baked bread on the baking sheets to cool.

PER SERVING:_CALORIES 176 (From Fat 52); Fat 6g (Saturated 1g); Cholesterol 40mg; Sodium 280mg; Carbohydrate 26g (Dietary Fiber 1g); Protein 4g._

TIP: Store in an airtight container or bread box at room temperature for 3 to 5 days.

TIP: Challah bread makes for a decadent French toast or bread pudding.

TIP: Serve with fresh jam, whipped honey butter, or go savory with cream cheese and chives.

English Muffins

PREP TIME: 15 MIN PLUS 1 HR 15 MIN FOR RISING | BAKE TIME: 20 MIN | YIELD: 12 SERVINGS

INGREDIENTS

325 grams (1⅓ cup) milk

28 grams (2 tablespoons) unsalted butter

5 grams (1¾ teaspoons) active dry yeast

12 grams (1 tablespoon) sugar

1 egg

480 grams (4 cups) bread flour

82 grams (½ cup) semolina flour

DIRECTIONS

1 In a microwave-safe bowl, heat the milk on high for 1½ minutes.

2 Add the unsalted butter to the milk to cool the milk and melt the butter.

3 In the bowl of a stand mixer with a dough hook attached, mix together the yeast, warm milk mixture, and sugar. Let the mixture rest for 5 minutes.

4 Add in the egg and bread flour. Mix on speed 2 for 5 minutes.

5 Cover the bowl with a damp tea towel and allow the mixture to rise for 1 hour in a warm, draft-free spot.

6 Place the parchment paper onto a baking sheet and sprinkle with semolina flour.

7 Lightly dust a flat surface with flour.

8 Place the dough onto the floured surface and divide into 12 equal parts.

9 Roll each piece of dough into a ball and press between the palm of your hands to a 4-inch circle.

10 Place the pieces of pressed dough onto the semolina flour, flipping to coat both sides.

11 Cover the dough and let them rise for 15 minutes.

12 Place a heavy griddle or cast-iron skillet on the stovetop. Heat over low for 5 minutes.

13 Working in batches, cook the English muffins for 10 minutes on each side, until an internal temperature of 190 to 200 degrees is reached. If your English muffins are sticking to the griddle, add more semolina flour or lightly coat with canola oil. If your English muffins are beginning to brown too much before the internal temperature shows they're done cooking, heat your oven to 325 degrees and bake for 10 minutes or until done.

14 Serve hot or cool for 1 hour before slicing.

PER SERVING: *Calories 213 (From Fat 36); Fat 4g (Saturated 2g); Cholesterol 25mg; Sodium 19mg; Carbohydrate 36g (Dietary Fiber 1g); Protein 7g.*

TIP: Store in an airtight container at room temperature for up 2 days. You can also preslice and store your English muffins in the freezer. Pop them in the toaster for a quick and breakfast any day of the week!

TIP: Serve these sliced and toasted with your favorite butter and jam.

Twisted Semolina Breadsticks

PREP TIME: 15 MIN PLUS 1 HR FOR RISING	BAKE TIME: 15 MIN	YIELD: 18 SERVINGS

INGREDIENTS

8 grams (2½ teaspoons) active dry yeast

352 (1½ cups) warm water

4 grams (1 teaspoon) sugar

163 grams (1 cup) semolina flour

300 grams (2½ cups) all-purpose flour

12 grams (2 teaspoons) sea salt

65 grams (½ cup) extra-virgin olive oil, divided

25 grams (¼ cup) grated Parmesan cheese

2 grams (2 teaspoons) dried oregano

1 gram (½ teaspoon) crushed red pepper flakes (optional)

DIRECTIONS

1 In the bowl of a stand mixer with a dough hook attached, mix together the yeast, water, and sugar. Let the mixture rest for 5 minutes.

2 Add in the semolina flour, all-purpose flour, sea salt, and ¼ cup of the extra virgin olive oil. Mix on speed 2 for 5 minutes.

3 Cover the bowl with a damp tea towel and allow the mixture to rise for 1 hour in a warm, draft-free spot.

4 Slightly press down on the dough to release the air.

5 Lightly dust a flat surface with flour.

6 Place the dough on the floured surface, flipping over to coat lightly with flour.

7 Roll out the dough into a 9-x-12-inch square.

8 Using a pizza cutter, cut the dough in 1-x-6-inch pieces.

9 Roll each piece of dough into a 10- to 12-inch snakelike piece.

10 Place parchment paper onto 2 heavy baking sheets.

11 Take a breadstick in your two hands and twist the breadstick 2 to 3 times to create a twist.

12 Place the twisted breadsticks 2 inches apart on the baking sheet.

13 Using a pastry brush, brush the breadsticks with the remaining olive oil.

14 Sprinkle the breadsticks with Parmesan cheese, dried oregano, and crushed red pepper flakes (if desired).

15 Preheat the oven to 400 degrees.

16 Place the breadsticks in the oven and reduce the heat to 350 degrees.

17 Bake the breadsticks for 15 to 20 minutes.

18 Serve hot or at room temperature.

PER SERVING: *Calories 133 (From Fat 39); Fat 4g (Saturated 1g); Cholesterol 1mg; Sodium 259mg; Carbohydrate 20g (Dietary Fiber 1g); Protein 4g.*

NOTE: Store in an airtight container at room temperature for up to 2 days.

VARY IT! Mix up your toppings with grated Romano, Pecorino, or Mozzarella cheeses. Top with fresh, chopped basil or parsley after baking for a fresh pop of color and flavor.

Wheat Bagels

PREP TIME: 15 MIN PLUS 12 HR FOR RISING | BAKE TIME: 20 MIN | YIELD: 10 SERVINGS

INGREDIENTS

5 grams (2 teaspoons) active dry yeast

350 grams (1¼ cup) warm water

35 grams (5 teaspoons) honey, divided

170 grams (1½ cups) whole-wheat flour

300 grams (2½ cups) all-purpose flour

12 grams (2 teaspoons) kosher salt

14 grams (1 tablespoon) safflower or canola oil

Everything bagel seasoning or steak seasoning mix (optional)

Sesame seeds (optional)

Poppy seeds (optional)

DIRECTIONS

1 In the bowl of a stand mixer with a dough hook attached, mix together the yeast, water, and 15 grams (2 teaspoons) honey. Let the mixture rest for 5 minutes.

2 Add in the whole-wheat flour, all-purpose flour, and salt. Mix on speed 2 for 5 minutes.

3 Place the oil in a glass bowl.

4 Place the dough into the bowl and coat with the oil.

5 Cover the bowl with plastic wrap and refrigerate 8 to 12 hours.

6 Line a baking sheet with parchment paper.

7 Place 10 cups of water into a stock pot with 20 grams honey (3 teaspoons) and begin to heat to a boil.

8 Meanwhile, on a flat surface dusted with flour, divide the dough into 10 equal balls (roughly 100 grams each) and roll each ball out into a 4-inch-diameter circle.

9 Wet your hands. Using your fingers, pierce the center of the dough and stretch and rotate the center eyelet in the dough to form a hole.

10 Place the dough back onto the lightly floured surface and continue working with each ball of dough.

11 Place the oven rack in the center position. Preheat the oven to 425 degrees.

12 Boil the bagels 2 to 3 at a time for 3 minutes, stirring once or twice to ensure the bagels are not sticking to the bottom of the pot.

13 Place the boiled bagels onto the parchment paper and top with desired seasonings. Continue until all bagels are parboiled.

14 Bake for 20 to 25 minutes or until they reach an internal temperature of 180 to 190 degrees.

15 Let cool for 1 hour before slicing or serve hot.

PER SERVING: *Calories 192 (From Fat 19); Fat 2g (Saturated 0g); Cholesterol 0mg; Sodium 428mg; Carbohydrate 38g (Dietary Fiber 3g); Protein 6g.*

NOTE: Store in an airtight container at room temperature for up to 2 days. If you use salt on the surface, the bagels may weep and stale faster.

TIP: Serve these whole-wheat bagels with cream cheese, smoked salmon, sliced red onions, capers, and lemon slices.

Franzi's Pretzels (Brezeln)

PREP TIME: 45 MIN PLUS 12 HR 20 MIN FOR RISING	BAKE TIME: 12 MIN	YIELD: 9 SERVINGS

INGREDIENTS

2 grams (¾ teaspoon) active dry yeast

100 grams (½ cup) warm water

15 grams (2 teaspoons) honey

110 grams (½ cup plus 2 tablespoons) whole milk

500 grams (2½ cups) cake or pastry flour

80 grams (⅓ cup or 1 medium) boiled and mashed potato

10 grams (1¾ teaspoon) salt

26 grams (2 tablespoons) unsalted butter

18 grams of food-grade lye crystals

470 grams (2 cups) cold water

Coarse salt

Water, for spraying pretzels after baking

DIRECTIONS

1   In the bowl of a stand mixer with a dough hook attached, mix together the yeast, warm water, and honey. Let the mixture rest for 5 minutes. Add in the milk, flour, potato, salt, and butter. Knead together for 6 minutes. The dough should be elastic and smooth, not sticking to the side of the bowl. Cover and let rise in the refrigerator overnight for 10 to 12 hours.

2   The next morning, place the dough on an unfloured surface and cut into 9 cylindrical pieces. Each piece should weigh approximately 95 to 100 grams. Roll each piece into a snake-like piece, tapered at each end. Cover and let rest for 5 minutes.

3   Begin stretching out each piece of dough in 3 stages. This allows the dough to stretch and relax. Starting with your hands in the middle, roll the dough outward to a length of 8 inches so that the middle is thick and the ends are thin and long. Repeat with the other pieces. Then, return to the first one and using the same rolling technique, and leaving a thicker center, roll out to 16 inches; repeat with the remaining pieces. Finally, roll the dough out to around 30 inches; the ends will be tapered off and much thinner than the rest of the dough, with the center still thicker.

4   Form the pretzel: Holding one end in each hand, carefully lift the dough and twist around two times quickly; then set it down over the dough, exposing the bulge of the center (see Figure 9-3). Press each loose end on top of each side in a typical pretzel form. Stretch the form out a bit and place it on parchment paper. Cover and let the dough rest for 2 hours.

5   Place the pretzels in the refrigerator for 15 minutes uncovered (this will create a skin or crust on the surface).

6   Put on protective eyewear and gloves. In a large bowl, combine the lye crystals and cold water.

7 Preheat the oven to 500 degrees. Prepare double-lined parchment paper or silicone-lined baking sheets.

8 Using a large skimmer or wooden tongs, dip each pretzel form into the lye solution for 4 to 5 seconds. Then place the pretzel onto the clean parchment paper or silicone. Repeat with the remaining 8 pretzels. Clean any metal tools immediately after dipping all the pretzels in warm, soapy water. *Warning:* Be sure to wear gloves and safety glasses! Always use parchment paper when working with lye — it will corrode any metal surface it touches. If you prefer not to use lye, check out the Tip at the end of this recipe for an alternative.

9 Using a sharp serrated knife or bread lame, make a ¼-inch cut on top of the thickest part of the pretzel (between where you pressed each end). Sprinkle the pretzels with coarse salt. Place the pretzels in the oven and lower the heat to 445 degrees. Bake for 12 to 15 minutes.

10 Immediately after taking out of the oven, use a water-filled, food-safe spray bottle and spritz the pretzels with water. This gives the crust a shinier look.

PER SERVING: *Calories 243 (From Fat 29); Fat 3g (Saturated 2g); Cholesterol 7mg; Sodium 578mg; Carbohydrate 47g (Dietary Fiber 1g); Protein 5g.*

TIP: Store in an airtight container at room temperature for up to 2 days. If you want to keep them longer, omit the salt and store in the freezer. (Salt will make the surface weep with moisture, turning the pretzels stale quicker.)

TIP: If you prefer to avoid lye, you can use a baking soda solution instead. Make a strong baking soda solution by adding 60 grams of baking soda to 1 liter (4¼ cups) of water; stir and bring to a boil. Then dip the pretzels into the solution one at a time for 30 seconds each. You'll end up with a browner and less shiny pretzel than you can achieve with a lye solution.

NOTE: To dispose of lye, simply dilute the lye mixture with an additional 8 cups of water before dumping in a drain.

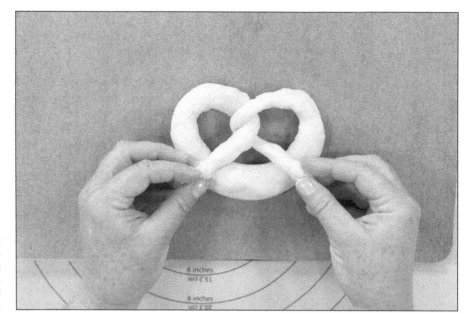

FIGURE 9-3:
Place the ends to the sides of the bigger bottom, creating a pretzel shape.

Chapter **10**

Going Global

Have you had the chance to travel the world and try different breads? Even if a vacation is out of the question, you can still transport yourself to other worldly places through bread! From French baguettes to Turkish flatbreads, you can excite your senses with breads of the world, all from the comfort of your own home. While living in Europe, I gained a new perspective on artisan breads and secrets to making really good bread, secrets I share in this chapter.

TIP

Some of these recipes call for a "well-fed starter." This refers to feeding your starter twice daily for at least two days prior to baking. It helps make the starter happy, healthy, and active! Some recipes require making a *poolish*, also referred to as *levain, biga,* or *madre bianca* around the globe. This is also called a *pre-ferment,* where you basically take your starter, feed it with a certain type of flour/water blend, and let it rise prior to mixing it with the remaining ingredients, for sometimes hours or even days. These small details are what make artisan breads so special. These differences yield incredible results, which can't be imitated with commercial yeast.

In Europe, neighbors often bring a gift of salt and bread to new neighbors or newly married couples. Why? So that they always have a full pantry and have the necessities of life. Such an endearing gift of welcome. Bread is the gift that keeps on giving. Share a loaf with a neighbor soon!

French Baguettes

| PREP TIME: 15 MIN PLUS 2 HR 30 MIN FOR RISING | BAKE TIME: 18 MIN | YIELD: 10 SERVINGS |

INGREDIENTS

290 grams (1¼ cups) warm water

7 grams (2¼ teaspoons or 1 packet) active dry yeast

450 grams (4¾ cups) bread flour

9 grams (1½ teaspoons) salt

DIRECTIONS

1 In the bowl of a stand mixer with a dough hook attached, place the water, yeast, and flour.

2 Mix the ingredients on low speed for 1 minute.

3 Sprinkle in the salt and continue mixing on speed 2 or 3 for 6 minutes or until the dough is smooth and elastic.

4 Cover and let the dough rest for 1½ hours.

5 Press on the dough to release the gas.

6 Roll out the dough into 2 small baguettes about 10 inches long or 1 large baguette about 18 inches long (or as long as your baking sheet will allow).

7 Line a baking sheet with parchment paper.

8 Place the rolled baguette onto the parchment paper.

9 Cover and let the dough rest for an additional hour or until the dough has doubled in size.

10 Preheat the oven to 450 degrees with a rack positioned at the center of the oven.

11 Using a lame or serrated knife, score the dough diagonally every 3 inches on the large baguette, or simply down the center for smaller baguettes.

12 Place the bread onto the center rack of the oven and immediately reduce the temperature to 400 degrees.

13 Bake for 18 to 22 minutes or until golden brown in color.

PER SERVING: *Calories 165 (From Fat 7); Fat 1g (Saturated 0g); Cholesterol 0mg; Sodium 350mg; Carbohydrate 33g (Dietary Fiber 1g); Protein 6g.*

TIP: Use baguettes within 1 day or par-bake and freeze for later.

NOTE: This recipe is simple and one you can double or even triple if needed. You can also *parbake* (bake for 15 minutes), and then remove from the oven and cool. Wrap tightly and place the parbaked bread into the freezer. Now you can have freshly baked baguettes any night of the week! Simply bake for 5 to 8 minutes at 400 degrees right out of the freezer.

TIP: Refer to the Spelt Baguettes (Chapter 7) for tips on rolling out baguettes.

German Twisted Baguettes

PREP TIME: 1 HR 15 MIN PLUS 2 HR 30 MIN FOR RISING	BAKE TIME: 30 MIN	YIELD: 12 SERVINGS

INGREDIENTS

570 grams (1¼ cup plus 2 tablespoons plus 3⅓ cups) all-purpose flour, divided

2.9 grams (⅓ teaspoon plus 1 teaspoon) active dry yeast, divided

40 grams (2 tablespoons) rye-fed sourdough starter

420 grams (3 cups) water, divided

30 grams (¼ cup plus 1 tablespoon) rye flour

12 grams (2½ teaspoons) salt

DIRECTIONS

1 In a medium bowl, mix together 170 grams (1¼ cups plus 2 tablespoons) of the all-purpose flour, 0.5 gram (⅓ teaspoon) of the yeast, 40 grams (2 tablespoons) of the starter, and 140 grams (1 cup) of the water.

2 Cover and let rise at room temperature for at least 1 hour or a maximum of 5 hours.

3 In the bowl of a stand mixer with a dough hook attached, place the mixture from Step 1.

4 Add the remaining 400 grams (3⅓ cups) of all-purpose flour, the rye flour, the salt, the remaining 2.4 grams (1 teaspoon) of yeast, and the remaining 280 grams (2 cups) of water.

5 Knead for 5 to 10 minutes or until the dough is smooth and elastic.

6 Cover and let rise at room temperature for about 1 hour and 30 minutes.

7 Place the dough on a lightly floured work surface and divide into three equal pieces.

8 Line a baking sheet with parchment paper.

9 Carefully form each piece into a baguette (a long, snakelike shape).

10   Holding one end of the baguette, twist the other end until the strand looks twisted.

11   Place the twisted dough onto the baking sheet.

12   Repeat with the other two pieces of dough.

13   Cover and let the 3 baguettes rise for about 1 hour.

14   Preheat the oven to 500 degrees.

15   Bake for 5 minutes.

16   Lower the temperature to 400 degrees and bake for another 25 minutes. The baguettes should be golden in color.

17   Serve warm or let cool to room temperature for easier slicing.

PER SERVING: *Calories 189 (From Fat 5); Fat 1g (Saturated 0g); Cholesterol 0mg; Sodium 389mg; Carbohydrate 40g (Dietary Fiber 2g); Protein 5g.*

TIP: Store tightly wrapped at room temperature or in a bread box for up to 3 days.

NOTE: You can tightly twist the dough to give this bread a fun, twisted shape or keep the dough loosely twisted for a relaxed baguette appearance. In Germany, you'll often find baguettes more tightly twisted.

German Everyday Rolls

PREP TIME: 72 HR PLUS 2 HR 45 MIN FOR RISING	BAKE TIME: 20 MIN	YIELD: 9 SERVINGS

INGREDIENTS

500 grams (¾ cup plus 2⅔ cups) all-purpose flour, divided

80 grams (⅓ cup) water

4 grams (1½ teaspoons) active dry yeast, divided

11 grams (½ teaspoon plus 1⅓ teaspoons) salt, divided

120 grams (½ cup) warm water

95 grams (⅓ cup) whole milk

20 grams (2 tablespoons) sesame seeds, poppy seeds, sunflower seeds, or pumpkin seeds

DIRECTIONS

1 In a medium bowl, mix 120 grams (¾ cup) of the flour, the 80 grams (⅓ cup) of water, 2 grams (¾ teaspoon) of the yeast, 3 grams (½ teaspoon) of the salt.

2 Cover and let rise in the refrigerator for 3 days.

3 In the bowl of a stand mixer with a dough hook attached, place the mixture from Step 1.

4 Add the remaining 380 grams (2⅔ cups) of flour, the 120 grams (½ cup) of warm water, the milk, the remaining 2 grams (¾ teaspoon) of the yeast, and the remaining 8 grams (1⅓ teaspoons) of salt.

5 Knead for 7 minutes or until elastic and smooth.

6 Cover and let rest at room temperature for 90 minutes.

7 Place the dough on a lightly floured work surface and divide into 9 pieces (approximately 90 grams each).

8 Roll each piece into a ball.

9 Cover and let rest for 10 to 15 minutes.

10 Lightly flour the pieces and press them flat; then fold them inward.

11 Cover the formed rolls upside down on a slightly floured work surface and let them rise for 45 to 60 minutes.

12 Preheat the oven to 450 degrees.

13 Spray the top of the rolls with water and dip them into the desired seeds.

14 Line a baking sheet with parchment paper.

15 Place the rolls on the baking sheet and spray with water again.

16 Bake for about 20 minutes.

PER SERVING: *Calories 210 (From Fat 8); Fat 1g (Saturated 0g); Cholesterol 1mg; Sodium 480mg; Carbohydrate 43g (Dietary Fiber 2g); Protein 1g.*

TIP: Store in an airtight container at room temperature for 2 to 3 days.

NOTE: This is a standard German roll, often made into sandwiches or served with butter and jam in the mornings. The shape is similar to a Kaiser roll.

German Braided Sweet Breads

PREP TIME: 15 MIN PLUS 1 HR 45 MIN FOR RISING	BAKE TIME: 25 MIN	YIELD: 16 SERVINGS

INGREDIENTS

550 grams (3¾ cups) all-purpose flour

3 grams (2⅓ teaspoons) active dry yeast

430 grams (1¾ cups) whole milk, divided

80 grams (⅓ cup) unsalted butter

1 egg

192 grams (⅓ cup plus 1 tablespoon plus ½ cup) sugar, divided

1.25 grams (¼ teaspoon) salt

8.4 grams (2 teaspoons) vanilla extract, divided

250 grams (2 cups) ground hazelnuts

5.28 grams (½ teaspoon) cinnamon

1 egg yolk

30 grams (2 tablespoons) coarse sugar

DIRECTIONS

1 In the bowl of a stand mixer with a dough hook attached, place the flour, the yeast, 250 grams (1 cup) of the milk, the butter, the egg, 92 grams (⅓ cup plus 1 tablespoon) of the sugar, the salt, and 4.2 grams (1 teaspoon) of the vanilla.

2 Knead for 6 to 8 minutes or until elastic and smooth.

3 Cover and let rise for about 1 hour at room temperature.

4 Place the dough on a lightly floured work surface.

5 Roll out the prepared dough into a rectangle (approximately 12 x 20 inches).

6 In a bowl, mix together the hazelnuts, the remaining 100 grams (½ cup) of the sugar, 150 grams (10 tablespoons) of the milk, the cinnamon, and the remaining 4.2 grams (1 teaspoon) of the vanilla.

7 Spread the nut filling on the dough.

8 Roll up the dough and cut the roll in half lengthwise.

9 Twist the two halves together so the filling faces the top.

10 Place in a buttered pan or on a baking sheet lined with parchment paper and let rise for 30 to 45 minutes.

11 Preheat the oven to 350 degrees.

12 In a small bowl, mix together the egg yolk and the remaining 30 grams (2 tablespoons) of milk.

13 Brush onto the braided loaf.

14 Sprinkle with the coarse sugar.

15 Bake for approximately 25 to 30 minutes.

PER SERVING: *Calories 332 (From Fat 138); Fat 15g (Saturated 4g); Cholesterol 40mg; Sodium 48mg; Carbohydrate 42g (Dietary Fiber 2g); Protein 7g.*

TIP: Wrap tightly in a towel and store in a brown paper bag or in a bread box at room temperature for up to 2 days.

NOTE: Don't be fooled by the word *sweet* in the name of this recipe. Many of the sweeter baked goods in Europe are far less sweet than the traditional American baked goods. Many Europeans enjoy an afternoon coffee or tea with a sweet bread like this one. Try serving this at a brunch or on a holiday.

TIP: You can coat this bread with a sugar glaze after baking if you like.

Meme's Swedish Brown Bread

PREP TIME: 20 MIN PLUS 2 HR FOR RISING	BAKE TIME: 45 MIN	YIELD: 16 SERVINGS

INGREDIENTS

500 grams (2 cups) whole milk

470 grams (2 cups) water

14 grams (5 teaspoons) active dry yeast

245 grams (¾ cup) molasses

100 grams (½ cup) sugar

416 grams (4 cups) rye or whole-wheat flour

240 grams (2 cups) bread flour

28 grams (2 tablespoons) shortening, butter, or bacon drippings

11 grams (2 teaspoons) salt

Oil

DIRECTIONS

1 In a microwave-safe bowl, heat the milk for 2 minutes.

2 In the bowl of a stand mixer with a dough hook attached, mix together the milk, water, yeast, molasses, and sugar.

3 Let sit for 5 minutes.

4 Add in the whole-wheat flour; the bread flour; the shortening, butter, or bacon drippings; and the salt.

5 Knead for 6 to 8 minutes. The dough should be stiff but not too dry.

6 Oil a glass bowl.

7 Place the dough into the bowl, cover, and let rise for 1 to 2 hours or until doubled in size.

8 Place the dough on a lightly floured surface and hand knead for 3 minutes.

9 Divide the dough into 3 equal pieces.

10 Roll each piece into a loaf (square, then roll up while tucking in the edges).

Dark Rye Bread (Chapter 6)

Golden Honey Wheat Sourdough (Chapter 7)

WENDY JO PETERSON

WENDY JO PETERSON

Chocolate Swirled Bread (Chapter 11)

Spelt Baguettes (Chapter 7), Sun-Dried Tomato Hummus (Chapter 14), Olive and Pine Nut
Spread (Chapter 14), and Sweet Potato and Pumpkin Seed Spread (Chapter 14)

Sun-Dried Tomato and Olive Bread (Chapter 8)

WENDY JO PETERSON

French Baguettes (Chapter 10)

WENDY JO PETERSON

Franzi's Pretzels (Brezeln) (Chapter 9)

Salted Pecan Cinnamon Rolls (Chapter 11)

WENDY JO PETERSON

Rustic Sourdough (Chapter 7)

WENDY JO PETERSON

European Muesli Bread (Chapter 11)

Josh's Texas Klobasneks (Chapter 12)

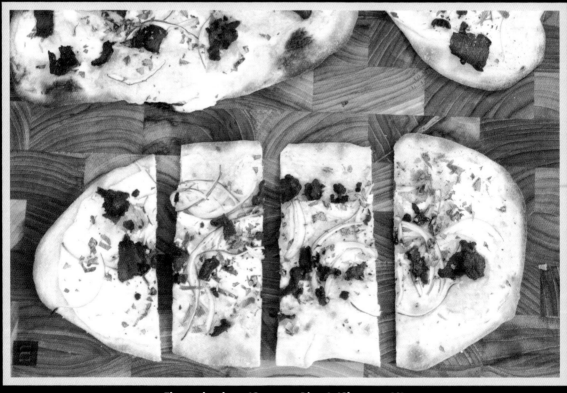

Flammkuchen (German Pizza) (Chapter 12)

Cheesy Kinder Crackers (Chapter 13)

Salted Dark Chocolate Brownies (Chapter 13)

WENDY JO PETERSON

WENDY JO PETERSON

WENDY JO PETERSON

Glazed Doughnuts (Chapter 11)

WENDY JO PETERSON

Baked Dutch Oven Pancakes (Chapter 13)

11 Spray 3 bread pans with cooking spray and line with parchment paper.

12 Place the dough into each bread pan.

13 Cover and let rise for 1½ hours.

14 Preheat the oven to 350 degrees.

15 Bake for 40 to 45 minutes or until an internal temperature of 180 to 190 degrees is reached.

16 Let cool for 2 hours prior to slicing or serve warm.

PER SERVING: *Calories 196 (From Fat 23); Fat 3g (Saturated 1g); Cholesterol 6mg; Sodium 230mg; Carbohydrate 39g (Dietary Fiber 3g); Protein 5g.*

TIP: Store in an airtight container at room temperature for up to 3 days.

NOTE: This bread has a slightly sweet taste to it. Meme, my Swedish grandmother, would make this for my family using whatever flour or fat she had on hand, and it was always delicious. You can make it with what you have on hand, too!

TIP: Traditionally, Meme baked these in old coffee cans, which have a nostalgic look to them. You can bake these as mini loaves or in standard bread pans.

NOTE: The dough can be rolled into rolls and loaves. Keep the rolls to about 50 grams per roll.

Nordic Sunflower Bread

PREP TIME: 15 HR PLUS 1 HR 45 MIN FOR RISING	BAKE TIME: 40 MIN	YIELD: 12 SERVINGS

INGREDIENTS

190 grams (⅔ cup plus 1⅛ cups) rye flour, divided

7 grams (1 teaspoon) rye sourdough starter

270 grams (⅓ cup plus ¾ cup) water, divided

250 grams (1⅛ cups plus ½ cup) sunflower seeds, divided

100 grams (½ cup) cold water

12 grams (2 teaspoons) salt

300 grams (2⅛ cups) all-purpose flour

3 grams (1 teaspoon) active dry yeast

14 grams (1 tablespoons) unsalted butter

DIRECTIONS

1   In a large bowl, mix together 70 grams (⅔ cup) of the rye flour, the rye sourdough starter, and 7 grams (⅓ cup) of the water.

2   Cover and let rise at room temperature for 15 to 20 hours.

3   In a small skillet, heat 150 grams (1⅛ cups) of the sunflower seeds over medium heat (without oil) for 1 to 2 minutes, until the seeds become fragrant, but do not brown.

4   In a small bowl, mix the roasted seeds with the cold water and salt.

5   Cover with plastic wrap or a towel and let soak for at least 5 hours.

6   In the bowl of a stand mixer with a dough hook attached, the polish from Step 2, the seeds from Step 5, the remaining 120 grams (1⅛ cups) rye flour, the all-purpose flour, the yeast, and the remaining 200 grams (¾ cup) water.

7   Knead together on level 2 for 5 to 7 minutes.

8   Cover and let rise at room temperature for about 45 minutes.

9   Place the dough on a lightly floured work surface.

10   Stretch and fold the dough into the length of a loaf pan.

11 Sprinkle the dough with water (or rub with wet hands) and roll it in the remaining 100 grams (½ cup) of sunflower seeds.

12 Grease the bread pan with the butter and put the dough into the pan.

13 Cover and let rise at room temperature for 60 to 90 minutes.

14 Preheat the oven to 475 degrees.

15 Bake for 5 minutes.

16 Lower the temperature to 400 degrees and bake for another 35 to 45 minutes.

17 Cool the bread in the pan for 10 minutes. Remove and continue to cool for 1 hour before slicing.

PER SERVING: *Calories 278 (From Fat 110); Fat 12g (Saturated 2g); Cholesterol 3mg; Sodium 391mg; Carbohydrate 36g (Dietary Fiber 4g); Protein 9g.*

TIP: Wrap tightly in a towel and store in a brown paper bag or in a bread box at room temperature for up to 3 days.

NOTE: If you travel throughout Scandinavia, Germany, Austria, Poland, or Switzerland, you'll surely note the love of sunflower seeds, especially in breads. This bread is delicious as a sandwich bread or toasted and topped with butter and jam.

VARY IT! Swap out the sunflower seeds with pumpkin seeds if you like.

Swabian Farmhouse Bread

PREP TIME: 30 MIN PLUS 3 HR FOR RISING	BAKE TIME: 45 MIN	YIELD: 12 SERVINGS

INGREDIENTS

350 grams (3 cups) bread flour

75 grams (½ cup) all-purpose flour

75 grams (¾ cup) rye flour

2.5 grams (1 teaspoon) active dry yeast

15 grams (1 tablespoon) well-fed sourdough starter

75 grams (1 medium) boiled potato, mashed and cooled

7 grams (1 teaspoon) honey

10 grams (1⅔ teaspoons) salt

400 grams (1¾ cups) water

DIRECTIONS

1 In the bowl of a stand mixer with a dough hook attached place the bread flour, all-purpose flour, rye flour, yeast, starter, potato, honey, salt, and water.

2 Knead on speed 2 for 15 to 20 minutes, until elastic and smooth. The dough will be very soft.

3 Cover and let rise for 3 hours at room temperature.

4 After 2½ hours, place a baking sheet in the oven and preheat the oven to 500 degrees.

5 With wet hands, round and tighten the dough into a boule shape.

6 Place the boule on a piece of parchment paper and immediately transfer to the hot baking sheet in the oven. Bake for 15 minutes.

7 Lower the temperature to 375 degrees and bake for another 30 minutes.

PER SERVING: *Calories 160 (From Fat 6); Fat 1g (Saturated 0g); Cholesterol 0mg; Sodium 324mg; Carbohydrate 33g (Dietary Fiber 2g); Protein 5g.*

TIP: Wrap tightly in a towel and store in a brown paper bag or in a bread box at room temperature for up to 3 days.

NOTE: This is a staple bread throughout Southern Germany. It works great as a rustic bread with soups or stews or with sliced meats and cheeses.

German Potato Bread

PREP TIME: 30 MIN PLUS 13 HR FOR RISING	BAKE TIME: 45 MIN	YIELD: 12 SERVINGS

INGREDIENTS

150 grams (1 large) boiled potato, mashed and cooled

400 grams (3⅓ cups) all-purpose flour

50 grams (½ cup) rye flour

320 grams (1⅓ cups) water

11 grams (1¾ teaspoons) salt

50 grams (¼ cup) well-fed sourdough starter

DIRECTIONS

1   In the bowl of a stand mixer with a dough hook attached place the potato, all-purpose flour, rye flour, water, salt, and starter.

2   Knead on level 2 for 6 minutes or until the dough is elastic.

3   Cover and let rise overnight for 10 to 12 hours at room temperature.

4   Place the dough on a floured work surface.

5   Stretch, fold, and round the dough into a boule shape.

6   With the closure on the bottom, place the dough in a well-floured banneton or fermenting basket (or see the Note below), cover, and let rise for 1 hour.

7   After 30 minutes, place a Dutch oven into the oven and pre-heat to 475 degrees.

8   After another 30 minutes, take the Dutch oven out of the oven and place the dough into the pot.

9   Put the lid on the Dutch oven, and place it into the oven.

10   Lower the temperature to 450 degrees and bake for 45 minutes.

PER SERVING: *Calories 155 (From Fat 4); Fat 0g (Saturated 0g); Cholesterol 0mg; Sodium 357mg; Carbohydrate 33g (Dietary Fiber 2g); Protein 4g.*

TIP: Wrap tightly in a towel and store in a brown paper bag or in a bread box at room temperature for up to 3 days.

NOTE: If you don't have a fermenting basket or banneton, place a piece of parchment paper into a large bowl, and rub the dough with flour. Then place the dough, seam-side down, on the parchment paper.

TIP: Serve with brats or stew. This bread is a rustic bread that is a real crowd pleaser!

Italian Focaccia

PREP TIME: 20 MIN PLUS 3 HR FOR RISING	BAKE TIME: 20 MIN	YIELD: 16 SERVINGS

INGREDIENTS

Semolina Mix:

150 grams (¾ cup) semolina flour

600 grams (2½ cups) boiling water

Main dough ingredients:

650 grams (4½ cups) all-purpose flour

15 grams (1¼ tablespoon) sugar

25 grams (1 tablespoon plus 1 teaspoon) salt

10 grams (1 tablespoon plus ½ teaspoon) active dry yeast

80 grams (½ cup) extra-virgin olive oil, divided

2.8 grams (½ teaspoon) sea salt

2.24 grams (2 teaspoons) minced dried rosemary

DIRECTIONS

1 In the bowl of a stand mixer with a dough hook attached, mix the semolina flour and the boiling water. Let cool.

2 Add in the all-purpose flour, the sugar, the salt, the yeast, and 40 grams (¼ cup) of the olive oil.

3 Knead together for 8 minutes. The dough will appear somewhat crumbly at the beginning but becomes smooth and elastic as it's kneaded.

4 When the dough is smooth and elastic in texture, cover and let rise at room temperature for about 1½ hours.

5 Spread the remaining 40 grams (¼ cup) of olive oil on the baking sheet.

6 Place the dough on the baking sheet and flip it over once so that the top is also covered with oil.

7 Use oily fingers to stretch the dough to the size of the baking sheet without kneading it. The air should remain in the dough.

8   If desired, add a little more olive oil to the top of the dough.

9   Sprinkle with sea salt and rosemary and let rest for 15 to 30 minutes.

10   Preheat the oven to 425 degrees.

11   Bake the focaccia for about 20 to 24 minutes.

12   Serve immediately or at room temperature.

PER SERVING: *Calories 231 (From Fat 50); Fat 6g (Saturated 1g); Cholesterol 0mg; Sodium 675mg; Carbohydrate 39g (Dietary Fiber 2g); Protein 6g.*

TIP: Focaccia doesn't store well. Eat it the day you make it — you won't be able to resist anyway!

Turkish Flatbread

PREP TIME: 15 MIN PLUS 2 HR 15 MIN FOR RISING	BAKE TIME: 10 MIN	YIELD: 8 SERVINGS

INGREDIENTS

30 grams (2 tablespoons) well-fed sourdough starter

500 grams (4 cups) all-purpose flour

50 grams (3 tablespoons plus 2 teaspoons) extra-virgin olive oil

4 grams (1¼ teaspoons) active dry yeast

10 grams (1½ teaspoons) salt

280 grams (1¼ cups) water

7 grams (1 tablespoon) black caraway seeds

9 grams (1 tablespoon) sesame seeds (black or white)

DIRECTIONS

1 In the bowl of a stand mixer with a dough hook attached, place the starter, flour, olive oil, yeast, salt, and water.

2 knead for 5 to 7 minutes or until elastic and smooth.

3 Cover and let rise at room temperature for 90 minutes.

4 Place the dough on a lightly floured work surface and divide into 8 equal pieces.

5 Stretch, fold, and round each piece of dough.

6 Cover and let rise for 45 to 60 minutes.

7 Preheat the oven to 475 degrees.

8 Press each piece of dough to a diameter of approximately 8 inches.

9 With oiled fingers, make irregular indentations, being sure not to break through and create a hole in the dough.

10 Sprinkle with the caraway seeds and sesame seeds and place in the oven.

11 Bake for 5 minutes.

12 Lower the temperature to 375 degrees and bake for another 5 to 10 minutes or until golden in color.

PER SERVING: *Calories 301 (From Fat 68); Fat 8g (Saturated 1g); Cholesterol 0mg; Sodium 487mg; Carbohydrate 50g (Dietary Fiber 2g); Protein 7g.*

TIP: These flatbreads are best eaten the same day they're made.

TIP: Flatbreads make for a great accompaniment to kebabs, curry, or your favorite salad.

VARY IT! Before baking, try topping them with sliced olives and tomatoes, or garlic and herbs.

Japanese Milk Bread

PREP TIME: 45 MIN PLUS 3 HR FOR RISING	BAKE TIME: 30 MIN	YIELD: 8 SERVINGS

INGREDIENTS

50 grams (3 tablespoons plus 1 teaspoon) water

250 grams (½ cup plus 1 tablespoon plus 1⅔ cups) bread flour, divided

3 grams (1 teaspoon) active dry yeast

15 grams (1 tablespoon) sugar

150 grams (½ cup plus 2 tablespoons) whole milk

15 grams (1 tablespoon) unsalted butter, cut into small cubes

200 grams (1⅔ cups) bread flour

5 grams (1 teaspoon) salt

5 grams (1 teaspoon) vegetable oil

DIRECTIONS

1 In a medium saucepan, heat the water until boiling.

2 Turn off the heat and stir in 50 grams (½ cup plus 1 tablespoon) of the bread flour with a fork.

3 Let the *tangzhong* cool to room temperature, cover with plastic wrap, and then place in the refrigerator for 4 to 12 hours. The longer the *tangzhong* chills in the refrigerator, the better the performance of the *tangzhong*.

4 In the bowl of a stand mixer with a dough hook attached, mix together the *tangzhong,* yeast, sugar, milk, butter, and the remaining 200 grams (1⅔ cups) of bread flour.

5 Stir on speed 2 for 1 minute.

6 Cover and let rest for 30 minutes. This is to autolyze, or allow the flour to take up moisture before adding the salt.

7 Next, add in the salt.

8 Knead on speed 2 for 12 minutes.

9 Increase the speed to speed 6 and continue kneading for 10 more minutes.

10 Divide the dough into 3 equal parts.

11 Roll each part into a ball and then press gently to flatten.

12 Cover and let the dough rest for 20 minutes to relax the dough.

13   Spray a standard bread pan with cooking spray, and place a piece of parchment paper into the bread pan.

14   Using a rolling pin, roll each piece of dough into a 8-x-4-inch rectangle.

15   Fold in the long sides of each rectangle into the center, and then roll the dough into a 4-inch roll, tucking in the edges as you roll.

16   Pinch the seams closed on the bottom.

17   Place the 3 rolled doughs side-by-side and seam-side down into the bread pan.

18   Cover the bread with a damp tea towel and let the dough rise in the bread pan for 45 minutes.

19   Preheat oven to 400 degrees.

20   Brush the top of the bread with oil, then place the bread pan into the oven and bake for 5 minutes.

21   Reduce the temperature to 350 degrees and continue to bake for 25 minutes.

22   Using the parchment paper, lift the bread out of the bread pan and cool on the counter for at least 3 hours prior to slicing.

PER SERVING: *Calories 152 (From Fat 30); Fat 3g (Saturated 1g); Cholesterol 6mg; Sodium251mg; Carbohydrate 26g (Dietary Fiber 1g); Protein 5g.*

TIP: Store in an airtight container at room temperature for up to 5 days.

NOTE: Serve this bread as a soft sandwich bread.

YiaYia's Holiday Bread

PREP TIME: 45 MIN PLUS 3 HR FOR RISING	BAKE TIME: 30 MIN	YIELD: 20 SERVINGS

INGREDIENTS

490 grams (2 cups) milk, divided

396 grams (2 cups) sugar, divided

25 grams (3 tablespoons) active dry yeast

250 grams (1 cup) fresh squeezed orange juice

224 grams (1 cup) vegetable oil

6 eggs, divided

1,560 to 1,680 grams (13 to 14 cups) all-purpose flour, divided

13 grams (1 tablespoon) vanilla extract

6 grams (1 teaspoon) mastika (see Note)

15 grams (1 tablespoon) milk

71 grams (½ cup) sesame seeds

DIRECTIONS

1 In a medium saucepan, heat 160 grams (⅔ cup) of the milk over medium heat until the milk warms to 105 to 110 degrees. Immediately remove from the heat and stir in 13 grams (1 tablespoon) of the sugar and the yeast. Set this mixture aside to activate the yeast.

2 In another saucepan, heat the remaining 330 grams (1⅓ cups) of the milk and the remaining 383 grams (1¾ cup plus 3 tablespoons) of the sugar over low heat, stirring to dissolve the sugar. When the sugar is dissolved, add in the orange juice and oil.

3 In a medium bowl, whisk 6 of the eggs.

4 In the bowl of a stand mixer with a dough hook attached, add the yeast mixture, the milk and orange juice mixture, the whisked eggs, 1,560 grams (13 cups) of the flour, the vanilla, and the mastika.

5 Mix on level 2 for 8 minutes. The dough will be sticky. If it's too moist to handle, knead in the remaining flour 30 grams (¼ cup) at a time.

6 Coat your hands and a glass bowl with vegetable oil, and transfer the bread to the bowl.

7 Cover and let the dough rise for 2 hours, or until doubled in size.

8 Press down the risen dough.

9 Divide the dough into 9 equal pieces.

10 Roll each piece out into a snakelike shape, approximately 8 inches in length.

11 Braid the 3 pieces together for one loaf. Repeat with the remaining pieces to make 5 loaves in total.

12 Place parchment paper onto 2 baking sheets.

13 Place the braided doughs onto the baking sheets, 2 loaves on one sheet and 1 loaf on the other.

14 Cover and let the breads rise for 45 minutes to 1 hour.

15 In a small bowl, whisk together the remaining 1 egg and the milk.

16 After the bread has risen, brush the tops of the dough with the egg mixture and sprinkle with sesame seeds.

17 Preheat the oven to 325 degrees.

18 Bake the breads for 30 minutes or until an internal temperature of 200 degrees is reached.

PER SERVING: *Calories 535 (From Fat 150); Fat 17g (Saturated 2g); Cholesterol 77mg; Sodium 39mg; Carbohydrate 83g (Dietary Fiber 3g); Protein 12g.*

TIP: After the bread is cooled, wrap it tightly in a tea towel and store in a brown paper bag for up to 3 days.

NOTE: Mastika, a traditional Greek spice from the resin of the Mastic tree, is traditional in this recipe. You can purchase this spice online or order from a market called Titans in Astoria, New York (www. titanfoods.net).

NOTE: This is a traditional holiday bread throughout Greece shared by my dear friend Hope Damergis. It was her mother, Eleni's recipe. Typically, it's baked with red eggs in the center or 3 boiled eggs pressed into the dough. Sometimes families wrap a coin in foil and place it into the dough for children to find and treasure.

NOTE: If the breads are browning too quickly, reduce the heat to 300 degrees.

Sahar's Yemeni Roti

PREP TIME: 15 MIN PLUS 1 HR 30 MIN FOR RISING	BAKE TIME: 25 MIN	YIELD: 8 SERVINGS

INGREDIENTS

294 grams (1¼ cups) warm water

6 grams (2 teaspoons) active dry yeast

4 grams (1 teaspoon) sugar

3 grams (½ teaspoon) salt

360 grams (3 cups) bread flour

60 grams (¼ cup) extra-virgin olive oil

DIRECTIONS

1 In the bowl of a stand mixer with a dough hook attached, place the water, yeast, sugar, salt, and flour.

2 Knead for 5 to 7 minutes or until elastic and smooth. The dough shouldn't be dry or too sticky. If it's dry, add a small amount of water. If it's sticky, knead in more flour in Step 5, as needed.

3 Take the dough out and place it onto a lightly floured surface.

4 Divide the dough into 8 equal parts.

5 Roll each part into a ball, cover, and let rise on the same surface for 30 minutes.

6 Working with 1 ball at a time, using a rolling pin, roll out the dough into an 8-inch oval.

7 Roll up each piece of dough in a snakelike form. It should be 8 inches in length.

8 Where the seam is, pinch each piece of dough to close the seam.

9 Brush an 8-x-12-inch baking dish with some of the extra-virgin olive oil.

10 Place the pieces of dough, seam-sides down, into the dish, about ½ inch apart.

11 Brush the bread with the remaining olive oil.

12 Cover and let the dough rise for 1 hour or until doubled in size.

13 Preheat the oven to 425 degrees.

14 Bake for 25 to 30 minutes or until golden brown.

PER SERVING: *Calories 233 (From Fat 75); Fat 8g (Saturated 1g); Cholesterol 0mg; Sodium 147mg; Carbohydrate 33g (Dietary Fiber 1g); Protein 6g.*

TIP: This bread is best eaten the day it's prepared.

NOTE: This dough is traditionally baked in a roti pan, which looks like separate breadsticks, so it gets crispy on all sides while baking.

NOTE: This bread is traditionally served with beans or curried sauces.

Chapter **11**

Sweet Treats

Sweetened yeast breads have a special place in the United States, from cinnamon rolls to doughnuts. In Europe, you find slightly sweetened breads, like the European Muesli Bread in this chapter — a perfect way to jump-start your day. The breads consist of a richer dough, made with eggs, milk, butter, and sugars. These additions give the breads a tender crumb.

If you're craving a sourdough-based breakfast bread, try the California Fruit and Nut Sourdough, which is one of my family's favorites. This bread isn't as rich as traditional sweet yeast breads, but the longer ferment time softens the texture. If you enjoy sourdough breads, you'll want to give this one a try!

If you're looking for a perfect brunch or holiday addition, this chapter will enhance your menu options. A decadent addition is the Monkey Bread, but if you want something with a hint of sweetness, try the Chocolate Swirled Bread. French toast or bread pudding fans, rejoice! Many of these breads will shine dipped in an egg-and-milk mixture and cooked into French toast or bread puddings.

REMEMBER

Temperature matters. Yeast is alive, and if your home is warmer, the yeast will be more active and the breads will rise quicker. Be mindful of the time of year in which you're baking and watch how your bread rises over these exact times.

Diana's Babkallah

PREP TIME: 30 MIN PLUS 5 HR FOR RISING	BAKE TIME: 30 MIN	YIELD: 10 SERVINGS

INGREDIENTS

1 orange

Lukewarm water

8.4 grams (1 tablespoon) active dry yeast

84 grams (6 tablespoons) unsalted butter, softened

8 grams (2 teaspoons) vanilla extract

85 grams (¼ cup) honey

2 large eggs

1 large egg yolk

480 grams (4 cups) all-purpose flour

6 grams (1 teaspoon) salt

190 grams (⅔ cup) Nutella or Chocolate Hazelnut Spread (see Chapter 14)

1 large egg, beaten

15 grams (1 tablespoon) water

DIRECTIONS

1 Zest and juice the orange, reserving half the zest for the filling later. Put the orange juice into a liquid measuring cup and add enough lukewarm water to measure ½ cup. Put the water-and-juice mixture into the bowl of a stand mixer with a dough hook attached, and add the yeast, half of the zest, the butter, the vanilla, the honey, the eggs, the egg yolk, the flour, and the salt. Knead on speed 2 for about 5 minutes or until the dough is smooth and soft. It will still be a bit sticky. Cover the bowl and allow the dough to rest for about 1½ to 2 hours, or until it's slightly puffy. It won't necessarily double in size.

2 Gently deflate the dough, and transfer it to a lightly floured surface. Divide the dough in half as evenly as you can (or use a scale to be precise). Shape each piece of dough into a rough ball, cover with a towel, and allow to rest for about 15 minutes.

3 In a small bowl, combine the Nutella with the remaining orange zest.

4 Using a rolling pin, roll each ball of dough into a 15-x-12-inch rectangle. Spread the Nutella mixture evenly onto both rectangles. Starting with the 15-inch edge, roll the dough up (similar to cinnamon rolls) and seal the seams. Place both logs onto a tray, cover, and refrigerate for 1 to 2 hours. This dough is *very* soft and can be difficult to work with, so refrigerating the dough at this point will help with the next step of shaping.

5 Cut each log in half (along the long side), exposing the filling. You now have 4 half-circle logs. Place the pieces vertically onto a greased or parchment-lined sheet pan, slightly close together. This shape is challenging to move after it's together, so shape it directly on the pan you'll be baking it on. Pinch together the far ends and slightly fan out the closer ends.

6   For this braid, the left piece will be referred to as 1, and moving to the right for 2, 3, and 4. The number doesn't follow each strand. Whichever position the is piece in determines its number. Starting with 4, go 4 over 3, 2 over 3, and then 1 under 2. Keep repeating this pattern until the braid is shaped, pinching the ends together to seal.

7   Cover the dough and let rise until it's very puffy and doubled, about 1½ to 2 hours. If your dough was very chilled, this stage may take longer.

8   Preheat the oven to 375 degrees.

9   In a small bowl, mix together the beaten egg and the water. Brush the bread with the egg wash and bake for 20 minutes.

10   Tent the bread with aluminum foil, and bake for an additional 10 to 20 minutes (for a total of 30 to 40 minutes baking), until the loaf feels set and the internal temperature reaches at least 190 degrees.

11   Remove from the pan and cool at least 2 hours on a wire rack.

PER SERVING: *Calories 399 (From Fat 135); Fat 15g (Saturated 10g); Cholesterol 102mg; Sodium 265mg; Carbohydrate 57g (Dietary Fiber 3g); Protein 9g.*

TIP: Store in plastic wrap at room temperature for 2 to 3 days.

NOTE: My dear friend and chef, Diana, developed this recipe. She grew up in a Jewish home and decided that a challah and babka made for a perfect marriage in this recipe, while also combining her love of Nutella and orange zest.

TIP: If you have any bread leftover, slice it and use it to make French toast!

California Fruit and Nut Sourdough

PREP TIME: 9 HR PLUS 16 HR FOR RISING | BAKE TIME: 35 MIN | YIELD: 12 SERVINGS

INGREDIENTS

150 grams (1 cup) dried mango

50 grams (¼ cup) dried dates

100 grams (½ cup) dried apricots

40 grams (3 tablespoons) apple juice

300 grams (1¼ cups) warm water

50 grams (¼ cup) sourdough starter

200 grams (1⅔ cups) all-purpose flour

100 grams (¾ cup) bread flour

100 grams (1 cup) whole-wheat or whole-spelt flour

9 grams (1½ teaspoons) salt

7 grams (1 tablespoon) cocoa powder

100 grams (1 cup) chopped almonds

DIRECTIONS

1 Cut the dried mango, dates, and apricots into small pieces.

2 In a large bowl, mix the dried fruit with the apple juice.

3 Cover and let soak overnight at room temperature.

4 In a glass bowl, place the soaked fruit with the liquid, the water, the starter, the all-purpose flour, the bread flour, the whole-wheat flour, the salt, the cocoa powder, and the almonds.

5 Mix together until it resembles a shaggy dough.

6 Cover and let rest for 30 minutes.

7 Fold and stretch 4 times, turning with each fold.

8 Cover and repeat the folding and stretching 3 more times over the next 2 hours.

9 Bulk ferment the dough for 6 to 8 more hours.

10 Place the dough into the refrigerator and chill for 8 to 18 hours.

11 Place the dough onto a lightly floured surface.

12 Press the dough into a 12-x-12-inch square.

13 Using a bench scraper or dough blade, cut the dough into 3-x-4-inch bars.

14 Line a baking sheet with parchment paper.

15 Place the bars on the parchment paper, about 1 inch apart, and cover.

16 Preheat the oven to 450 degrees.

17 Place the baking sheet into the oven and immediately reduce the temperature to 400 degrees.

18 Bake for 35 to 40 minutes or until an internal temperature of 180 degrees is reached.

PER SERVING: *Calories 294 (From Fat 45); Fat 5g (Saturated 0g); Cholesterol 0mg; Sodium 296mg; Carbohydrate 47g (Dietary Fiber 4g); Protein 7g.*

TIP: Store in an airtight container at room temperature for up to 3 days or in the freezer for up to 1 month.

NOTE: These are perfect for the trail or any sporting event. They'll keep you full during all your favorite outings.

VARY IT! Any dried fruit will work well in this recipe. Try dried cherries with orange zest or dried blueberries.

Apple Cinnamon Bread

PREP TIME: 30 MIN PLUS 1 HR 45 MIN FOR RISING	BAKE TIME: 45 MIN	YIELD: 10 SERVINGS

INGREDIENTS

245 grams (1 cup) whole milk

114 grams (½ cup) unsalted butter

48 grams (¼ cup) sugar

7 grams (2 teaspoons) active dry yeast

480 grams (4 cups) all-purpose flour

2 eggs

8 grams (1½ teaspoons) kosher salt

Filling:

1 large Granny Smith apple, chopped small

100 grams (½ cup) packed brown sugar

5 grams (1 teaspoon) cinnamon

42 grams (3 tablespoons) melted, unsalted butter

DIRECTIONS

1 Place the milk in a microwave-safe bowl and microwave on high for 1 minute.

2 Pour the hot milk into the bowl of a stand mixer with a dough hook attached.

3 Add in the butter and sugar and stir to cool the milk to warm.

4 Add in the yeast, and let this mixture rest for 5 minutes.

5 Add in the flour, eggs, and salt.

6 Mix on speed 2 for 8 minutes.

7 Cover the bowl with a damp tea towel and allow the mixture to rise for 1 hour in a warm, draft-free spot.

8 In a small bowl, stir together the chopped apple, brown sugar, and cinnamon.

9 Line a bread pan with parchment paper.

10 Place the dough on a floured surface.

11 Using a rolling pin, roll out the dough into an 8-x-16-inch rectangle.

12 Brush the dough with the melted butter.

13 Sprinkle the filling mixture over the melted butter.

14 Roll the loaf up along the 8-inch edge, leaving an 8-inch loaf.

15 Place the loaf into the prepared bread pan.

16 Cover and let the dough rise for 45 minutes.

17 Preheat the oven to 350 degrees.

18 Bake the bread for 45 minutes or until golden brown and an internal temperature of 190 degrees is reached.

19 Allow the bread to cool for at least 1 hour prior to slicing.

PER SERVING: *Calories 386 (From Fat 135); Fat 15g (Saturated 9g); Cholesterol 78mg; Sodium 341mg; Carbohydrate 56g (Dietary Fiber 2g); Protein 7g.*

TIP: Store at room temperature, wrapped in plastic wrap, for 2 to 3 days.

NOTE: This bread is perfect for the toaster or used to make French toast.

Cinnamon Raisin Bread

PREP TIME: 30 MIN PLUS 1 HR 45 MIN FOR RISING	BAKE TIME: 45 MIN	YIELD: 10 SERVINGS

INGREDIENTS

245 grams (1 cup) whole milk

114 grams (½ cup) unsalted butter

100 grams (½ cup) sugar

7 grams (2 teaspoons) active dry yeast

480 grams (4 cups) all-purpose flour

1 egg

8 grams (1½ teaspoons) kosher salt

75 grams (½ cup) raisins

5 grams (1 teaspoon) cinnamon

DIRECTIONS

1 Place the milk into a microwave-safe bowl and microwave on high for 1 minute.

2 Pour the hot milk into the bowl of a stand mixer with a dough hook attached.

3 Add in the butter and sugar and stir to cool the milk to warm.

4 Add the yeast, and let this mixture rest for 5 minutes.

5 Add in the flour, egg, and salt.

6 Mix on speed 2 for 4 minutes.

7 Add in the raisins and cinnamon and continue to mix on speed 2 for 2 minutes.

8 Cover the bowl with a damp tea towel and allow the mixture to rise for 1 hour in a warm, draft-free spot.

9 Spray a bread pan with cooking spray and line with parchment paper.

10 Place the dough on a floured surface.

11 Using a rolling pin, roll out the dough into an 8-x-8-inch rectangle.

12 Roll the loaf up along the 8-inch edge, leaving an 8-inch loaf.

13 Place the loaf into the prepared bread pan.

14 Cover and let the dough rise for 45 minutes.

15 Preheat the oven to 350 degrees.

16 Bake the bread for 45 minutes or until golden brown and an internal temperature of 190 degrees is reached.

17 Allow the bread to cool for at least 1 hour prior to slicing.

PER SERVING: *Calories 342 (From Fat 100); Fat 11g (Saturated 7g); Cholesterol 48mg; Sodium 331mg; Carbohydrate 54g (Dietary Fiber 2g); Protein 7g.*

TIP: Store at room temperature, wrapped in plastic wrap, for 2 to 3 days.

VARY IT! If you're not a raisin fan, the bread can be made without raisins or with another dried fruit.

TIP: If you have any bread left over, slice it and use it to make French toast!

Orange Cranberry Bread

PREP TIME: 30 MIN PLUS 1 HR 45 MIN FOR RISING	BAKE TIME: 45 MIN	YIELD: 10 SERVINGS

INGREDIENTS

123 grams (½ cup) whole milk

50 grams (½ cup) fresh squeezed orange juice

100 grams (½ cup) dried cranberries

8 grams (1 tablespoon) active dry yeast

10 grams (1 tablespoon plus 2 teaspoons) orange zest, divided

150 grams (¾ cup) sugar, divided

112 grams (3 tablespoons plus ⅓ cup) unsalted butter, softened, divided

6 grams (1 teaspoon) salt

1 large egg

390 grams (3¼ cups) all-purpose flour

2 grams (½ teaspoon) vanilla extract

DIRECTIONS

1 Place the milk in a microwave-safe bowl and microwave on high for 1 minute.

2 Pour the hot milk into the bowl of a stand mixer with a dough hook attached.

3 Add in the orange juice and dried cranberries.

4 Let this mixture rest for 5 minutes.

5 Add in the yeast, 6 grams (1 tablespoon) of the orange zest, 50 grams (¼ cup) of the sugar, 42 grams (3 tablespoons) of the unsalted butter, the salt, the egg, and the flour.

6 Mix on speed 2 for 8 minutes.

7 Cover the bowl with a damp tea towel and allow the mixture to rise for 1 hour in a warm, draft-free spot.

8 In a small bowl, stir together the remaining 100 grams (½ cup) of the sugar, the remaining 4 grams (2 teaspoons) of the orange zest, and the vanilla extract for the filling.

9 Spray two bread pans with cooking spray and line with parchment paper.

10 Place the dough on a floured surface.

11 Divide the dough in half.

12 Using a rolling pin, roll out each piece of dough into an 8-x-16-inch rectangle.

13 Spread the remaining 70 grams (⅓ cup) of butter across the surfaces of the dough.

14 Sprinkle the filling mixture across the butter.

15 Roll each loaf up along the 8-inch edge, leaving two 8-inch loaves.

16 Place the loaves into the prepared bread pans.

17 Cover and let the dough rise for 45 minutes.

18 Preheat the oven to 350 degrees.

19 Bake the breads for 45 minutes or until golden brown and an internal temperature of 190 degrees is reached.

20 Allow the breads to cool for at least 1 hour prior to slicing.

PER SERVING: *Calories 341 (From Fat 99); Fat 11g (Saturated 6g); Cholesterol 48mg; Sodium 248mg; Carbohydrate 54g (Dietary Fiber 2g); Protein 6g.*

TIP: Store tightly wrapped in plastic at room temperature for 3 days.

NOTE: You can make this recipe with half whole-wheat flour, but it will yield a denser bread.

TIP: Slice, toast, and serve with whipped cream cheese. Or serve with a powdered sugar and orange juice glaze.

Chocolate Swirled Bread

PREP TIME: 30 MIN PLUS 1 HR 45 MIN FOR RISING	BAKE TIME: 45 MIN	YIELD: 10 SERVINGS

INGREDIENTS

245 grams (1 cup) whole milk

142 grams (½ cup plus 2 tablespoons) unsalted butter, divided

48 grams (¼ cup) sugar

7 grams (2 teaspoons) active dry yeast

510 grams (4¼ cups) all-purpose flour, divided

3 eggs, divided

8 grams (1½ teaspoons) kosher salt

50 grams (¼ cup) packed light brown sugar

4 grams (2 teaspoons) instant coffee or espresso powder

2 grams (¼ teaspoon) salt

262 grams (1½ cups) semisweet chocolate chips

DIRECTIONS

1 Place the milk into a microwave-safe bowl and microwave on high for 1 minute.

2 Pour the hot milk into the bowl of a stand mixer with a dough hook attached.

3 Add in 114 grams (½ cup) of the butter and the sugar and stir to cool the milk to warm.

4 Add in the yeast, and let this mixture rest for 5 minutes.

5 Next add in 480 grams (4 cups) of the flour, 2 of the eggs, and kosher salt.

6 Mix on speed 2 for 8 minutes.

7 Cover the bowl with a damp tea towel and allow the mixture to rise for 1 hour in a warm, draft-free spot.

8 In a small bowl, whisk together the remaining 30 grams (¼ cup) of flour, the brown sugar, the instant coffee, and the salt.

9 In a microwave-safe bowl, microwave on high the chocolate chips and the remaining 28 grams (2 tablespoons) of butter, stirring every 15 seconds until melted, about 1 to 2 minutes. Let this mixture cool for 3 minutes.

10 Next, stir in the flour mixture and the remaining egg just until combined.

11 Line two bread pans with parchment paper.

12 Place the dough on a floured surface. Divide dough in half.

13 Using a rolling pin, roll out each dough into an 8-x-16-inch rectangles.

14 Spread the filling mixture across the doughs.

15 Roll the loaves up along the 8-inch edge, leaving two 8-inch loaves.

16 Place the loaves into the prepared bread pans.

17 Cover and let the doughs rise for 45 minutes.

18 Preheat the oven to 350 degrees.

19 Bake the breads for 45 minutes or until golden brown and an internal temperature of 190 degrees is reached.

20 Allow the breads to cool for at least 1 hour prior to slicing.

PER SERVING: *Calories 490 (From Fat 200); Fat 22g (Saturated 13g); Cholesterol 96mg; Sodium 427mg; Carbohydrate 67g (Dietary Fiber 3g); Protein 9g.*

TIP: Store tightly wrapped in plastic wrap at room temperature for up to 2 days.

NOTE: Serve this chocolatey bread with a strong cup of coffee, and sit and savor the day.

TIP: The chocolate filling used in this recipe can also be used to make chocolate croissants.

TIP: If you want to dress these loaves up a bit, braid them instead of rolling. Check out the Spinach and Artichoke Stuffed Bread recipe in Chapter 12 for braiding instructions.

Peach Kolaches

PREP TIME: 45 MIN PLUS 5 HR 30 MIN FOR RISING	BAKE TIME: 20 MIN	YIELD: 9 SERVINGS

INGREDIENTS

245 grams (1 cup) whole milk

83 grams (¼ cup plus 2 tablespoons) unsalted butter

60 grams (¼ cup) warm water

150 grams (¾ cup) sugar, divided

3 grams (1 teaspoons) active dry yeast

530 grams (4½ cups) all-purpose flour, divided

6 grams (1 teaspoon) salt

1 large egg

225 grams (1 cup) chopped fresh or frozen and defrosted peaches

325 grams (1 cup) peach jam

DIRECTIONS

1 Place the milk into a microwave-safe bowl and microwave on high for 1 minute.

2 Pour the hot milk into the bowl of a stand mixer with a dough hook attached.

3 Add in 55 grams (¼ cup) of the butter, the water, and 100 grams (½ cup) of the sugar.

4 Stir to cool the milk.

5 When the milk has cooled to warm, add in the yeast.

6 Stir and let the mixture sit for 5 minutes.

7 Add in 500 grams (4¼ cups) of the flour, the salt, and the egg.

8 Mix on speed 2 for 8 minutes.

9 Spray a glass bowl with cooking spray.

10 Transfer the dough to the bowl.

11 Cover the bowl with plastic wrap and allow the mixture to rise for 1 to 2 hours in a warm, draft-free spot until the dough can hold an indentation when a finger is pressed into the dough.

12 Press the dough until the air deflates.

13 Cover the bowl again with plastic wrap and refrigerate for 4 to 12 hours.

14 Spray a 9-x-12-inch casserole pan with cooking spray.

15 In a small bowl, stir together the chopped peaches and peach jam.

16 In another bowl, mix together the remaining 30 grams (¼ cup) of flour, the remaining 50 grams (¼ cup) of sugar, and the remaining 28 grams (2 tablespoons) of butter for the streusel topping.

17 Use your fingers to break apart the butter into pea-size crumbs.

18 Place the dough onto a flat surface.

19 Working with oiled hands, divide the dough into 9 equal parts.

20 Roll each round into a ball, pinching and tucking the dough on the bottom as you work it into a ball.

21 Flatten each ball gently in your palm.

22 Place the dough balls 3 across by 3 down in the casserole pan.

23 Use a tablespoon to press into the center of the dough, forming a deep well for the filling.

24 Divide the filling among the rolls, about 4 tablespoons each.

25 Sprinkle the streusel mixture over the top of all the kolaches.

26 Cover with plastic wrap and let rise for 30 minutes.

27 Preheat the oven to 375 degrees.

28 Bake for 25 to 30 minutes or until golden brown and internal temperature of 190 degrees is reached.

29 Allow to cool for at least 30 minutes prior to serving.

PER SERVING: *Calories 491 (From Fat 86); Fat 10g (Saturated 6g); Cholesterol 46mg; Sodium 292mg; Carbohydrate 90g (Dietary Fiber 2g); Protein 8g.*

TIP: Store covered with plastic wrap at room temperature for up to 3 days.

VARY IT! These are a popular sweet throughout Central Texas. You can find them made sweet with peaches, poppy seed filling, and many other fruit combinations. If you want to try a savory kolache, check out Chapter 12 for Josh's Texas Klobasneks.

Salted Pecan Cinnamon Rolls

PREP TIME: 35 MIN PLUS 1 HR 45 MIN FOR RISING	BAKE TIME: 25 MIN	YIELD: 9 SERVINGS

INGREDIENTS

245 grams (1 cup) whole milk

114 grams (½ cup) unsalted butter

48 grams (¼ cup) sugar

7 grams (1½ teaspoons) active dry yeast

480 grams (4 cups) all-purpose flour

2 eggs

5 grams (1 teaspoon) kosher salt

11 grams (1 teaspoon plus 1 tablespoon) cinnamon, divided

114 grams (½ cup) unsalted butter, softened

200 grams (1 cup) packed brown sugar

114 grams (1 cup) chopped pecans

6 grams (1 teaspoon) sea salt

DIRECTIONS

1 Place the milk in a microwave-safe bowl and microwave on high for 1 minute and 30 seconds.

2 Pour the hot milk into the bowl of a stand mixer with a dough hook attached.

3 Add in the butter and stir until the butter has melted and the milk has cooled.

4 Next, add in the sugar and yeast.

5 Let the mixture rest for 5 minutes.

6 Add in the flour, eggs, kosher salt, and 3 grams (1 teaspoon) of the cinnamon.

7 Mix on speed 2 for 8 minutes.

8 Cover the bowl with a damp tea towel and allow the mixture to rise for 1 hour in a warm, draft-free spot.

9 Spray a 9-x-9-inch casserole dish or large Dutch oven with cooking spray.

10 In a small bowl, stir together the softened butter, brown sugar, and the remaining 8 grams (1 tablespoon) of cinnamon to create a paste.

11 Place the dough onto a lightly floured surface.

12   Using a rolling pin, roll out the dough into a 9-x-18-inch rectangle.

13   Spread the brown sugar mixture over the dough.

14   Sprinkle with pecans and sea salt.

15   Roll the dough from the 9-inch edge.

16   Using a bench scraper or sharp serrated knife, cut the dough into 1-inch rounds.

17   Place the cinnamon rolls, cut side down, into the prepared baking dish.

18   Cover the cinnamon rolls with a towel and allow the breads to rise for 45 minutes.

19   Preheat the oven to 350 degrees.

20   Bake the cinnamon rolls for 25 to 30 minutes or until golden brown and an internal temperature of 190 degrees is reached.

PER SERVING: *Calories 603 (From Fat 290); Fat 32g (Saturated 15g); Cholesterol 104mg; Sodium 511mg; Carbohydrate 71g (Dietary Fiber 3g); Protein 9g.*

TIP: To store, cover with plastic wrap and refrigerate for up to 3 days.

TIP: These rolls are perfect for the freezer. Roll and place them into a casserole dish, cover, and freeze. To bake, defrost in the refrigerator overnight and then bake as directed.

Monkey Bread

PREP TIME: 45 MIN PLUS 2 HR FOR RISING	BAKE TIME: 35 MIN	YIELD: 12 SERVINGS

INGREDIENTS

245 grams (1 cup) whole milk

228 grams (1 cup) unsalted butter, divided

148 grams (¾ cup) sugar, divided

7 grams (2 teaspoons) active dry yeast

480 grams (4 cups) all-purpose flour

2 eggs

8 grams (1½ teaspoons) kosher salt

5 grams (2 teaspoons) cinnamon

2 grams (1 teaspoon) ground nutmeg

66 grams (⅓ cup) packed brown sugar

1 grams (½ teaspoon) vanilla extract

DIRECTIONS

1 Place the milk into a microwave-safe bowl and microwave on high for 1 minute and 30 seconds.

2 Pour the hot milk into the bowl of a stand mixer with a dough hook attached.

3 Add in 114 grams (½ cup) of the unsalted butter and stir until the butter has melted and the milk has cooled.

4 Add in 48 grams (¼ cup) of the sugar and the yeast.

5 Let the mixture rest for 5 minutes.

6 Add in the flour, eggs, and kosher salt.

7 Mix on speed 2 for 8 minutes.

8 Cover the bowl with a damp tea towel and allow the mixture to rise for 1½ hours in a warm, draft-free spot.

9 Spray a Bundt pan with cooking spray.

10 In a small bowl, mix together the remaining 100 grams (½ cup) of sugar, the cinnamon, and the nutmeg.

11 Pull off a small piece of dough and roll it into a 1-inch ball.

12 Dip the ball into the melted butter, and then dip it into the granulated sugar mixture to coat the ball.

13 Place the ball into the Bundt pan.

14 Repeat with the remaining dough.

15 Add the brown sugar and vanilla to the remaining 114 grams (½ cup) of butter and add the granulated sugar mixture to this mixture, stirring to combine.

16 Pour this mixture over the top of the dough balls.

17 Cover the pan with foil and let the dough rest for 30 minutes.

18 Preheat the oven to 350 degrees.

19 Bake covered with foil for 10 minutes.

20 Remove the foil and continue baking for 30 to 35 minutes or until an internal temperature of 190 degrees is reached. If the top looks like it's getting too brown, return the foil over the top.

21 Let the monkey bread cool for 10 minutes. Then place a plate over the top and invert the Bundt cake pan.

22 Let the bread cool for an additional 10 minutes. Then remove the cake pan and serve.

PER SERVING: *Calories 377 (From Fat 156); Fat 17g (Saturated 10g); Cholesterol 78mg; Sodium 284mg; Carbohydrate 50g (Dietary Fiber 1g); Protein 6g.*

TIP: You can enjoy this bread up to 2 days, but it's best the day it's made.

VARY IT! Add in chopped pecans or walnuts for a little crunch.

Glazed Doughnuts

PREP TIME: 45 MIN PLUS 10 HR FOR RISING | BAKE TIME: 4 MIN | YIELD: 12 SERVINGS

INGREDIENTS

245 grams (1 cup) whole milk

114 grams (½ cup) unsalted butter

45 grams (¼ cup) sugar

6 grams (2 teaspoons) active dry yeast

2 eggs

150 grams (2 tablespoons plus ½ cup) water, divided

420 grams (3½ cups) all-purpose flour

2 grams (½ teaspoon) salt, divided

1 gram (½ teaspoon) ground nutmeg

900 grams (4 cups) peanut oil or safflower oil

240 grams (2 cups) powdered sugar

1 gram (½ teaspoon) vanilla extract

DIRECTIONS

1   Place the milk into a microwave-safe bowl and microwave on high for 1 minute and 30 seconds.

2   Pour the hot milk into the bowl of a stand mixer with a dough hook attached.

3   Add in the butter and stir until the butter has melted and the milk has cooled.

4   Add in the sugar and yeast.

5   Let the mixture rest for 5 minutes.

6   Add in the eggs, 30 grams (2 tablespoons) of water, flour, 1 gram (¼ teaspoon) of salt, and nutmeg.

7   Mix on speed 2 for 8 minutes.

8   Cover the bowl with plastic wrap and allow the mixture to rest in the refrigerator for 8 to 18 hours.

9   Place the dough onto a floured surface and roll out to about ¼ inch thick.

10   Using a small circular cookie cutter and a large circular cookie cutter, cut out doughnuts and doughnut holes.

11   Line a baking sheet with parchment paper.

12   Place the doughnuts and doughnut holes onto the baking sheet.

13   Reform the dough and cut until all the dough is used.

14   Cover the doughnuts with a towel and let them rise for 1½ to 2 hours in a warm, draft-free spot.

15 In a large, heavy Dutch oven, heat the oil to 375 degrees.

16 Fry the doughnuts 3 to 4 at a time, making sure to keep the oil at 375 degrees. Cook the doughnuts for 1 to 2 minutes on each side or until golden.

17 Transfer the cooked doughnuts to paper towels or brown paper bags to drain and cool.

18 Return the oil to 375 degrees prior to cooking the remaining doughnuts.

19 In a medium bowl, whisk together the powder sugar, the remaining 1 gram (¼ teaspoon) salt, and the vanilla. Add in a little of the remaining 120 grams (½ cup) water a little at a time until smooth. Make a glaze thicker with less water or thinner with more water.

20 Dip the doughnuts into the glaze and serve warm.

PER SERVING: *Calories 455 (From Fat 230); Fat 26g (Saturated 7g); Cholesterol 58mg; Sodium 87mg; Carbohydrate 52g (Dietary Fiber 1g); Protein 6g.*

NOTE: Doughnuts are best the day they're prepared. If you prefer to freeze cooked doughnuts, don't glaze them. You can keep unglazed doughnuts in the freezer for up to 1 month. Reheat them in an air fryer for 2 minutes at 400 degrees or in the oven for 4 to 6 minutes at 400 degrees.

TIP: Try to handle the dough very little or the last batch may be tougher in texture.

NOTE: If you prefer a creamier glaze, use half-and-half in place of water.

VARY IT! If you prefer a cinnamon sugar instead of glaze, mix together ½ cup sugar with 1 tablespoon ground cinnamon. Roll the hot doughnuts in the cinnamon-and-sugar mixture and serve.

VARY IT! If you love a good blueberry doughnut, add ½ cup dried wild blueberries to the dough.

European Muesli Bread

PREP TIME: 15 MIN PLUS 1 HR 30 MIN FOR RISING	BAKE TIME: 15 MIN	YIELD: 12 SERVINGS

INGREDIENTS

250 grams (2 cups) all-purpose flour

2 grams (1 teaspoon) active dry yeast

180 grams (¾ cup) water

7 grams (1 teaspoon) honey

1 pinch of salt

50 grams (½ cup) oats

50 grams (⅓ cup) chopped hazelnuts

50 grams (¼ cup) dried cranberries

50 grams (¼ cup) dried tart or Bing cherries

46 grams (3 tablespoons) plain yogurt

DIRECTIONS

1 Place the flour, yeast, water, honey, salt, and oats into the bowl of a stand mixer with a dough hook attached.

2 Knead on speed 2 for 4 minutes.

3 Sprinkle in the hazelnuts, cranberries, and cherries.

4 Continue to knead on speed 2 for 2 more minutes.

5 Cover and let rise at room temperature for 1 hour.

6 Place the dough on a lightly floured flat surface and divide into 12 equally sized pieces (approximately 50 to 55 grams each).

7 Line a baking sheet with parchment paper.

8 Form a ball with each piece of dough and place it on the baking sheet.

9 Cover and let rise at room temperature for 90 minutes.

10 Preheat the oven to 425 degrees.

11 Using a pastry brush, brush the rolls with yogurt and bake for 15 to 18 minutes.

PER SERVING: *Calories 138 (From Fat 28); Fat 3g (Saturated 0g); Cholesterol 0mg; Sodium 17mg; Carbohydrate 24g (Dietary Fiber 2g); Protein 4g.*

TIP: Store at room temperature, wrapped in plastic wrap, for 2 to 3 days.

NOTE: These rolls are perfect for a breakfast on the go, a brunch, or a mid-exercise snack.

VARY IT! Any fruit-and-nut combination can work. Try walnuts with dried blueberries or almonds with dried apricots.

Chapter **12**

Hearty Stuffed Breads

Stuffed breads are a favorite in our home, and after diving into this chapter, I hope they will be in yours, too! You can transport yourself to Italy with Pepperoni and Cheese Calzones or try a couple of German favorites, like Flammkuchen (German Pizza) or German Potato Pie. Breads can shine bright as a main meal, whether stuffed, rolled, or topped with your favorite additions. Simply add a side dish, and your meal is complete.

This chapter highlights hearty and savory breads, from Quick Pizza Margherita to Spinach and Artichoke Stuffed Bread, which are fairly simple, as far as bread skills go. If you're looking for a stuffed breakfast bread for a brunch, try the Southern Sausage Bread. If you want finger food for a party, try the Texas Klobasneks.

Get creative with these recipes! If you have a favorite filling, try it out! A richer dough, more like a crescent bread, is found in the Spinach and Artichoke Stuffed Bread and the Texas Klobasneks recipes. If you want a simple French-style bread dough recipe to fill, look to the Quick Pizza Margherita and Pepperoni and Cheese Calzones. Stuffed breads are fun to make and are perfect for weeknight meals.

TIP

If you're trying to add a bit more nutrition to your meals, try swapping out half of the flour with whole-wheat flour or whole-spelt flour. Just remember that the dough will be denser. You can also stir in or top any of the breads with seeds to boost the overall nutrition.

Southern Sausage Bread

PREP TIME: 30 MIN PLUS 1 HR 30 MIN FOR RISING	BAKE TIME: 50 MIN	YIELD: 12 SERVINGS

INGREDIENTS

313 grams (1⅓ cups) warm water

6 grams (2 teaspoons) active dry yeast

12 grams (1 tablespoon) granulated sugar

420 grams (3½ cups) all-purpose flour

12 grams (2 teaspoons) salt

28 grams (2 tablespoons) extra-virgin olive oil, divided

1 green bell pepper, finely diced

1 medium yellow onion, finely diced

8 ounces (½ pound) ground sausage

DIRECTIONS

1 In a bowl of a stand mixer with a dough hook attached, mix together the water, yeast, and sugar. Let the mixture rest for 5 minutes.

2 Add in the flour, salt, and 14 grams (1 tablespoon) of the olive oil.

3 Knead the dough on speed 2 for 8 minutes.

4 Coat a glass bowl with cooking spray.

5 Make a ball with the dough and place the dough in the glass bowl.

6 Cover the bowl with plastic wrap and let rest for 1 hour.

7 Meanwhile, in a large skillet, heat the remaining 14 grams (1 tablespoon) of olive oil over medium-high heat.

8 Add in the bell peppers and onions, and sauté for 5 minutes.

9 Place the cooked onions and peppers onto a plate.

10 Add the ground sausage to the skillet, and cook for 10 minutes or until fully browned and cooked through.

11 Stir in the onions and bell peppers, and set aside to cool.

12 Line a baking sheet with parchment paper.

13 On a lightly floured surface, roll out the dough into a 16-x-8-inch rectangle.

14 Transfer the dough to the baking sheet.

15 Spread the meat filling across the surface of the dough.

16 From the long, 16-inch edge, roll up the loaf and pinch the seams to seal on the ends and underneath.

17 Place the rolled bread, seam side down, onto the baking sheet.

18 Cover with a tea towel and let rest for 30 minutes.

19 Meanwhile, preheat the oven to 325 degrees.

20 Bake the bread for 50 minutes, or until the internal temperature reaches 190 to 200 degrees. Cover with foil if the surface gets too brown.

21 Allow the loaf to rest 15 minutes before slicing and serving.

PER SERVING: *Calories 222 (From Fat 70); Fat 8g (Saturated 2g); Cholesterol 14mg; Sodium 511mg; Carbohydrate 30g (Dietary Fiber 1g); Protein 7g.*

TIP: Store in an airtight container at room temperature for up to 5 days, in the refrigerator for up to 1 week, or in the freezer for up to 3 months.

TIP: This bread is delicious as a breakfast bread or as a main course. Serve with scrambled eggs or a side salad to complete the meal.

VARY IT! Use any variety of ground meat or sausage. We've tried this with turkey and vegetarian sausage with success.

Pepperoni and Cheese Calzones

PREP TIME: 30 MIN PLUS 1 HR FOR RISING	BAKE TIME: 30 MIN	YIELD: 4 SERVINGS

INGREDIENTS

352 grams (1½ cups) warm water

12 grams (1 tablespoon) sugar

9 grams (1 tablespoon) active dry yeast

480 grams (4 cups) all-purpose flour

12 grams (2 teaspoons) salt

28 grams (2 tablespoons) extra-virgin olive oil, divided

4 ounces pepperoni slices

200 grams (2 cups) shredded mozzarella

22 grams (¼ cup) grated Parmesan cheese

75 grams (1 cup) thinly sliced mushrooms

1 gram (1 teaspoon) dried oregano

1 gram (¼ teaspoon) crushed red pepper flakes

450 grams (2 cups) marinara sauce, for dipping

DIRECTIONS

1 In a bowl of a stand mixer with a dough hook attached, mix together the water, sugar, and yeast. Let the mixture rest for 5 minutes.

2 Add in the flour, salt, and 14 grams (1 tablespoon) of the olive oil.

3 Knead the dough on speed 2 for 7 minutes.

4 Coat a glass bowl with cooking spray.

5 Make a ball with the dough and place it in a glass bowl.

6 Cover the bowl with plastic wrap and let rest for 1 hour.

7 On a lightly floured surface, divide the dough into 4 equal pieces.

8 Roll out each piece to an 8-inch circle.

9 Cover and let the dough rest for 5 minutes.

10 Roll out the rounds into 12-inch circles.

11 Line 2 baking sheets with parchment paper.

12 Place the rounds onto the baking sheets.

13 Divide the pepperoni slices, mozzarella, Parmesan, mushrooms, oregano, and red pepper flakes evenly between each round, making sure to place the toppings on one-side of each round, leaving ½ inch of an edge without any toppings. This will allow you to fold over the edge without any toppings and seal the calzone.

14 Fold over the halves without filling to sandwich the filling.

15 Using a fork, seal the edges by crimping them closed with the tines of the fork.

16 Poke the fork tines through the top surface of each calzone to create vent holes.

17 Brush the top of each calzone with the remaining 14 grams (1 tablespoon) of olive oil.

18 Meanwhile, preheat the oven to 375 degrees.

19 Bake for 30 to 35 minutes. Cover with foil if the surface gets too brown.

20 Meanwhile, in a small saucepan, heat the marinara sauce over low heat.

21 Serve the calzones with warm marinara sauce for dipping.

PER SERVING: *Calories 836 (From Fat 275); Fat 31g (Saturated 11g); Cholesterol 66mg; Sodium 1459mg; Carbohydrate 102g (Dietary Fiber 5g); Protein 36g.*

TIP: Store in an airtight container in the refrigerator for up to 3 days.

VARY IT! Try any of your favorite pizza toppings inside these calzones.

Josh's Texas Klobasneks

PREP TIME: 30 MIN PLUS 2 HR 15 MIN FOR RISING	BAKE TIME: 18 MIN	YIELD: 16 SERVINGS

INGREDIENTS

242 grams (1 cup) half-and-half

8 tablespoons (1 stick) unsalted butter, divided

9 grams (1 tablespoon) active dry yeast

50 grams (¼ cup) sugar

3 grams (½ teaspoon) kosher salt

420 to 480 grams (3½ to 4 cups) all-purpose flour, divided

50 grams (¼ cup) active sourdough starter

28 grams (2 tablespoons) vegetable oil

2 egg yolks

56 grams (½ cup) grated colby jack cheese

1 jar (32 slices) pickled jalapeños

1 pound smoked kielbasa sausage, cut into 16 pieces (2 inches long and quartered lengthwise)

DIRECTIONS

1 In a microwave-safe measuring cup, heat the half-and-half for 1 minute 30 seconds. Add 4 tablespoons of the butter and stir to cool the milk slightly.

2 In the bowl of a stand mixer with a dough hook attached, stir together the yeast, sugar, salt, and 1½ cups of the flour.

3 Pour in the warm cream mixture and sourdough starter.

4 Mix until the ingredients come together.

5 Cover and let rest for 30 minutes.

6 Add in the oil and egg yolks, and blend until fully incorporated.

7 Slowly stir in enough of the remaining 2 to 2½ cups flour until the dough comes together and is not sticky.

8 Knead on speed 2 for 6 minutes, or until smooth. The dough will be soft and not stiff.

9 Place the dough in a lightly oiled bowl and cover.

10 Allow to rise until doubled in size, 1 to 2 hours.

11 Line a baking sheet with parchment paper.

12 After the dough has risen, press out the gas and divide into 16 even pieces (45 to 50 grams per roll).

13 Roll each piece of dough into balls and then flatten them into 3-inch circles.

14 In the center of each piece of dough, place ½ tablespoon of the cheese, 1 slice of jalapeño, and a piece of sausage.

15 Fold one side of the dough over the other and roll; then seal by pinching all seams together.

16 Place on the baking sheet 1 inch apart, seam side down.

17 Cover and allow to rise for 45 more minutes.

18 Preheat the oven to 375 degrees.

19 In a microwave-safe dish, melt the 4 tablespoons of butter in the microwave on high for 1 minute.

20 With a pastry brush, brush the tops of the klobasneks with melted butter and top with an additional jalapeño slice on top of each.

21 Bake, uncovered, for 18 minutes or until golden.

PER SERVING: *Calories 311 (From Fat 171); Fat 19g (Saturated 8g); Cholesterol 69mg; Sodium 387mg; Carbohydrate 27g (Dietary Fiber 1g); Protein 8g.*

TIP: Store in an airtight container in the refrigerator for up to 3 days.

NOTE: My dear friend, Chef Josh Brown, shared this Czech-rooted recipe. If you're ever in Central Texas, there's a good chance you'll see these in bake shops. They're definitely a crowd pleaser!

Quick Pizza Margherita

PREP TIME: 25 MIN PLUS 1 HR FOR RISING	BAKE TIME: 10 MIN	YIELD: 4 SERVINGS

INGREDIENTS

176 grams (¾ cup) warm water

4 grams (1 teaspoon) sugar

8 grams (2½ teaspoons) active dry yeast

250 grams (2 cups) bread flour

28 grams (2 tablespoons) extra-virgin olive oil, divided

6 grams (1 teaspoon) salt

41 grams (¼ cup) cornmeal or semolina

225 grams (1 cup) pizza or marinara sauce (see Chapter 14 for Roasted Tomato Pizza Sauce)

10 basil leaves

8 ounces fresh mozzarella, thinly sliced

DIRECTIONS

1   In the bowl of a stand mixer with a dough hook attached, mix together the water, sugar, and yeast. Let the mixture rest for 5 minutes.

2   Add in the bread flour, 14 grams (1 tablespoon) of the olive oil, and the salt.

3   Knead on speed 2 for 6 minutes.

4   Make a ball with the dough and coat with the remaining olive oil.

5   Cover the dough in plastic wrap and let rest for 1 hour.

6   At this point, you can either make the pizza, freeze the dough, or refrigerate for up to 3 days prior to shaping and baking.

7   To shape the dough, place it on a lightly floured surface.

8   Roll out the dough into a 12-inch pizza for a thicker crust or 16- to 18-inch crust for a thinner crust.

9   Sprinkle a pizza stone with cornmeal or semolina or line with parchment paper.

10   Place the dough onto the pizza stone or baking sheet.

11 Spread the marinara sauce thinly across the top of the dough.

12 Top with 10 whole basil leaves or thinly slice the basil and sprinkle over the top.

13 Lay the mozzarella slices over the top, not fully covering the sauce.

14 Preheat the oven to 550 degrees, or as high as your oven can go.

15 Bake for 10 to 20 minutes, depending on the desired brownness of your crust and cheese. If you prefer a less crispy pizza, you can bake at 450 degrees for 12 to 15 minutes.

PER SERVING: *Calories 371 (From Fat 84); Fat 9g (Saturated 2g); Cholesterol 3mg; Sodium 699mg; Carbohydrate 60g (Dietary Fiber 4g); Protein 11g.*

TIP: Store in an airtight container in the refrigerator for up to 2 days.

NOTE: A true Italian pizza is made with Type 0 or 00 flour and fermented with very little yeast for 24 hours. If you'd like to experiment with this dough, start with a 24-hour cold ferment in the refrigerator, then bake. Next, you can experiment using less yeast (about 0.5 gram of sourdough starter or $\frac{1}{16}$ teaspoon of active dry yeast) and fermenting on the counter for 24 hours.

NOTE: This recipe makes 1 pizza. You can double or triple this recipe. You can also make extra dough and keep in the freezer for up to 1 month.

TIP: If you prefer a classic American pizza, use a shredded mozzarella cheese.

Flammkuchen (German Pizza)

PREP TIME: 25 MIN PLUS 8 HR 15 MIN FOR RISING	BAKE TIME: 8 MIN	YIELD: 6 SERVINGS

INGREDIENTS

300 grams (2½ cups) all-purpose flour

3 grams (1 teaspoon) active dry yeast

11 grams (1¾ teaspoons) salt

30 grams (2¼ tablespoons) extra-virgin olive oil

140 grams (½ cup) water

500 grams (2 cups) crème fraîche or sour cream

2 grams (1 teaspoon) ground black pepper

12 grams (4 tablespoons) chopped chives

12 slices cooked bacon, finely chopped

1 large red onion, thinly sliced

DIRECTIONS

1 In the bowl of a stand mixer with a dough hook attached, place the flour, yeast, 5 grams (¾ teaspoon) of the salt, the olive oil, and the water.

2 Knead together all the ingredients on speed 2 for 6 to 8 minutes until elastic and smooth.

3 Cover and let rise in the refrigerator for 8 to 12 hours.

4 The next day, cut the dough into 6 equally sized pieces.

5 Hand-knead each piece of dough for 2 minutes, round each dough piece, and press it flat.

6 Cover the dough with a tea towel and let rest for about 15 minutes.

7 Meanwhile, preheat the oven to 500 to 550 degrees.

8 Line 2 baking sheets with parchment paper.

9 Roll the dough out very thin, about ¼ inch in thickness.

10 Place the dough onto the prepared baking sheets.

11 Spread ⅓ cup crème fraîche or sour cream over the surface of the dough.

12 Sprinkle with the remaining 6 grams (1 teaspoon) of salt, pepper, chives, and bacon, and then equally distribute the onion slices.

13 Immediately place the prepared flammkuchen into the hot oven and bake for 8 minutes.

PER SERVING: *Calories 500 (From Fat 264); Fat 29g (Saturated 14g); Cholesterol 55mg; Sodium 1141mg; Carbohydrate 44g (Dietary Fiber 2g); Protein 14g.*

TIP: Store in an airtight container in the refrigerator for up to 2 days.

NOTE: Flammkuchen is a specialty from the Alsace and Lorraine regions of France, but it's also made in Saarland, Pfalz, and Baden in Germany. There are countless variations. The classic topping is made with cream, sour cream, or crème fraîche; raw (red) onions; and bacon (speck).

VARY IT! For popular variations of this pizza, check out the nearby sidebar.

VARIATIONS ON A THEME

Here are popular variations to try:

Leek and cheese (with or without diced bacon)

- Cream topping as in the classic version
- Thinly sliced leek
- Shredded Swiss cheese

Vegetarian with goat cream cheese

- Cream topping as in the classic version
- Goat cream cheese
- Thinly sliced (red) onion

Potato and rosemary

- Cream topping as in the classic version
- Sliced boiled potatoes
- Rosemary, olive oil, and salt (optional) for sprinkling

German Potato Pie

PREP TIME: 25 MIN PLUS 1 HR FOR RISING | BAKE TIME: 20 MIN | YIELD: 8 SERVINGS

INGREDIENTS

200 grams (1⅔ cups) all-purpose flour

2 grams (½ teaspoon) active dry yeast

125 grams (½ cup) whole milk

4.5 grams (¾ teaspoon) salt

30 grams (2 tablespoons) unsalted butter, softened or at room temperature

500 grams (3⅓ cups) boiled and peeled potatoes

130 grams (½ cup) sour cream

130 grams (1½ cup) whipping cream

1 egg yolk

1 gram (½ teaspoon) ground black pepper

4.5 grams (2 teaspoons) caraway seeds, optional

DIRECTIONS

1 In the bowl of a stand mixer with a dough hook attachment, knead together the flour, yeast, milk, 1.5 grams (¼ teaspoon) of the salt, and the butter for 5 minutes on speed 2.

2 Cover and let rise at room temperature for about 1 hour.

3 Boil the potatoes and peel them while they're still warm.

4 Press the potatoes through a potato press or mash with a potato masher in a medium bowl.

5 Add in the sour cream, whipping cream, and egg yolk. Season to taste with the remaining 3 grams (½ teaspoon) of salt and the pepper.

6 Preheat the oven to 425 degrees.

7 Spray a pie or tart pan with cooking spray.

8 Roll out the dough until about ¼ inch thick.

9 Press into the pie or tart pan, cutting off excess dough around edges. Pour in the potato mixture and smooth the top. If using, sprinkle the surface with caraway seeds.

10 Bake for 20 to 25 minutes or until golden on top.

PER SERVING: *Calories 282 (From Fat 126); Fat 14g (Saturated 8g); Cholesterol 65mg; Sodium 244mg; Carbohydrate 34g (Dietary Fiber 2g); Protein 6g.*

TIP: Store in an airtight container in the refrigerator for up to 2 days.

NOTE: In Germany, this dish would be called *Kartoffelkuchen* (potato cake), but for an American eye it looks more like a pie or a tart. My dear friend Marina Bauer made this for us in Germany, and it quickly became one of my favorite dishes. Her mother-in-law, Helga, teaches cooking, and this is her recipe that she has shared.

VARY IT! Another popular way to serve this dish is with sauerkraut on top. Perfect for Octoberfest celebrations!

Ham and Cheese Rolled Bread

PREP TIME: 20 MIN PLUS 1 HR 30 MIN FOR RISING	BAKE TIME: 50 MIN	YIELD: 16 SERVINGS

INGREDIENTS

470 grams (2 cups) warm water

25 grams (2 tablespoons) sugar

6 grams (2 teaspoons) active dry yeast

720 grams (6 cups) all-purpose flour

8 grams (1¼ teaspoon) salt

8 ounces (8 slices) deli ham slices

200 grams (2 cups) shredded cheddar cheese

DIRECTIONS

1 In the bowl of a stand mixer with a dough hook attached, mix together the water, sugar, and yeast. Let the mixture rest for 5 minutes.

2 Add in the flour and salt.

3 Knead the dough on speed 2 for 5 minutes.

4 Coat a glass bowl with cooking spray.

5 Make a ball with the dough and place it in the glass bowl.

6 Cover the bowl with plastic wrap and rest for 1 hour.

7 Line a baking sheet with parchment paper.

8 On a lightly floured surface, roll out the dough into a 16-x-8-inch rectangle.

9 Transfer the dough to the baking sheet.

10 Spread the ham slices across the dough and top with cheese.

11 From the long, 16-inch edge, roll up the loaf and pinch the seam to seal the ends and underneath.

12 Cover with a tea towel and let rest for 30 minutes.

13 Meanwhile, preheat the oven to 325 degrees.

14 Bake for 50 minutes, until the internal temperature reaches 190 to 200 degrees. Cover with foil if the surface gets too brown.

15 Allow the loaf to rest 15 minutes before slicing and serving.

PER SERVING: *Calories 244 (From Fat 52); Fat 6g (Saturated 3g); Cholesterol 21mg; Sodium 455mg; Carbohydrate 37g (Dietary Fiber 1g); Protein 10g.*

TIP: Store in an airtight container in the refrigerator for up to 3 days.

NOTE: This bread is a great alternative to traditional sandwiches, and perfect for a picnic or potluck. Serve with a green salad to complete the meal.

VARY IT! You can use any variety of lunch meat or cheese combination in place of ham and cheddar.

Spinach and Artichoke Stuffed Bread

PREP TIME: 25 MIN PLUS 1 HR 30 MIN FOR RISING	BAKE TIME: 45 MIN	YIELD: 16 SERVINGS

INGREDIENTS

293 grams (1¼ cups) warm water

6 grams (2 teaspoons) active dry yeast

4 grams (1 teaspoon) sugar

25 grams (2 tablespoons) extra-virgin olive oil

420 grams (3½ cups) all-purpose flour

85 grams (¾ cup) grated cheddar cheese

9 grams (1½ teaspoons) salt

4 ounces cream cheese, softened

82 grams (⅓ cup) sour cream

2 cloves garlic, minced

100 grams (1 cup) mozzarella cheese, divided

45 grams (½ cup) fresh shredded Parmesan cheese

312 grams (2 cups) frozen chopped spinach, defrosted and squeezed dry

240 grams (1 cup) marinated artichoke hearts, drained and chopped

DIRECTIONS

1 In a bowl of a stand mixer with a dough hook attached, mix together the water, yeast, and sugar. Let the mixture rest for 5 minutes.

2 Add in the olive oil, flour, cheese, and salt. Knead the dough on speed 2 for 7 minutes.

3 Coat a glass bowl with cooking spray. Make a ball with the dough and place it in the glass bowl. Cover the bowl with plastic wrap and let rest for 1 hour.

4 Meanwhile, in a large bowl, mix together the cream cheese, sour cream, garlic, mozzarella, Parmesan, spinach, and artichoke hearts with a wooden spoon or rubber spatula.

5 On a lightly floured surface, roll out the dough into a 16-x-8-inch rectangle. Line a baking sheet with parchment paper, and place the dough onto the baking sheet.

6 On the long, 16-inch edge, cut a 2-inch slit every 1 inch on both sides (see Figure 12-1). In the 4-inch center, place the filling.

7 Starting at the top, fold in the left dough piece, then the right overlapping to create a braided effect (see Figure 12-2). Continue down the length of the dough (see Figure 12-3). Cover with a tea towel and let rest for 30 minutes.

8 Meanwhile, preheat the oven to 350 degrees.

9 Bake for 45 minutes or until the bread is golden brown and the filling is bubbly. Slice and serve warm.

PER SERVING: *Calories 216 (From Fat 97); Fat 11g (Saturated 4g); Cholesterol 14mg; Sodium 394mg; Carbohydrate 22g (Dietary Fiber 2g); Protein 8g.*

TIP: Store in an airtight container in the refrigerator for up to 3 days.

TIP: Make sure you fill and braid the bread on the baking sheet, or it will be very difficult to transfer.

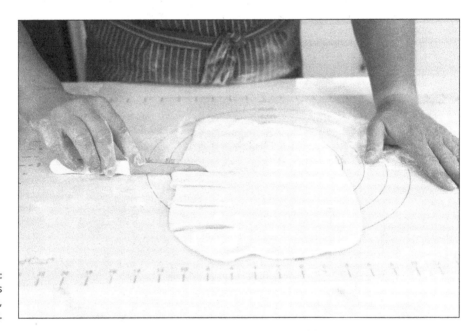

FIGURE 12-1: Making slits in the dough, prior to filling.

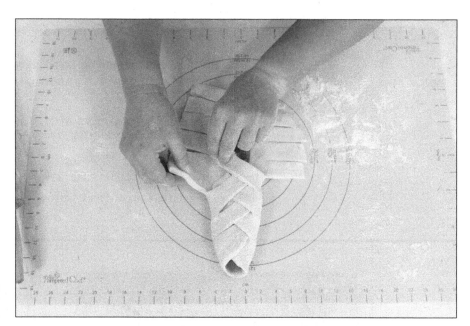

FIGURE 12-2:
Braiding over
the filling.

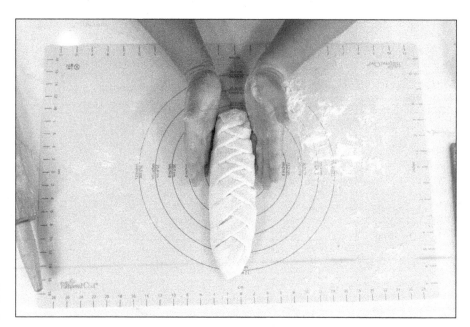

FIGURE 12-3:
The braided and
stuffed bread.

Chapter **13**

Sourdough Discard Recipes

Quick, before you dump your discard, this is the chapter you need! One of the most frequent complaints I hear about making sourdough breads is about all the wasted or tossed discard. Let me assure you, I'm a no-waste gal, and I prefer using up the discard in other recipes.

Discard contains flour, water, and, yes, yeast. So, it has a little rise, a slightly sour taste, and thickening powers. When you're trying to manipulate a recipe and throw in your sourdough discard, you want to think about it like this: 120 grams of discard is 60 grams of flour and 60 grams of water, so about ½ cup of flour and ¼ cup of water. This is what it needs to replace in an existing recipe in order to be used successfully. Many people realize that discard works great in muffins and quick breads, but I'm excited to share some more unusual ways to use it, like Beer-Battered Vegetable Tempura and Cheesy Kinder Crackers. In this chapter, you find some sweet and savory ways to upcycle your leftover discard.

TIP Remove the starter from the refrigerator. Let the starter revitalize and bubble to double in size. Pull what you need for a bread recipe. Then take 50 grams to feed and restart another jar of starter (50 grams of starter, 50 grams of flour, and 50 grams of water). The remaining amount you can creatively use in another recipe.

Griddle Pancakes

PREP TIME: 5 MIN | BAKE TIME: 15 MIN | YIELD: 4 SERVINGS

INGREDIENTS

240 grams (2 cups) all-purpose flour

9.6 grams (2 teaspoons) baking powder

5 grams (1 teaspoon) baking soda

13 grams (1 tablespoon) packed brown sugar

3 grams (½ teaspoon) salt

227 grams (1 cup) sourdough starter

368 grams (1½ cups) whole milk

4 grams (1 teaspoon) vanilla extract

1 egg

26 grams (2 tablespoons) canola or coconut oil, divided

DIRECTIONS

1 In a medium bowl, whisk together the flour, baking powder, baking soda, brown sugar, and salt.

2 In another bowl, whisk together the starter, milk, vanilla, egg, and 1 tablespoon of the oil.

3 Make a well in the dry ingredients.

4 Pour the wet ingredients into the well and stir to combine. (Some small clumps are okay.)

5 Rub a large skillet with 1 teaspoon of oil.

6 Heat the skillet over medium-high heat. Hold your hand near the skillet; if it's hot, the skillet is ready to begin cooking the pancakes. (Obviously, be careful not to touch the skillet with your hand.)

7 Pour the batter into small piles, ¼ cup per pile, making however many your pan can fit without crowding the pan.

8 When the pancakes start to bubble, flip the pancakes. If the pancakes are browning too fast, reduce the heat to medium or medium-low.

9 Let the pancakes cook on the other side for 1 to 2 minutes or until they rise and are browned on the underside. Recoat with oil, as needed.

10 Repeat with the remaining batter.

11 Serve warm.

PER SERVING: *Calories 474 (From Fat 107); Fat 12g (Saturated 3g); Cholesterol 62mg; Sodium 959mg; Carbohydrate 77g (Dietary Fiber 4g); Protein 14g.*

TIP: Store in an airtight container at room temperature for up to 5 days, in the refrigerator for up to 1 week, or in the freezer for up to 3 months.

Baked Dutch Oven Pancakes

PREP TIME: 5 MIN | BAKE TIME: 20 MIN | YIELD: 6 SERVINGS

INGREDIENTS

57 grams (¼ cup) unsalted butter

6 eggs

454 grams (2 cups) sourdough starter

82 grams (⅓ cup) milk

4 grams (1 teaspoon) vanilla extract

13 grams (1 tablespoon) sugar

3 grams (½ teaspoon) salt

DIRECTIONS

1 Preheat the oven to 400 degrees.

2 In a large Dutch oven, heat the butter over medium heat.

3 Meanwhile, in a large bowl, whisk together the eggs, sourdough starter, milk, vanilla, sugar, and salt. (Keep an eye on the butter as it melts to make sure it isn't burning.)

4 When the oven has heated, add the pancake mix to the melted butter and swirl around in the Dutch oven.

5 Remove from the heat and bake for 20 minutes or until puffy and golden brown.

6 Serve immediately.

PER SERVING: *Calories 303 (From Fat 125); Fat 14g (Saturated 7g); Cholesterol 233mg; Sodium 273mg; Carbohydrate 34g (Dietary Fiber 3g); Protein 12g.*

TIP: Store these pancakes in the refrigerator for up to 2 days.

NOTE: Feeding your starter with rye flour will give these pancakes a unique and interesting flavor.

TIP: Serve with fresh berries and maple syrup or sprinkle with powdered sugar.

VARY IT! Add lemon zest to the batter and serve with fresh blueberries and a drizzle of lemon sauce (made with lemon juice and powdered sugar).

Sourdough Flatbread

PREP TIME: 15 MIN PLUS 1 HR FOR RISING	BAKE TIME: 6 MIN	YIELD: 6 SERVINGS

INGREDIENTS

227 grams (2 cups) all-purpose flour

6 grams (1 teaspoon) salt

2 grams (½ teaspoon) baking powder

113 grams (½ cup) sourdough starter

82 grams (⅓ cup) plain yogurt

60 grams (¼ cup) canola oil, divided

28 grams (2 tablespoons) butter

DIRECTIONS

1 In a large bowl, whisk together the flour, salt, and baking powder.

2 Stir in the starter, yogurt, and 2 tablespoons of the canola oil.

3 Form the dough into a ball.

4 Sprinkle about ¼ cup to ½ cup of flour on a flat surface.

5 Place the dough onto the floured surface, and knead in more flour, as needed. The dough should be pliable, neither dry nor wet.

6 Knead about 5 times.

7 Cover the dough with plastic wrap and let it sit for 1 hour.

8 Divide the dough into 6 equal pieces.

9 Roll each piece of dough into a circular or oblong shape (whichever you prefer). For a thinner flat bread, roll out to 10 inches; for a thicker flat bread, roll out to 8 inches.

10 In a small heat-safe bowl, melt the butter and mix with the remaining 2 tablespoons of canola oil.

11 Heat a large Dutch oven over medium-high heat.

12 Brush the tops of the bread with the butter-and-oil mixture.

13 Cook each flat bread for 2 to 3 minutes on each side or until it puffs up and begins to brown with bubbles.

PER SERVING: *Calories 296 (From Fat 122); Fat 14g (Saturated 3g); Cholesterol 11mg; Sodium 435mg; Carbohydrate 38g (Dietary Fiber 2g); Protein 6g.*

TIP: Flatbreads are best consumed the day they're prepared.

NOTE: The range in flour for kneading is based on the starter. Some starters are more wet, due to humidity in the air. The dough should feel like pizza dough.

TIP: Serve with hummus, grilled meats, or as part of a charcuterie board.

VARY IT! Add roasted garlic and chopped herbs (cilantro, parsley, or thyme) for a pop of flavor.

Fluffy Biscuits

PREP TIME: 15 MIN | **BAKE TIME: 12 MIN** | **YIELD: 12 SERVINGS**

INGREDIENTS

240 grams (2 cups) all-purpose flour

14 grams (1 tablespoon) baking powder

5 grams (1 teaspoon) baking soda

6 grams (1 teaspoon) salt

113 grams (½ cup) cold unsalted butter

454 grams (2 cups) sourdough starter

28 grams (2 tablespoons) salted butter, melted

DIRECTIONS

1 In a medium bowl, whisk together the flour, baking powder, baking soda, and salt.

2 Using a pastry cutter or your fingers, cut the cold butter into the flour mixture until the small butter crumbles.

3 Add in the sourdough starter and stir to combine.

4 Preheat the oven to 450 degrees.

5 On a lightly floured flat surface, place the biscuit dough.

6 Knead the dough 3 times and flatten into a 12-x-12-inch square.

7 Brush the tops with the melted butter.

8 Cut the dough into 12 biscuits, about 2 x 2 inches.

9 Line a baking sheet with parchment paper.

10 Place the biscuits on the parchment paper.

11 Place the baking sheet in the oven and immediately reduce the heat to 425 degrees.

12 Bake for 12 to 15 minutes or until golden brown and cooked through.

PER SERVING: *Calories 231 (From Fat 91); Fat 10g (Saturated 6g); Cholesterol 25mg; Sodium 448mg; Carbohydrate 31g (Dietary Fiber 2g); Protein 5g.*

TIP: Store in an airtight container at room temperature for up to 2 days.

NOTE: Biscuits perform better when everything is cold. If it's a hot day, place all the dry ingredients in the refrigerator and let them chill before adding in the starter.

TIP: Serve with fresh jam and whipped honey butter, like Honey Cardamom Butter (Chapter 14).

VARY IT! Craving a savory biscuit? Add 1 tablespoon fresh thyme leaves and ½ teaspoon garlic powder.

Cheesy Kinder Crackers

PREP TIME: 15 MIN PLUS 1 HR FOR RISING	BAKE TIME: 25 MIN	YIELD: 8 SERVINGS

INGREDIENTS

100 grams (¾ cup plus 1 tablespoon) whole-spelt flour or whole-wheat flour

170 grams (¾ cup) sourdough starter discard

50 grams (¼ cup) room-temperature unsalted butter

3 grams (1 tablespoon) chopped thyme leaves

4 grams (¾ teaspoon) salt

Extra-virgin olive oil, for brushing or spraying the surface of the crackers

58.7 grams (¼ cup) grated Parmesan

DIRECTIONS

1 In a medium bowl, mix together the flour, starter, butter, thyme, and salt.

2 Knead the dough into a ball.

3 Divide the dough in half and tightly wrap each rounded dough with plastic wrap.

4 Place the wrapped dough in the refrigerator for 1 hour.

5 Lightly flour a flat surface.

6 Working with one piece of dough at a time, roll out the dough into a square, about 1/8-inch thick.

7 Place a piece of parchment paper on a baking sheet.

8 Place the dough on top of the parchment paper.

9 Brush or spray the top of the dough with olive oil and sprinkle with 2 tablespoons grated Parmesan cheese.

10 Using a pizza cutter or a sharp knife, cut the dough into 1-inch squares. (It's okay if the squares aren't perfectly shaped.)

11 Preheat the oven to 325 degrees.

12 Bake for 20 to 25 minutes or until golden brown.

13 While the first batch of crackers is baking, roll out the second batch of dough.

14 Place a piece of parchment paper on a baking sheet.

15 Place the dough on top of the parchment paper.

16 Brush or spray the top of the dough with olive oil and sprinkle with 2 tablespoons grated Parmesan cheese.

17 Using a pizza cutter or a sharp knife, cut the dough into 1-inch squares.

18 After you've removed the first batch from the oven, place the second batch in the oven and bake for 20 to 25 minutes or until golden brown.

PER SERVING: *Calories 142 (From Fat 58); Fat 6g (Saturated 4g); Cholesterol 16mg; Sodium 244mg; Carbohydrate 18g (Dietary Fiber 2g); Protein 4g.*

TIP: Store in an airtight container at room temperature for up to 5 days.

TIP: Serve with thinly sliced apples, tomatoes, or salami for an afternoon snack.

VARY IT! Add in ¼ cup sesame seeds and cracked black pepper for a savory spin.

Savory Bacon and Cheddar Scones

PREP TIME: 10 MIN | BAKE TIME: 20 MIN | YIELD: 8 SERVINGS

INGREDIENTS

188 grams (1½ cups) all-purpose flour

12 grams (1 teaspoon) sugar

15 grams (1 tablespoon) baking powder

3 gram (½ teaspoon) kosher salt

70 grams (2 tablespoons) cold unsalted butter, cubed

6 slices cooked bacon, crumbled or chopped

50 grams (½ cup) finely grated cheddar cheese

227 grams (1 cup) sourdough starter discard

120 grams (½ cup) half-and-half

DIRECTIONS

1 In a medium bowl, mix together the flour, sugar, baking powder, and salt.

2 Cut in the butter until small crumbs appear.

3 Stir in the crumbled bacon and grated cheese.

4 Make a well in the center of the dry ingredients.

5 Pour the starter and half-and-half into the well and stir until combined.

6 Preheat the oven to 425 degrees.

7 Lightly flour a flat surface.

8 Place the scone mixture onto the floured surface and knead 5 times or until the mixture comes together and is not too moist.

9 Flatten the dough into an 8-inch circular disk.

10   Cut the dough into 8 wedges.

11   Place a piece of parchment paper on a baking sheet.

12   Place the scones on top of the parchment paper, about 1 inch apart.

13   Bake the scones for 20 to 22 minutes, or until golden brown.

PER SERVING: *Calories 286 (From Fat 124); Fat 14g (Saturated 8g); Cholesterol 38mg; Sodium 438mg; Carbohydrate 32g (Dietary Fiber 2g); Protein 9g.*

TIP: Store baked scones in an airtight container in the refrigerator for up to 3 days. You can also store the raw scones or baked scones in an airtight wrapping in the freezer for up to 1 month.

TIP: Preshredded cheese and precooked bacon help this scone recipe come together in minutes.

VARY IT! Add in fresh herbs like chives, chopped rosemary, or dried oregano. You can use whole milk in place of half-and-half for a less rich dough.

Beer-Battered Vegetable Tempura

| PREP TIME: 30 MIN | BAKE TIME: 2 MIN | YIELD: 4 SERVINGS |

INGREDIENTS

872 grams (4 cups) avocado or grapeseed oil, for frying

454 grams (2 cups) sourdough starter discard

2 eggs

1 gram (½ teaspoon) paprika

1 gram (½ teaspoon) black pepper

3 grams (½ teaspoon) salt

8 asparagus spears

16 green beans

1 sweet onion, thickly sliced into rings

1 medium sweet potato, roasted and cooled and sliced into ½-inch circles

120 grams (½ cup) ranch dressing, for dipping

DIRECTIONS

1 In a Dutch oven or deep skillet, heat the oil to 355 degrees.

2 Meanwhile, in a medium bowl, mix together the starter, eggs, paprika, pepper, and salt.

3 Place the asparagus, green beans, onion, and sweet potato into the batter and toss to lightly coat.

4 Place a brown paper bag or paper towels on a baking sheet.

5 When the oil has heated, work in small batches to cook the tempura vegetables. Add 4 to 6 vegetable pieces in at a time and cook the vegetables for 2 to 3 minutes, or until golden brown, flipping the vegetables periodically as they fry.

6 Remove the vegetables to the baking sheet to cool.

7 Return the oil temperature to 355 degrees and then add in the next batch of vegetables.

8 Check the seasoning, and salt if needed.

9 Serve the tempura vegetables with the ranch dip.

PER SERVING: *Calories 448 (From Fat 162); Fat 18g (Saturated 2g); Cholesterol 106mg; Sodium 348mg; Carbohydrate 62g (Dietary Fiber 7g); Protein 13g.*

TIP: These are best consumed the day they're prepared.

NOTE: To preroast the sweet potato, slice it into rings and roast at 400 degrees for 15 to 20 minutes or until slightly tender. The idea is that the sweet potato is mostly cooked, because it won't be fried long enough to fully cook the vegetable.

VARY IT! You can use a variety of vegetables, like mushrooms, squash, zucchini, broccoli, or potatoes. Pre-cook harder vegetables by blanching, boiling, microwaving, or roasting. This is a fun way to repurpose leftover vegetables!

Salted Dark Chocolate Brownies

PREP TIME: 15 MIN	BAKE TIME: 45 MIN	YIELD: 9 SERVINGS

INGREDIENTS

150 grams (5.3 ounces) dark chocolate (65% to 70% cocoa solids), broken into small pieces

50 grams (¼ cup) unsalted butter

40 grams (¼ cup) canola oil

6 grams (1 large) orange, zested

36 grams (3 tablespoons) brewed coffee or espresso

3 grams (½ teaspoon) salt

2 grams (½ teaspoon) vanilla extract

120 grams (½ cup plus 2 tablespoons) sourdough starter

150 grams (⅔ cup) sugar

110 grams (½ cup, packed) light brown sugar

25 grams (¼ cup) unsweetened cocoa powder

25 grams (¼ cup) all-purpose flour

3 eggs

3 grams (½ teaspoon) coarse sea salt, for topping

DIRECTIONS

1 In a microwave-safe bowl, place the chocolate and butter, and microwave on high for 1 minute, stirring after 30 seconds.

2 Stir to melt the remaining chocolate chunks.

3 Add the canola oil, orange zest, coffee, salt, and vanilla to the melted chocolate, and stir.

4 When the chocolate feels slightly warm, mix in the starter, sugar, light brown sugar, cocoa powder, flour, and eggs.

5 Preheat the oven to 350 degrees.

6 Spray a 9-x-9-inch baking sheet or glass casserole dish with cooking spray.

7 Pour the batter into the dish and bake for 45 to 50 minutes or until an internal temperature of 190 degrees has been reached.

8 Sprinkle the sea salt on top as the brownies cool.

PER SERVING: *Calories 353 (From Fat 158); Fat 18g (Saturated 8g); Cholesterol 83mg; Sodium 289mg; Carbohydrate 47g (Dietary Fiber 3g); Protein 5g.*

NOTE: Store in an airtight container in the refrigerator for up to 3 days.

VARY IT! Add in chopped pecans or walnuts for a little crunch.

Blueberry Sourdough Coffeecake

PREP TIME: 20 MIN	BAKE TIME: 45 MIN	YIELD: 12 SERVINGS

INGREDIENTS

480 grams (4 cups) all-purpose flour, divided

298 grams (1½ cup) sugar, divided

100 grams (½ cup) packed brown sugar

1 gram (½ teaspoon) ground cardamom

6 grams (1 teaspoon) salt, divided

170 grams (¾ cup) unsalted butter, melted

113 grams (½ cup) room-temperature unsalted butter

2 large eggs

4 grams (1 teaspoon) vanilla extract

227 grams (1 cup) sourdough starter discard

61 grams (¼ cup) whole milk

5 grams (1 teaspoon) baking powder

2.5 grams (½ teaspoon) baking soda

150 grams (1½ cups) fresh or frozen whole blueberries

DIRECTIONS

1 To make the streusel topping, in a medium bowl, stir together 240 grams (2 cups) of the flour, 100 grams (½ cup) of the sugar, the brown sugar, the cardamom, and 3 grams (½ teaspoon) of the salt.

2 Pour in the melted butter and use your fingers or a fork to crumble the topping into pea-size crumbs.

3 To make the cake batter, in the bowl of a stand mixer with a whisk or paddle attachment, beat together the room-temperature butter and the remaining 198 grams (1 cup) of the sugar for 4 minutes or until creamy.

4 Add in 1 egg at a time, mixing for 1 minute after adding each egg.

5 Add the vanilla, starter, and milk, and mix to combine.

6 In a medium bowl, whisk together the remaining 240 grams (2 cups) of flour, the baking powder, the baking soda, and the remaining 3 grams (½ teaspoon) of salt.

7 Run the mixer at speed 2 and slowly add in the flour mixture.

8 Remove the whisk attachment and stir in the blueberries.

9 Preheat the oven to 350 degrees.

10 Spray a 9-x-13-inch casserole dish with cooking spray.

11 Pour the cake batter into the dish.

12 Crumble the topping over the top of the batter.

13 Bake for 45 to 50 minutes, or until golden brown, with the sides pulling away from the edge. The internal temperature should be between 200 and 205 degrees.

PER SERVING: *Calories 501 (From Fat 187); Fat 21g (Saturated 13g); Cholesterol 86mg; Sodium 304mg; Carbohydrate 74g (Dietary Fiber 2g); Protein 7g.*

NOTE: Store tightly wrapped at room temperature for 3 to 5 days.

TIP: To boost the fiber content of this recipe, use white whole-wheat flour instead of all-purpose flour.

VARY IT! Mix in chopped walnuts in the crumb topping for a fun crunch.

Chapter **14**

Dip It, Spread It, Top It

M any breads taste amazing with just a dip of olive oil or a smear of butter. You can also elevate your favorite toasted bread or sandwich with sauces or spreads. My absolute favorite — the Sweet Potato and Pumpkin Seed Spread — may shock your taste buds. My dear friend Franzi introduced this to me, and we topped it with lemon-dressed arugula and goat cheese. Instantly, it became my new favorite way to use up leftover roasted sweet potatoes.

If you love pizza, skip jarred sauce and try my Roasted Tomato Pizza Sauce, which takes me back to my travels in Italy. If red sauce isn't your thing, try dollops of the Olive and Pine Nut Spread instead.

Next time you make a charcuterie board, wow your guests with this combination: Spelt Baguettes (Chapter 7), crackers, grapes, dried apricots, Chia Apricot Jam (recipe in this chapter) over goat cheese, Indian Spiced Lentil Dip (recipe in this chapter), and toasted almonds and walnuts.

TIP

Most dips and sauces can be made in advance and stored in the refrigerator for at least five days. Perfect for party planning and prepping in advance — and the best way to complement your delicious breads!

Compound Herbed Butter

INGREDIENTS

30 grams (½ cup) chopped parsley

4 cloves garlic

2 grams (1 tablespoon) chopped mint

6 grams (2 tablespoons) thyme leaves

16 ounces (2 cups) unsalted butter

1 gram (½ teaspoon) white ground pepper

6 grams (1 teaspoon) sea salt

1 lemon, zested

DIRECTIONS

1 In the bowl of a food processor, place the parsley, garlic, mint, and thyme. Pulse for 1 minute.

2 Slice the butter into tablespoons and add to the food processor.

3 Sprinkle with white pepper, salt, and lemon zest. Pulse for 2 to 3 minutes or until the butter softens with the herbs and gets infused.

4 Cut a piece of parchment paper in half.

5 Place half the butter mixture in a snakelike strip, about 2 x 5 inches, on one side of the parchment paper.

6 Repeat on the other piece of parchment paper with the remaining butter mixture.

7 Roll up the butter and twist the ends to secure the compound butter.

8 Place the butter in the refrigerator or freezer.

9 Chill for at least 1 hour before slicing and serving.

PER SERVING: *Calories 204 (From Fat 207); Fat 23g (Saturated 15g); Cholesterol 61mg; Sodium 125mg; Carbohydrate 0g (Dietary Fiber 0g); Protein 0g.*

TIP: Store in an airtight container in the refrigerator for up to 1 week or in the freezer for up to 6 months.

TIP: Serve on grilled baguettes or toast, toss with roasted vegetables, or serve on cooked meats or seafood.

Sweet Potato and Pumpkin Seed Spread

PREP TIME: 55 MIN	YIELD: 12 SERVINGS

INGREDIENTS

2 medium sweet potatoes, cubed

73 grams (¼ cup plus 1 tablespoon) extra-virgin olive oil, divided

3 grams (½ teaspoon) sea salt

3 grams (½ teaspoon) garlic powder

1 gram (¼ teaspoon) onion powder

60 grams (½ cup) hulled pumpkin seeds, divided

43 grams (3 tablespoons) fresh lime juice

1 gram (¼ teaspoon) ground cumin

DIRECTIONS

1 Preheat the oven to 400 degrees.

2 Line a baking sheet with parchment paper.

3 In a bowl, toss the sweet potatoes with 1 tablespoon of the olive oil, the salt, the garlic powder, and the onion powder.

4 Transfer to the parchment paper and bake for 30 minutes or until golden brown and soft.

5 Let the sweet potatoes cool completely, about 20 minutes.

6 Place 6 tablespoons of the pumpkin seeds into a food processor and pulse for 30 seconds to 1 minute, until a coarse texture is reached.

7 Add in the sweet potatoes, lime juice, and cumin.

8 Pulse while slowly adding the remaining olive oil until the desired consistency is reached.

9 Top with the remaining 2 tablespoons of pumpkin seeds for serving.

PER SERVING: *Calories 376 (From Fat 354); Fat 39g (Saturated 21g); Cholesterol 81mg; Sodium 245mg; Carbohydrate 5g (Dietary Fiber 1g); Protein 2g.*

TIP: Store in an airtight container in the refrigerator for up to 5 days.

TIP: Serve this savory sweet potato dip on toast with fresh arugula and goat cheese on top, or dip your favorite crackers into the savory spread.

VARY IT! Make this spread Spanish-style, using paprika and lemon juice instead of cumin and lime juice.

Mashed Avocado Spread

PREP TIME: 5 MIN   YIELD: 8 SERVINGS

INGREDIENTS

2 large ripe avocados, peeled and pitted

½ lemon, juiced (about 3 tablespoons)

61 grams (¼ cup) sour cream

2 grams (¼ cup) chopped dill

3 grams (½ teaspoon) sea salt

9 grams (1 tablespoon) sesame seeds, for garnish

DIRECTIONS

1 Place the avocados in a bowl.

2 Using a fork, mash the avocados until they're chunky.

3 Add in the lemon juice, sour cream, dill, and salt. Adjust the salt as desired.

4 To serve, top with sesame seeds.

PER SERVING: *Calories 103 (From Fat 85); Fat 9g (Saturated 2g); Cholesterol 4mg; Sodium 156mg; Carbohydrate 5g (Dietary Fiber 4g); Protein 1g.*

TIP: Store in an airtight container at room temperature for up to 5 days, in the refrigerator for up to 1 week, or in the freezer for up to 3 months.

TIP: Everyone makes guacamole for toast, but why not try this fresh spin on a crusty baguette or toasted sourdough? Top with smoked salmon, thinly sliced lemon, thinly sliced red onion, and capers for a complete lunch.

VARY IT! Spice up this recipe with a dash of ground ginger. Craving a crunch? Add chopped almonds, walnuts, or pecans.

Sun-Dried Tomato Hummus

PREP TIME: 10 MIN YIELD: 16 SERVINGS

INGREDIENTS

14 grams (¼ cup) sun-dried tomatoes, canned in oil

One 16-ounce can garbanzo beans (chickpeas)

61 grams (¼ cup) garbanzo bean liquid from the can

10 grams (2 teaspoons) tahini

14 grams (1 tablespoon) lemon juice

3 grams (½ teaspoon) kosher salt

75 grams (⅓ cup) extra-virgin olive oil

DIRECTIONS

1 Place the sun-dried tomatoes in a food processor.

2 Pulse the tomatoes for about 1 minute.

3 Add in the garbanzo beans, the liquid from the can, the tahini, the lemon juice, and the salt.

4 Pulse until mixed.

5 While running the food processor, drizzle in the olive oil until the desired consistency is reached.

PER SERVING: *Calories 84 (From Fat 52); Fat 6g (Saturated 1g); Cholesterol 0mg; Sodium 161mg; Carbohydrate 7g (Dietary Fiber 1g); Protein 2g.*

NOTE: Store in an airtight container in the refrigerator for up to 1 week.

TIP: Saving the water from the garbanzo bean can is a great way to thin out hummus without it becoming too oily.

TIP: Serve with your favorite crackers, sandwiches, or smeared onto crusty bread.

VARY IT! Hummus has many variations where you can add almost any addition, from olive to beets. Get creative and have fun with combinations like pumpkin seeds or artichokes.

Roasted Tomato Pizza Sauce

INGREDIENTS

56 grams (¼ cup) extra-virgin olive oil

6 garlic cloves, minced

Two 14.5-ounce cans fire-roasted tomatoes

12 grams (1 tablespoon) sugar

2 grams (1 teaspoon) black pepper

2 grams (2 teaspoons) dried oregano

6 grams (1 teaspoon) sea salt

DIRECTIONS

1 In a small skillet, heat the olive oil over medium heat.

2 Add the garlic and sauté for 2 minutes. Do not allow the garlic to brown or burn. Immediately remove from the heat.

3 Transfer the olive oil and garlic to a blender or food processor.

4 Add the tomatoes, sugar, pepper, oregano, and salt.

5 Blend for 1 minute or until smooth.

6 Transfer the sauce to a large skillet and heat over medium-low heat for 10 minutes.

7 Remove from the heat.

PER SERVING: *Calories 85 (From Fat 68); Fat 8g (Saturated 1g); Cholesterol 0mg; Sodium 359mg; Carbohydrate 5g (Dietary Fiber 1g); Protein 1g.*

TIP: Store in an airtight container in the refrigerator for up to 1 week or in the freezer for up to 6 months.

TIP: This sauce can be used for 2 to 4 pizzas, depending on whether you prefer a thicker or thinner sauce.

VARY IT! Stir in chopped olives, capers, or fresh parsley for Greek-style pizza.

Olive and Pine Nut Spread

INGREDIENTS

67 grams (½ cup) pine nuts

90 grams (½ cup) canned black or green olives (pitted)

60 grams (1 cup) fresh parsley leaves

1 garlic clove

⅛ teaspoon crushed red pepper (optional)

43 grams (3 tablespoons) olive oil

DIRECTIONS

1 In a small skillet, toast the pine nuts over medium-low heat until fragrant, about 2 minutes.

2 Transfer the pine nuts to a food processor.

3 Add the olives, parsley, garlic, and red pepper.

4 Pulse a few times to roughly chop.

5 Add the olive oil, 1 tablespoon at a time, while pulsing, until the desired consistency is reached.

PER SERVING: *Calories 118 (From Fat 108); Fat 12g (Saturated 1g); Cholesterol 0mg; Sodium 104mg; Carbohydrate 3g (Dietary Fiber 1g); Protein 2g.*

TIP: Store in an airtight container in the refrigerator for up to 2 weeks.

NOTE: If you prefer a smooth consistency, process for 2 minutes. For a chunkier consistency, pulse for 30 seconds.

TIP: Stir into olive oil and vinegar for a quick vinaigrette, add on top of pizza for a salty addition, or spread onto your favorite Greek- or Italian-inspired sandwich.

VARY IT! If you're looking for a tapenade, add anchovies and capers to this mix. It's a fun twist on an Italian classic!

Roasted Garlic and Lemon Dip

PREP TIME: 40 MIN	BAKE TIME: 35 MIN	YIELD: 10 SERVINGS

INGREDIENTS

1 whole head of garlic

109 grams (½ cup) extra-virgin olive oil, divided

1 lemon, zested and juiced

30 grams (½ cup) finely chopped parsley leaves

3 grams (½ teaspoon) sea salt

15 grams (1 tablespoon) red wine vinegar

DIRECTIONS

1 Preheat the oven to 350 degrees.

2 Cut off the top of the head of garlic, just to expose the start of the cloves inside.

3 Place the head of garlic in the center of a piece of foil, about 8 x 8 inches in size.

4 Drizzle 1 tablespoon of olive oil over the top of the garlic.

5 Enclose the foil around the garlic head.

6 Place the garlic in the oven and roast for 35 minutes. When you can squeeze the garlic with ease, you know it's cooked.

7 Remove from the oven and cool completely before handling.

8 In a small bowl, squeeze out the roasted garlic; the pulp should squeeze out with ease, leaving the skins behind.

9 Stir in the remaining olive oil, the lemon juice and zest, the parsley, the sea salt, and the vinegar.

PER SERVING: *Calories 112 (From Fat 108); Fat 12g (Saturated 2g); Cholesterol 0mg; Sodium 118mg; Carbohydrate 1g (Dietary Fiber 0g); Protein 0g.*

TIP: Store in an airtight container in the refrigerator for up to 3 weeks or in the freezer for up to 6 months.

TIP: If you love dipping bread into olive oil, you'll love this recipe! It also makes for a great salad dressing or a sauce for grilled meats or shrimp.

TIP: Prepare multiple heads of garlic at one time and freeze the garlic you don't use. Just put the pulp in an airtight container or freezer-safe plastic bag.

Smoked Salmon Spread

INGREDIENTS

4 ounces cream cheese

4 ounces plain Greek yogurt

9 grams (1 tablespoon) capers

3 grams (2 tablespoons) chopped parsley

1 grams (½ teaspoon) black pepper

½ lemon, zested and juiced

4 ounces smoked salmon, flaked or chopped

1 gram (¼ teaspoon) salt, or to taste

DIRECTIONS

1 In the bowl of a stand mixer with a paddle attachment, stir together the cream cheese, yogurt, capers, parsley, pepper, lemon juice, and lemon zest for 3 minutes or until creamy.

2 Add in the smoked salmon and stir until combined.

3 Season with salt to taste.

PER SERVING: *Calories 107 (From Fat 66); Fat 7g (Saturated 4g); Cholesterol 27mg; Sodium 330mg; Carbohydrate 3g (Dietary Fiber 0g); Protein 8g.*

TIP: Store in an airtight container in the refrigerator for up to 3 days.

NOTE: Be careful not to oversalt this recipe. The smoked salmon and capers can quickly add salt to this dish.

TIP: Try the Nordic Sunflower Bread (Chapter 10) with this creamy spread. Top with thinly sliced onions and lemon slices. This dip also makes for a perfect vegetable dip on your favorite charcuterie board.

VARY IT! If you don't have Greek yogurt, try using sour cream instead.

Indian Spiced Lentil Dip

PREP TIME: 50 MIN | YIELD: 8 SERVINGS

INGREDIENTS

200 grams (1 cup) uncooked lentils

450 grams (2 cups) water

1 bay leaf

½ lemon, juiced

1 garlic clove, finely chopped

15 grams (¼ cup) chopped cilantro

2 gram (½ teaspoon) curry powder

2 grams (1 teaspoon) ground cumin

39 grams (3 tablespoons) extra-virgin olive oil

3 grams (½ teaspoon) salt

DIRECTIONS

1 In a small saucepan, add the lentils, water, and bay leaf.

2 Cook uncovered over medium heat for 20 minutes or until tender.

3 Drain the lentils.

4 In a medium bowl, stir together the lentils, lemon juice, garlic, cilantro, curry powder, cumin, olive oil, and salt.

5 Cover with plastic wrap and refrigerate for 30 minutes.

6 Adjust the seasonings as desired and serve.

PER SERVING: *Calories 132 (From Fat 46); Fat 5g (Saturated 1g); Cholesterol 0mg; Sodium 147mg; Carbohydrate 15g (Dietary Fiber 8g); Protein 6g.*

TIP: Store in an airtight container in the refrigerator for up to 1 week or in the freezer for 3 months.

TIP: This dip is great when serving flatbread, Indian food, or a Mediterranean charcuterie board. Lentils are dense with nutrition and perfect for vegetarians.

VARY IT! Add in harissa, grated carrot, and chopped preserved lemon for a more authentic flavor profile.

Honey Cardamom Butter

INGREDIENTS

8 ounces unsalted butter, at room temperature

14 grams (2 tablespoons) powdered sugar

85 grams (¼ cup) honey

2 grams (1 teaspoon) ground cardamom

18 grams (2 tablespoons) sesame seeds

1.5 gram (¼ teaspoon) sea salt

DIRECTIONS

1 In the bowl of a stand mixer with a paddle attachment, whip the butter and powdered sugar on speed 2 for 3 minutes or until it's beginning to get fluffy.

2 Add in the honey, cardamom, sesame seeds, and salt.

3 Continue to whip and scrape down the sides until light and fluffy.

PER SERVING: *Calories 171 (From Fat 145); Fat 16g (Saturated 10g); Cholesterol 41mg; Sodium 35mg; Carbohydrate 8g (Dietary Fiber 0g); Protein 0g.*

TIP: Store in an airtight container in the refrigerator for up to 3 weeks.

TIP: The sesame seeds and cardamom marry beautifully in this creamy butter. Serve on your favorite biscuits, breakfast bread, or toast.

VARY IT! Chopped pecans and cinnamon or chopped walnuts and orange zest are great combinations. The sky is the limit when it comes to home-made honey butters!

Chia Apricot Jam

PREP TIME: 8 HR 10 MIN | YIELD: 32 SERVINGS

INGREDIENTS

760 grams (4 cups) dried apricots

900 grams (4 cups) boiling water

1 gram (¼ teaspoon) almond extract

1 gram (½ teaspoon) ground cinnamon

36 grams (3 tablespoons) chia seeds

DIRECTIONS

1 In a heat-safe bowl, add the apricots and boiling water.

2 Cover and let them reconstitute for 20 minutes.

3 In the bowl of a food processor, add the reconstituted apricots and pulse for 1 minute.

4 If the mixture seems too thick, add 1 tablespoon of the apricot water until it thins to the consistency of yogurt.

5 Add the almond extract and cinnamon and pulse for 30 seconds.

6 Add the chia seeds and pulse for 30 seconds.

7 Pour the jam into 4-ounce jars and refrigerate for 8 hours.

PER SERVING: *Calories 62 (From Fat 4); Fat 0g (Saturated 0g); Cholesterol 0mg; Sodium 3mg; Carbohydrate 15g (Dietary Fiber 2g); Protein 1g.*

NOTE: Store in an airtight container in the refrigerator for up to 2 weeks or in the freezer for up to 6 months.

TIP: You can use this jam on biscuits, on toast, or stirred into plain yogurt. Our favorite is over goat cheese with Cheesy Kinder Crackers (Chapter 13).

VARY IT! Chia jam is so simple! You can make this with fresh, frozen, or dried fruit. If you want it thicker, add another tablespoon of chia seeds. Adjust the sweetness with honey or maple syrup.

Chocolate Hazelnut Spread

PREP TIME: 20 MIN | **YIELD: 16 SERVINGS**

INGREDIENTS

8 ounces (1¾ cups) hazelnuts

28 grams (2 tablespoons) coconut oil

1 grams (¼ teaspoon) salt

25 grams (¼ cup) cocoa powder

120 grams (1 cup) powdered sugar

DIRECTIONS

1 Preheat the oven to 325 degrees.

2 Place the parchment paper onto a baking sheet.

3 Spread the hazelnuts onto the parchment paper.

4 Roast the hazelnuts for 15 minutes. They should be toasted, but not browned.

5 Pour the hazelnuts onto a tea towel.

6 Rub the nuts with the towel to remove the outer skins.

7 Place the hazelnuts into the bowl of a food processor.

8 Pulse the nuts for 3 minutes, scraping down the sides as needed.

9 Add in the coconut oil and salt and blend for 3 to 5 minutes or until it starts to become creamy.

10 Meanwhile, in a small bowl, stir together the cocoa powder and powdered sugar.

11 Add the sugar mixture to the nuts and blend until creamy and incorporated.

PER SERVING: *Calories 137 (From Fat 96); Fat 11g (Saturated 2g); Cholesterol 0mg; Sodium 25mg; Carbohydrate 1g (Dietary Fiber 2g); Protein 2g.*

NOTE: Store in an airtight container in the refrigerator for up to 3 weeks.

NOTE: This spread is a bit thick. If you prefer a creamy hazelnut sauce, opt for melted chocolate (about 1 cup semisweet chips, melted in the microwave for 1 to 2 minutes, stirring frequently).

NOTE: Serve on toast, stirred into yogurt, or with Sharon's Challah Bread (Chapter 9).

VARY IT! You can also make this spread with almonds or peanuts.

3

The Part of Tens

Find ten tips for bread-making success.

Discover the tricks of sourdough bread making.

Prepare creative sandwiches with delicious homemade breads.

Create crowd-pleasing recipes with stale bread.

Chapter **15**

Ten Tips for Successful Bread Making

E very baker — from novice to professional — does, at some point, have a bread-baking flop. As I developed recipes for this book, I had some flops, too. I forgot my salt, it was too hot one night and my bread over-proofed, and I forgot to set a timer for one loaf and it got mighty charred. It happens to us all! Some people have them more often, though, so if you find your trouble is not a one-time thing, it's time to dive deeper and look at some common mistakes that can cause trouble in baking bread.

Use a Digital Scale

There is a reason why grams are listed before volumetric measurements in the recipes in this book: Weight measurements are more accurate than cups. Whether you consider yourself a beginner or an advanced baker, scaled measurements are better. A good digital scale is a $12 to $15 investment, and it'll make all the difference in the quality of your breads!

Use a Digital Thermometer

A digital thermometer will help you make sure your bread is baked. After years of baking, I still pull out my thermometer and check. Oven temperatures can waiver, especially over time, and the result can be disastrous.

My favorite times to use my digital thermometer are when I'm making sweet stuffed or rolled breads, because fillings can quickly make breads behave differently. No one wants an uncooked bread. A good digital thermometer will run you about $20 and save you plenty of heartache.

Use a Stand Mixer with a Dough Hook

A stand mixer with a dough hook *is* an investment, but kneading dough by hand, although very satisfying and a great workout, can put your dough at risk for under-developing the gluten. With a stand mixer, you can mix a dough in 5 to 20 minutes, as opposed to about 10 to 30 minutes by hand. I'm exhausted just writing it!

There are many brands to choose from, including top-rated KitchenAid, budget-friendly Hamilton Beach, ever-popular Cuisinart, and the new rising star, Swedish-made Ankarsrum. You don't have to break the bank buying a stand mixer, but less expensive models may have a shorter lifespan. My current KitchenAid mixer is over 20 years old and still going strong.

Use the Right Flour

The recipes in this book have been tested with the ingredients listed, but if you find yourself in a crazy situation — like, oh, for example, a pandemic — and the only flour you can find are low-protein flours, grab a bag of vital wheat gluten flour and add it to lower-protein flours to give them the gluten structure you need for a successful loaf. Vital wheat gluten flour is also a useful product to use if you want to make 100 percent whole einkorn or Khorasan breads, which are lower in gluten.

TIP

A good rule of thumb is 1 to 2 tablespoons of vital wheat gluten flour for every 2 to 3 cups of flour.

Use Less Flour

This lesson was probably the hardest one for me to learn. I had been raised hearing that bread should pull from the sides of the mixing bowl and create a slapping sound on the sides. For many breads, yes, but for enriched breads, I haven't found this to be the case.

Actually, in many of the sweet and enriched bread recipes in this book, I tell you to refrigerate the dough before you work with it. That's a good tip to keep in your mind if the dough you're working with is moister and harder to handle. Let the dough rise until it doubles in size. Then press out the air and try to shape it. Then put it in a bowl topped with plastic wrap and refrigerate for a couple hours or overnight. The chilling of the dough can really help with shaping.

TIP

Many bakers recommend kneading with wet hands, instead of adding more flour. This helps keep the dough from sticking to your hands and from surfaces.

REMEMBER

The more bread you bake, the better you'll get at identifying these subtle tricks of the trade.

Pay Attention to the Weather

Bread behaves differently in cold weather than it does in hot, dry climates than it does in humid weather. And altitude affects bread, too.

REMEMBER

Yeast is *alive*, and because it's a living, breathing thing, bakers need to understand how to work with dough in varying conditions. Here are my suggestions:

>> **Temperature:** As temperatures creep up, you may find your dough doubling in size quickly, or your sourdough starter may bubble over the top, or your breads may look over-proofed. In hot weather, yeast gets more active. There are a couple things you can do:

- Reduce the amount of yeast or sourdough starter you use. Cut it in half and see how quickly the bread responds.

- Check your dough frequently to make sure it hasn't doubled in size too fast. Cut the time to 1 hour in traditional yeast breads and maybe just 6 to 8 hours for a sourdough bulk ferment.

Alternatively, in cold weather, things really may slow down. You may need to rise your bread for 4 hours in a cold house or put it into an oven with the heat off and light on to warm the space. Typically, I don't recommend adding in more yeast, but if you find yourself in a hurry that may be the solution you need.

>> **Humidity:** Humidity may require you to bake your breads longer to evaporate the moisture. On the other hand, in dry, arid climates you may find your breads overbake quickly. Where I live, in the summer, the humidity goes up, so I cut back on water and just use wet hands to knead to help address this situation. If you're having trouble, take notes on the temperature and humidity on the day you're baking, and try a single recipe multiple times until you figure out what's best. After all, baking is a science!

>> **Altitude:** If you live high in the mountains, there's a good chance you've already discovered the frustrating reality that breads made at altitude behave differently. The recipes in this book have been tested at sea level, so if you live above 3,000 feet, you'll have to make adjustments. Some facts to consider:

- Water boils faster at altitude.

- Moisture evaporates quicker at altitude, which is also why the air is often drier.

- Gas expands more rapidly at altitude, so your bread may be fluffier.

To adjust for these conditions, you may need to:

- Heat your water longer.

- Add more water (working with wet hands helps).

- Keep your flours fresher.

- Bake longer or increase the oven temperature and bake less.

- Use less yeast.

- Use a higher-protein flour or add in vital wheat gluten flour.

- Decrease rise times.

Search the web for "high-altitude bread baking" and see if you can find a recipe baked in your area. This can help you get an idea of how to adjust the recipes you find in this book. Whatever you do, don't give up! You *can* bake bread at altitude — and it's worth the effort to get it right.

Use High-Quality Baking Pans

A cast-iron Dutch oven and a heavy baking sheet are my go-to picks for baking. Cast iron can handle very high heat (well above 700 degrees), so you'll be safe using these products. I have a cast-iron baking sheet and Dutch oven that I use primarily in baking. I recommend avoiding nonstick pans, because the coating is often not safe when heated to high temperatures like the kind used in bread baking. Stoneware is best with temperatures less than 450 degrees. Aluminum is safe in household ovens with temperatures below 600 degrees. Find a high-quality baking vessel and take good care of it.

TIP

My method of keeping my cast iron seasoned and in top shape is to season it by frying thinly sliced potatoes until black. (Clearly, I don't serve these potatoes to anyone.) Also, any time I use the pan, I clean it with oil and coarse salt, not soapy water. I may rinse with water, but I never use soap. When in doubt, check with the manufacturer of your cast iron to see how they recommend you care for it.

Experiment with Flours

Using white or wheat flours is easy, but the depth of flavor you get with grains like spelt, rye, and einkorn is interesting to explore. These grains will give you a new respect for the way grains are grown, how they behave in recipes, and their unique flavor profiles. In my own kitchen, I regularly use spelt and rye, and I dabble with einkorn and Khorasan.

Don't Skip the Salt

Do you have health concerns that make you want to drop the salt? If you're thinking of cutting back on the salt, I don't recommend using less than 5 grams per loaf.

REMEMBER

Salt works with gluten and creating the ever-important matrix (see Chapter 1). To give your bread structure and flavor, you need salt.

Play with Different Baking Techniques

Steaming (putting boiling water in a hot pan as you place the bread in), using a bread stone, covering bread and then uncovering it halfway through the baking process, using a little sourdough starter and yeast combined, using less yeast and letting a dough rise longer, trying out a *tangzhong* or *yudane* to extend the shelf life (see Appendix C for more on these techniques). There are so many great ways to play with breads. My hope is that you work through many of the recipes in this book, find the one that fits you best, and then make it your own!

TIP

Before settling on just one favorite recipe, do your best to bake your way through this book and try new techniques. You may be surprised which techniques and recipes become your favorites.

Chapter **16**

Ten (Or So) Common Sourdough Questions

Sourdough can be so simple and yet so complex. Because your starter is alive, your dough is also alive, which means you have to treat it with care. Many variables, some of which I cover in Chapter 15, can apply to sourdough baking. But specific to sourdough there are some frequent questions I hear about from friends, colleagues, and fellow bakers. I answer those questions in this chapter.

This book isn't dedicated to sourdough baking, but sourdough is my favorite bread to bake and one I really hope you'll try and keep trying until you find the rhythm to love it, too.

Why Is My Bread Gummy?

If you're finding that your bread is gummy, make sure you've allowed it to cool completely before slicing into the loaf. Cutting into a warm loaf can create a gummy crumb.

TIP

If you really can't resist the taste of warm bread, bake your sourdough as rolls instead. Then you can allow some to cool completely and still savor the taste of warm bread.

Why Is My Loaf Flat?

A light, rounded loaf is typically the goal of sourdough, but even experienced bakers sometimes end up with a flat disk. Doing routine stretches and folds really helps add volume to a loaf. Make sure the temperature is about 70 to 75 degrees when it's bulk fermenting. Then be sure to get a tight shape. After you shape, place the dough into a well-floured banneton or into your parchment-lined Dutch oven and let it rise (covered) for 1 to 2 more hours or do a cold proof for up to 36 to 48 hours. Get your oven very hot. Then quickly score the bread and bake.

How Do I Know if My Starter Is Ready?

If you're not sure whether your starter is ready, feed it again and let it rise before using it. If your starter has sat in the refrigerator for a while, do twice-daily feedings for a couple days before baking with it. The more you bake, the happier your starter will be and the better it will perform.

In addition to feeding the starter regularly, consider feeding with rye flour. Rye flour naturally imparts a beautiful color and *tang* (sour notes) into the starter.

REMEMBER

The starter is alive! Treat it with care, feed it appropriately, and try not to neglect it.

What Do I Do If My Dough Is Too Sticky to Handle?

A dough scraper can be your best friend and help transfer dough from a bowl to a work surface. As you shape the dough, you'll feel it become more pliable and less sticky. If you're still struggling, use wet hands. Doughs with a higher level of hydration (more water than a standard loaf) can be trickier to work. Wet your hands and try your best to stretch and fold. If it seems impossible, place your dough in the refrigerator for a couple hours and then try again.

A wetter dough is actually preferred among sourdough bakers and will yield the desired airholes sourdough lovers crave. If you're a beginner in sourdough baking, you can use 50 to 100 grams less water, and see if the dough is easier to handle. The highest hydration loaf in this book is the Spelt Baguettes recipe in Chapter 7.

TECHNICAL STUFF

Baker's percentages calculate the percentage of water to flour in a loaf. This topic is a common point of discussion among serious sourdough bakers. You don't need to know baker's percentages in order to bake a successful loaf — my grandmother never did and most folks I know don't calculate it. However, most bakers understand higher- and lower-hydration loaves. If you'd like to learn more about baker's percentages, head over to King Arthur Flour's website at www.kingarthurflour.com/pro/reference/bakers-percentage and check out their excellent explanation about this complex topic.

How Do I Tighten the Dough after Bulk Rising?

Without the risk of sounding like your mother, practice makes perfect. Practice. Practice. Practice. When I first got started baking sourdough, I watched my friend shape and mold hers. Then I found videos on YouTube. And then I practiced on my own. With practice, I've figured out techniques that feel good to me, where I tuck and pull back on the dough, creating the desired tension. When I've rushed it, my bread tattled on me. The loaves that arch beautifully, have perfect crumb, and have great *spring* (when you press on the baked loaf after it has cooled and it springs back into shape) are letting you know that you're doing something right!

TIP

A double scraper is your friend. This nifty, flexible piece of plastic can help you transfer and work the dough. Use it to your advantage!

Why Is My Loaf So Dense?

There are a couple plausible explanations. Is your starter viable (that is, bubbly and healthy)? Is your dough too cold? Sourdough loves 70 to 75 degrees for the bulk ferment. If it's winter and your home is cold, try sticking the loaf in the oven with the light on (make sure the oven is turned off!), cover it, and see if this helps it double for a bulk ferment.

How Do I Get Those Fancy "Ears" or Lifts in the Crust of My Sourdough?

Many people long for the curved flap produced from scoring the bread at a certain angle and a perfect oven spring at the start of baking. My recommendation is to worry less about scoring and more about getting the taste and texture right. You can find many videos online, explaining how to score bread. If you feel artistic and you're ready to move toward that goal, seek out videos explaining the tricks of the trade.

TIP

To nail a good scoring, you need to have a tightened and shaped dough, a solid second rise, and a sharp scoring tool. Then practice, practice, practice!

Why Is My Bread Dense with Giant Holes?

Yes, holes are desired, but not *giant* holes! Generally, this can mean you've over-proofed your dough (in other words, you've let it rise too long).

Another possible reason can be your oven. Your oven may not be hot enough or you may not be baking your bread long enough. Set your oven temperature to 450 degrees and give it a solid hour to heat up. Rushed on time? Shoot for 30 minutes. This helps you know that your oven is truly hot and ready for the bread.

Use a thermometer to measure the internal temperature of your bread. Has it fully cooked? Aim for 190 to 210 degrees for sourdough. Bake your dough enclosed in a Dutch oven for the first 30 minutes; then uncover and continue baking until the desired color is achieved. Some folks really prefer a softer crumb and crust. If so, you'll want to not let the crust get as dark in color. But for a true artisan look, feel, and crunch, the crust will have a deep golden color and a classic crunchy sound when tapped.

Why Does My Bread Keep Burning on the Bottom?

Baking sheets are your friend. Placing a high-heat baking sheet under your Dutch oven can add a layer of protection so your loaf doesn't burn.

IN THIS CHAPTER

» **Discovering the perfect lunch, picnic, or dinner between two slices of bread**

» **Creating fun and unique sandwich combinations to pair with homemade bread**

Chapter **17**

Ten Trendy Sandwiches

Sandwiches are iconic, from peanut butter and jelly to the classic BLT (bacon, lettuce, and tomato). The key to a great sandwich, of course, is the bread. When you know how to make great bread, it's time to put your bread to good use. Whether it's for lunch or a party, sandwiches are delectable in every bite.

Everyone knows how to make a peanut butter and jelly sandwich, so instead of tackling the classics, this chapter explores some unique flavor combinations you may not have considered. These sandwiches are not only delicious, but also nutritious.

Sweet Potato and Arugula

Plant-based sandwiches are a great way to ramp up your vegetable servings and improve your health. This delicious combo can also be made into an open-faced sandwich or toast. To make this sandwich, follow these steps:

1. **Toast two slices of bread.**

   Great breads to try with this sandwich include Rustic Sourdough (Chapter 7), Pumpkin Seed Bread (Chapter 8), and Swabian Farmhouse Bread (Chapter 10).

TIP

2. **Spread 2 tablespoons of Sweet Potato and Pumpkin Seed Spread (Chapter 14) onto one slice of bread.**

3. In a bowl, toss 1 cup of arugula or spinach leaves with 2 teaspoons lemon juice.

4. Place the greens on top of the spread.

5. Drizzle with extra-virgin olive oil and season with salt and pepper to taste.

6. Top with the second slice of toasted bread.

Mighty Mediterranean

There's no denying the health benefits of the Mediterranean. If you're paying attention to heart health — or you just love delicious food! — be sure to try this sandwich. Follow these steps:

1. Spread Sun-Dried Tomato Hummus (Chapter 14) or your favorite store-bought hummus onto one slice of bread.

TIP

Great breads to try with this sandwich include Hearty Whole-Wheat Bread (Chapter 6), Sun-Dried Tomato and Olive Bread (Chapter 8), and Spelt Baguettes (Chapter 7).

2. Layer thin slices of sliced cucumbers, sliced tomatoes, and raw spinach on top of the hummus.

3. Top with canned, flaked tuna.

4. Season with sea salt and fresh cracked pepper.

5. Sprinkle with feta cheese and drizzle with extra-virgin olive oil.

6. Serve open-faced or top with another slice of bread.

TIP

The Mediterranean diet is rich with seafood, fruits, vegetables, nuts, and seeds. Check out one of my other books, *Mediterranean Diet Cookbook For Dummies* (Wiley), for more creative ideas to embrace the Mediterranean diet.

Chicken and Pesto

Here's another Mediterranean-inspired sandwich that uses up leftover chicken:

1. Thinly slice 3 ounces of grilled or roasted chicken breast.

2. In a bowl, toss the sliced chicken with 1 tablespoon pesto sauce (store bought or see the nearby recipe).

MAKE YOUR OWN PESTO!

TIP

If you'd like to make your own pesto, here's a simple recipe:

1. **Blanch 1 cup of fresh basil in boiling water for 2 seconds; then quickly transfer it to ice water for 30 seconds.**

2. **Pat the basil dry; then place it in a food processor.**

3. **Add the juice of ½ lemon, 2 tablespoons grated Parmesan cheese, 2 table-spoons pine nuts, and 1 clove garlic.**

4. **Blend for 1 minute, while streaming in extra-virgin olive until the desired consistency is reached.**

5. **Season with salt to taste.**

Store in an airtight container in the refrigerator with a layer of olive oil on the surface. It will keep up to 2 weeks.

3. **Layer the chicken breast on one slice of bread.**

TIP

Great breads to try with this sandwich include Ciabatta (Chapter 7), Wheat Bagels (Chapter 9), and French Baguettes (Chapter 10).

4. **Top with thin slices of tomato and fresh mozzarella (the kind stored in water).**

5. **Serve open faced or top with another slice of bread.**

Indian Spiced

Turmeric and lentils both have many heart-healthy attributes. Turmeric is a powerful spice that is touted for its anti-inflammatory properties. Lentils are loaded with fiber and protein and perfect for a vegetarian or plant-based enthusiast. To make this sandwich, follow these steps:

1. **In a bowl, combine 1 cup plain yogurt, 1 grated cucumber, 1 minced garlic clove, the juice of ½ lemon, and salt and pepper to taste; set aside.**

2. **Spread 2 to 3 tablespoons of Indian Spiced Lentil Dip (Chapter 14) on one slice of bread.**

Great breads to try with this sandwich include Turkish Flatbread (Chapter 10), Wheat Sandwich Bread (Chapter 6), and Sourdough Spelt and Sesame Bagels (Chapter 7).

TIP

3. **Top with 2 tablespoons of grated carrots and 2 tablespoons of shredded cabbage.**

4. **Drizzle 2 tablespoons of the cucumber yogurt sauce (from Step 1).**

   Store the rest of the sauce in an airtight container in the refrigerator up to 5 days.

5. **Serve open faced or top with another slice of bread.**

California Club

The California climate is similar to the Mediterranean. Avocados and almonds often take center stage on a California plate. Here's a fun way to serve up this heart-healthy duo:

1. **Thinly slice a ripe avocado.**

2. **Squeeze ½ lemon over the top of the avocado, and season with salt.**

3. **Layer the avocado slices onto one slice of bread.**

TIP

   Great breads to try with this sandwich include Oatmeal Bread (Chapter 6), Bakery Sandwich Rolls (Chapter 9), and German Everyday Rolls (Chapter 10).

4. **Top with baby *microgreens* (young, sprouted seedlings that are about 1 to 3 inches in length), like broccoli, radish, or alfalfa sprouts.**

5. **Chop up roasted almonds and sprinkle on the top of the greens.**

6. **Add a layer of thinly sliced red onions, smoked turkey, and crisp bacon.**

7. **Top with another slice of bread and serve.**

Scandinavian Style

Throughout Scandinavia, you'll find fatty fish served with sunflower seeds. Both of these ingredients boast omega-3 fatty acids and heart-healthy benefits. To make a Scandi-style sandwich, follow these steps:

1. **Thinly spread fermented butter, crème fraiche, or cream cheese on one slice of bread.**

TIP

   Great breads to try with this sandwich include Dark Rye Bread (Chapter 6), Nordic Sunflower Bread (Chapter 10), or Cottage Cheese and Dill Bread (Chapter 8).

2. Top with thin slices of smoked salmon, thinly sliced cucumbers, thinly sliced red onions, and chopped fresh dill.

3. Serve open faced.

Greek Yogurt Tuna Sandwiches

Swapping out mayonnaise with Greek yogurt is a great way to improve your diet with protein and *probiotics* (the healthy bacteria that promotes gut health). To make this healthy sandwich, follow these steps:

1. Drain 6 to 8 ounces of water-packed tuna fish.

2. In a small bowl, whisk together ¼ cup plain Greek yogurt, 1 minced shallot, 1 teaspoon Dijon or spicy mustard, 1 tablespoon lemon juice, and salt and pepper to taste.

3. Place half of the tuna mixture on one slice of bread.

TIP

Great breads to try with this sandwich include Rustic Sourdough (Chapter 7), Golden Honey Wheat Sourdough (Chapter 7), or German Potato Bread (Chapter 10).

4. Top with finely grated carrots and lettuce or sprouts.

5. Serve open faced or top with another slice of bread.

Lamb Burgers

Burgers are fun! You can change the toppings, the bread, and the meat to get creative combinations. Don't just think they need to be served on a bun! You can cook these lamb burgers as meatballs and wrap in flatbread or in a roll. Follow these steps:

1. In a bowl, mix 1 pound of ground lamb meat with 1 teaspoon dried oregano, 1 tablespoon fresh mint, ½ teaspoon garlic powder, ½ teaspoon onion powder, and salt and pepper to taste.

2. Form 4 patties and grill for 4 to 6 minutes on each side until an internal temperature of 160 degrees is reached.

3. **Place each patty on a slice of bread.**

TIP

   Great breads to try with this sandwich include Hamburger Buns (see the Hot Dog Buns recipe in Chapter 9 for a hamburger bun variation), Turkish Flatbread (Chapter 10), and Sahar's Yemini Roti (Chapter 10).

4. **Serve topped with lemon-juice-tossed arugula and drizzle with cucumber sauce (see the recipe in the "Indian Spiced" section, earlier in this chapter).**

5. **Top with crumbled feta cheese and another slice of bread before serving.**

TIP

Wonder why it's recommended to toss arugula or kale greens with citrus? The citrus has citric acid, which softens the greens without wilting them. Plus, citrus has vitamin C, which helps with iron absorption. A winning combination!

Spicy Shrimp

Ramp up your weekly seafood servings with this spicy addition:

1. **In a bowl, mix ½ cup plain Greek yogurt, 2 tablespoons mayonnaise, 1 to 2 teaspoons of Sriracha sauce, the juice of ½ lime, and salt to taste; set aside.**

2. **Season 1 pound raw shrimp with ½ teaspoon garlic powder, 1 teaspoon onion powder, ½ teaspoon ground cumin, and a pinch of ground chili pepper flakes.**

3. **Drizzle or spritz with extra-virgin olive oil.**

4. **Roast the shrimp at 400 degrees for 8 minutes.**

5. **To serve, place the shrimp on a slice of bread and then drizzle with the Sriracha mayo (from Step 1), thinly sliced avocados, and sprouts or shredded cabbage.**

TIP

   Great breads to try with this sandwich include Rustic Sourdough (Chapter 7), Bakery Sandwich Rolls (Chapter 9), and Sourdough Flatbread (Chapter 13).

6. **Serve open faced or top with another slice of bread.**

Breakfast Sandwich

This sandwich is delicious for breakfast, lunch, *or* dinner. It's a great way to use a bread that is starting to stale! Follow these steps:

1. **Fry an egg in extra-virgin olive oil, over easy or over medium; set aside.**

2. **In the same skillet, heat 1 tablespoon olive oil and 1 teaspoon butter.**

3. **Thickly slice the bread and toast both sides in the heated fats.**

TIP

Great breads to try with this sandwich include Sharon's Challah Bread (Chapter 9), German Everyday Rolls (Chapter 10), and Wheat Sandwich Bread (Chapter 6).

4. **Top the pan-toasted bread with the fried egg, grated or sliced sharp cheddar, thinly sliced ham, and thinly sliced avocado.**

5. **Serve open faced or top with another slice of bread.**

Chapter **18**

Ten Ways to Upcycle Stale Bread

As you bake your way through this book, you're bound to find yourself with more bread than you can eat. Before you toss it to the chickens, share it with your compost, or (gasp!) throw it away, consider some creative ways to make that stale bread taste fresh again.

You may note the European influence in many of these recipes. Bread is cherished in every country throughout Europe, and without using preservatives, their breads go stale fast. So, of course, Europeans are well-versed on upcycling breads. If you like gnocchi, try the German classic Spinat Knödel (Spinach Dumplings) — it's a family favorite in my home and created by my dear friend, Franzi. If you're craving something savory, check out the Breakfast Strata. Have a sweet tooth? Skip down to the Tropical Bread Pudding. Inspired by the Mediterranean diet? You'll definitely want to check out the Panzanella.

REMEMBER

Don't despair when you find yourself with excess bread! Instead, get creative with one of the dishes in this chapter.

Sweet and Savory Bread Crumbs

I'll start with something really simple: fresh bread crumbs. Stale bread is perfect for this job! (Just about any bread can be made into bread crumbs except for sweet breads.) Simply follow these steps:

1. **Cube your dry, stale bread and place it in a food processor.**

TIP

   If your bread is stale, but not very dry, try slicing it, placing it on a baking sheet, and putting the baking sheet in the turned-off oven overnight. The natural warmth of the oven will speed up the drying process, without your even having to turning it on.

2. **Pulse the crumbs until they resemble (wait for it) fine bread crumbs.**

TIP

To make the bread crumbs savory, add in dried spices and herbs, like garlic powder, onion powder, oregano, and parsley. To make them sweet, add in cinnamon, nutmeg, allspice, or cardamom.

You can use bread crumbs in lots of ways. For example, mix them into your meatballs, toss them on top of a pasta dish, or use them to bread chicken fingers. Try rolling banana slices in sweet bread crumbs, drizzling them with chocolate sauce, and freezing for a simple dessert.

Crunchy Croutons

The key to great croutons is to make them the same size, about ½-inch to 1-inch squares. The breads in Chapters 6, 7, and are perfect for croutons. When your bread has begun to stale, follow these steps:

1. **Preheat the oven to 375 degrees.**

2. **Cube the bread in equal pieces.**

3. **In a large bowl, toss together 6 cups of cubed bread with ½ cup extra-virgin olive oil; ½ teaspoon garlic powder; 1 tablespoon crushed dried parsley, thyme, oregano, or basil; and 1 teaspoon sea salt.**

TIP

   If you're using a flavored bread, toss with extra-virgin olive oil and skip the seasonings.

4. **Line a baking sheet with parchment paper, and spread the bread evenly on top.**

5. **Bake for 10 to 15 minutes or until golden brown and crisp, but not too dark.**

TIP

Stale bread browns faster, whereas fresher bread needs a bit more time to dry out.

Breakfast Strata

Cubed, stale bread gets a savory facelift with eggs, sausage, and cheese to make for a hearty breakfast addition. Any bread will work, but try the Sun-Dried Tomato and Olive Bread, the Onion Bread, the Rosemary Bread, or the Swiss Gruyère Bread (all in Chapter 8) for some variety. Just follow these steps:

1. **Cook ½ pound breakfast sausage and drain off the excess fat.**

2. **Cube enough stale bread to make 4 cups.**

3. **In a large bowl, mix together the 4 cups of cubed bread with 6 eggs, 2 cups milk, 1 cup grated cheddar cheese, ½ teaspoon salt, ½ teaspoon cracked pepper, ¼ teaspoon paprika, and the cooked sausage.**

4. **Spray a 9-x-13-inch casserole dish with cooking spray and pour the strata mixture into the baking dish.**

5. **Cover with foil and refrigerate overnight.**

6. **Remove from the refrigerator and preheat the oven to 350 degrees.**

7. **Bake the strata, covered, for 20 minutes. Uncover and continue baking for 20 to 25 minutes or until golden brown and the strata is set, not jiggling.**

8. **Cool for 10 minutes before serving.**

Panzanella

Panzanella is an Italian bread salad and the epitome of summer! Crusty white or whole-grain breads work beautifully in this dish. Just follow these steps:

1. **Preheat the oven to 400 degrees.**

2. **Cube enough stale bread to make 4 cups.**

3. **On a baking sheet, toss the bread with 2 tablespoons extra-virgin olive oil and roast for 10 minutes.**

4. Meanwhile, cut up 3 large, vine-ripe tomatoes; ½ red onion, thinly sliced; ¼ cup fresh basil, thinly sliced; and ½ cucumber, chopped.

5. In a small bowl, whisk together 2 tablespoons red wine vinegar, ½ cup extra-virgin olive oil, 1 teaspoon sea salt, ½ teaspoon cracked pepper, and ¼ cup chopped parsley.

6. In a serving bowl, toss together the tomato mixture with the toasted bread and the dressing.

7. Let the salad sit at room temperature for at least 30 minutes (or up to 6 hours) before serving.

French Toast Casserole

Challah and sweet breads, like the Chocolate Swirled Bread and Diana's Babkallah (both in Chapter 11) are simply decadent in this recipe, but you can also stick with a plain white or wheat bread, too. You mix this dish, refrigerate it, and bake it in the morning. Follow these steps:

1. Start with 350 grams of crusty, stale bread. Slice it about 1-inch thick.

   If your bread is not completely stale or dry, slice the bread and let the bread sit out to dry or dry it in the oven on 200 degrees for 30 minutes.

2. In a medium bowl, whisk together 5 eggs, 2½ cups milk, the zest of 1 orange, ¼ teaspoon ground nutmeg, 1 teaspoon cinnamon, and ¼ cup sugar.

3. Place the bread slices, slightly overlapping, in a 9-x-13-inch casserole dish.

4. Pour the milk mixture over the bread.

5. Cover with foil and refrigerate overnight.

6. In the morning, in a small bowl, crumble together ½ cup brown sugar, 3 tablespoons flour, and ¼ cup butter.

7. Sprinkle the sugar mixture over the French toast.

8. Bake the French toast, covered for 20 minutes.

9. Uncover and continue baking for 20 to 25 minutes or until golden brown and it's set, not jiggling.

10. Cool for 10 minutes before serving with fresh fruit, powdered sugar, or maple syrup.

Tropical Bread Pudding

Coconut, pineapple, and macadamia nuts are the perfect addition to a bread pudding. White breads, croissants, brioche, or sweet enriched breads work well with this recipe. Serve with coconut ice cream or whipped coconut cream for an elegant dessert. To prepare, follow these steps:

1. Preheat the oven to 350 degrees.

2. Cube enough stale bread to make 4 cups.

3. Butter a 9-x-9-inch casserole dish and pour the bread into the dish.

4. In a microwave-safe dish, combine 1 cup whole milk with 1½ cups half-and-half and microwave on high for 3 minutes.

5. In a double boiler (where you have a stock pot with water on the bottom and an empty bowl on top), whisk together 3 eggs and ⅓ cup sugar.

6. Over medium heat, heat the water to a low boil, whisking the eggs and sugar mixture constantly.

7. When the eggs slightly thicken, whisk in the heated milk, and continue to whisk for 3 minutes. Then remove from the heat.

8. Stir in ½ cup chopped and drained, canned pineapple and ¼ cup dried, unsweetened coconut.

9. Pour this mixture over the bread. Press the bread down to submerge it in the liquid.

10. Top the bread pudding with ½ cup chopped macadamia nuts and ¼ cup brown sugar.

11. Place the bread pudding casserole dish inside a larger roasting pan or high-edged baking sheet.

    You'll create a water bath around the casserole dish.

12. Pour water in the outer pan, about halfway up the side of the 9-x-9-inch casserole dish.

13. Bake the bread pudding for 45 minutes to 1 hour, or until golden brown and the internal temperature reaches 160 degrees.

Spinat Knödel (Spinach Bread Dumplings)

Throughout Europe, you will find these savory bread dumplings served in broth or steamed and pan-fried in butter. They're similar to gnocchi (potato dumplings), but much bigger in size. I serve these spinach dumplings with a sage butter and fresh Parmesan cheese. They're a family favorite!

Any savory or plain bread can be made into dumplings. In Europe, they stockpile their stale breads and mix whatever they have on hand for this dish. Just follow these steps:

1. In a saucepan, cook 1 chopped onion and 3 minced garlic cloves in ¼ cup olive oil for about 5 minutes on medium heat.

2. In a bowl, mix together ½ cup milk, 2 eggs, ½ teaspoon salt, ¼ teaspoon pepper, and ⅛ teaspoon ground nutmeg.

3. In a large bowl, place 40 grams grated Parmesan, 250 grams frozen and thawed spinach, and 250 grams finely chopped stale bread.

4. Pour the milk mixture over the bread and spinach mixture and stir. Let the mixture rest for 15 minutes.

5. With wet hands, form into 3-inch round dumplings (like baseballs).

   If the dough is too wet, add in more bread crumbs until you can form a dumpling and they hold together.

6. Steam for 35 minutes or braise in chicken stock until they rise to the surface, about 15 minutes.

   Braising is where little bubbles form, not a full boil.

7. Serve in broth or in a buttery sage sauce with grated Parmesan cheese.

Summery Bruschetta

If you have fresh tomatoes on hand you'll want to make this with your next batch of stale bread. French bread, crusty sourdough, ciabatta, or baguettes all work wonderfully here. Just follow these steps:

1. Thinly slice a crusty bread into ¼- to ½-inch slices.

2. Broil the bread for 2 to 3 minutes or until golden slightly.

3. Rub a raw garlic clove onto the surface of the toasted bread and set onto a serving platter.

4. In a small bowl, mix together 2 chopped tomatoes with ¼ cup thinly sliced basil, 2 teaspoons balsamic vinegar, and ¼ cup extra-virgin olive oil. Season with salt, to taste.

5. Serve garlic toasts with a couple tablespoons of the tomato mixture.

Savory Stuffing

A good bread stuffing is a holiday favorite. Often, this dish is overcomplicated, and I'm definitely of the mindset that simple is best. Here's my family's favorite stuffing recipe:

1. Butter a 9-x-13-inch baking dish.

2. Cube enough stale bread to get 8 cups.

   A mixture of white, wheat, and even rye breads can be delicious as stuffing. This mixture also works beautifully using up leftover buns and rolls.

3. Add the bread to the baking dish and bake for 15 minutes to dry out the bread if it isn't already dried out.

4. In a large skillet, heat ¼ cup olive oil with ¼ cup butter over medium heat.

5. Add in 2 cups chopped onion and 1 cup chopped celery and cook for 6 minutes.

6. Add in ¼ cup chopped parsley and 1 tablespoon chopped thyme leaves and sauté for 1 minute.

7. Remove from the heat and whisk in 1 cup chicken stock and ½ cup half-and-half. Season with salt and pepper.

8. Whisk together 1 cup chicken stock with 2 eggs and 1 cup grated Parmesan cheese. Add this mixture to the vegetables and stir.

9. Pour the vegetable mixture over the bread cubes. Make sure all the bread is coated. Press down on bread to submerge. Let this mixture rest for 30 minutes.

10. Preheat the oven to 350 degrees.

11. Bake the stuffing for 40 to 45 minutes or until it reaches 160 degrees internally.

4

Appendixes

Metric Conversion Guide

Note: The recipes in this book were developed and tested using metric measurements, and the ingredients lists include both metric and U.S. measurements, so you can use whichever you prefer. This appendix is included for your reference.

Common Abbreviations

Abbreviation(s)	What It Stands For
cm	Centimeter
C., c.	Cup
G, g	Gram
kg	Kilogram
L, l	Liter
lb.	Pound
mL, ml	Milliliter
oz.	Ounce
pt.	Pint
t., tsp.	Teaspoon
T., Tb., Tbsp.	Tablespoon

Volume

U.S. Units	Canadian Metric	Australian Metric
¼ teaspoon	1 milliliter	1 milliliter
½ teaspoon	2 milliliters	2 milliliters
1 teaspoon	5 milliliters	5 milliliters

U.S. Units	Canadian Metric	Australian Metric
1 tablespoon	15 milliliters	20 milliliters
¼ cup	50 milliliters	60 milliliters
⅓ cup	75 milliliters	80 milliliters
½ cup	125 milliliters	125 milliliters
⅔ cup	150 milliliters	170 milliliters
¾ cup	175 milliliters	190 milliliters
1 cup	250 milliliters	250 milliliters
1 quart	1 liter	1 liter
1½ quarts	1.5 liters	1.5 liters
2 quarts	2 liters	2 liters
2½ quarts	2.5 liters	2.5 liters
3 quarts	3 liters	3 liters
4 quarts (1 gallon)	4 liters	4 liters

Weight

U.S. Units	Canadian Metric	Australian Metric
1 ounce	30 grams	30 grams
2 ounces	55 grams	60 grams
3 ounces	85 grams	90 grams
4 ounces (¼ pound)	115 grams	125 grams
8 ounces (½ pound)	225 grams	225 grams
16 ounces (1 pound)	455 grams	500 grams (½ kilogram)

Length

Inches	Centimeters
0.5	1.5
1	2.5

Inches	Centimeters
2	5.0
3	7.5
4	10.0
5	12.5
6	15.0
7	17.5
8	20.5
9	23.0
10	25.5
11	28.0
12	30.5

Temperature (Degrees)

Fahrenheit	Celsius
32	0
212	100
250	120
275	140
300	150
325	160
350	180
375	190
400	200
425	220
450	230
475	240
500	260

Appendix B
Grain Mill Guide

Looking for local grain producers? I have you covered with great options across the United States. Local grain producers often have a greater variety of specialty grains, including organic options.

Grain Mills

Mill (Location)	Organic	Website
Barton Springs Mill (Texas)	No*	https://bartonspringsmill.com
Beck's Bakery (California)	Yes	www.becksbakery.com
Bluebird Grain Farms (Washington)	Yes	https://bluebirdgrainfarms.com
Bob's Red Mill (Oregon)	Yes	www.bobsredmill.com
Breslin Farms (Illinois)	Yes	https://breslinfarms.com
Camas Country Mill (Oregon)	Yes	www.camascountrymill.com
Carolina Ground (North Carolina)	Yes	https://carolinaground.com
Castle Valley Mill (Pennsylvania)	No	https://castlevalleymill.com
Central Milling Petaluma (California)	Yes	https://centralmilling.com
Community Grains (California)	No	www.communitygrains.com

Mill (Location)	Organic	Website
DaySpring Farms (Georgia)	Yes	www.dayspringfarmsga.com
Doubting Thomas Farms (Minnesota)	Yes	https://doubtingthomasfarms.com
Early Morning Harvest (Iowa)	Yes	https://earlymorningharvest.com
Farmer Ground Flour (New York)	Yes	www.farmergroundflour.com
Grist & Toll (California)	Most	www.gristandtoll.com
Ground Up Grain (Massachusetts)	Some	www.groundupgrain.com
Heartland Mill (Kansas)	Yes	www.heartlandmill.com
Janie's Mill (Illinois)	Yes	www.janiesmill.com
Josey Baker Bread (California)	Yes	www.joseybakerbread.com
King Arthur Baking Company (Vermont)	Some	www.kingarthurflour.com
Meadowlark Organics (Wisconsin)	Yes	www.meadowlarkorganics.com
Migrash Farm (Maryland)	Yes	www.migrashfarm.com
Songbird Farm (Maine)	Yes	www.songbirdorganicfarm.com
Sunrise Flour Mill (Minnesota)	Yes	www.sunriseflourmill.com
Swany White Flour Mills (Minnesota)	Yes	https://swanywhiteflour.com
Wade's Mill (Virginia)	No	www.wadesmill.com
Weisenberger Mills (Kentucky)	No	www.weisenberger.com
Wheat Montana Farms & Bakery (Montana)	Yes	www.wheatmontana.com
Wild Hive Farm (New York)	Yes	https://wildhivefarm.com

*Not certified organic, but uses organic practices.

Appendix C

Glossary

autolyze: Technically, to break down with enzymes. But when it comes to bread making, all you need to know is that when a recipe refers to autolyzing, it just means you're adding the flour and water together first, allowing the flour to become hydrated for 30 minutes to an hour. Then you add the remaining ingredients as described in a recipe. This technique forms a less sticky dough that's easier to work. If you're really interested in the chemical process involved in autolysis, check out "Using the Autolyse Method," a blog post from King Arthur Baking Company (www.kingarthurflour.com/blog/2017/09/29/using-the-autolyse-method). **Note:** You may see the term spelled *autolyse* in other places; that's the British spelling of the word.

banneton: A woven or braided basket that helps a loaf hold its shape and creates a desired design on the surface of the dough during its final proofing.

boule: The round shape many artisanal breads are shaped into.

bulk fermentation: The initial rising of the dough.

cold proofing: A second rising of the dough under refrigerated temperatures. This technique strengthens the sour notes of bread. Some breads can be cold proofed for 24, 48, or even 72 hours before baking.

crumb: The consistency of a loaf of bread. The structure of a loaf varies by bread type and technique. Typically, a yeast bread has a *closed crumb* with smaller holes, whereas a sourdough bread has an *open crumb,* with big, asymmetrical holes throughout the loaf.

fermentation: The process in which the yeast begins to feed on the carbohydrates, breaking down the sugars and expelling carbon dioxide and alcohol.

hard wheat: Wheat with a higher protein content.

hooch: Alcohol that sometimes forms on the surface of a sourdough starter. Hooch is a natural discard from yeast as it breaks down carbohydrates. When you see a hooch form, you know your starter needs to be fed — simply stir the hooch back into the thicker liquid and feed your starter by adding more flour and water (see Chapter 5).

hydration: The ratio of water to flour in a dough. The more hydrated a dough is, the more challenging it is to work. To calculate the hydration, divide the weight of the water by the weight of the flour. For example, if you're mixing 500 grams of flour with 350 grams of water, the hydration is 350 ÷ 500 = 0.7, or 70 percent. Working with doughs that are higher than 70 percent hydration takes patience and skill. Check out a detailed post titled "Bakers Percentage" on King Arthur Baking Company's blog, highlighting how to calculate hydration: www.kingarthurbaking.com/pro/reference/bakers-percentage.

knead: The process of developing the gluten in dough. Whether it's done with a dough hook or by hand, kneading creates a smooth, elastic ball of dough.

lame: A specific blade used in scoring or marking loaves of bread prior to baking. A serrated knife works just as well for beginners.

levain: A sourdough starter or a pre-starter. Some recipes actually have you create a starter specific to the recipe. You mix this starter and allow it to ferment prior to making the bread recipe. The term is French, and the pronunciation is sort of like leh-*vawn,* where you *barely* pronounce the *n* sound on the end of the word before tossing your beret in the air.

Maillard reaction: The chemical reaction between amino acids and sugars that gives the crust of breads their golden hues. The reaction gets its name from a French chemist, and *Maillard* is pronounced my-*yar.*

oven spring: The last bit of rising after a loaf of bread is put in the oven. In some recipes, the oven temperature is set higher for 10 minutes and then decreased. This is to help the bread rise before the crust hardens. You see a quick rise in bread when it hits the heat of the oven and the yeast is heated.

proofing: Allowing the dough to rise before baking. Also known as *proving. See also* cold proofing.

retarding: Slowing down the fermentation process at cold temperatures. Retarding adds to the tangy flavor many people love in a sourdough bread. *See also* cold proofing.

sponge: Flour, water, and yeast mixed together, as a pre-starter, and allowed to ferment before being added to the rest of the ingredients. This begins the development of flavor and alters the texture of the dough. It's an important step in many recipes, so be sure not to rush through it.

tangzhong: A newly popularized method of bread making from Japan in which the water and flour are heated, much like a roux, over low to medium heat, until a thickened slurry forms. The typical ratio of flour to water is 1:5 (for example, 10 grams of flour to 50 grams of water). This technique creates a tender and fluffy bread texture often desired in rolls and sandwich loaves. It also extends the shelf life of the bread.

windowpane test: A method of determining whether the gluten has been fully developed in the kneading process. Pull off a small piece of dough and stretch it between your fingers. If it holds its shape without tearing, you've passed the test. The dough should stretch and not break, illustrating the formation of long, elastic strands (known as the *gluten matrix*).

yudane: Another popularized method of bread making from Japan in which boiling water is added to flour to extend the shelf life of the bread. The typical ratio of flour to water is 1:1 (for example, 80 grams of flour to 80 grams of water). This technique creates a tender and fluffy bread texture often desired in rolls and sandwich loaves.

Index

A

all-purpose flour, 2, 12

altitude, 234

aluminum, baking with, 235

Apple Cinnamon Bread recipe, 164–165

apricots, Chia Apricot Jam recipe, 226

artichokes, Spinach and Artichoke Stuffed Bread recipe, 196–198

artisan breads, 40

arugula, Sweet Potato and Arugula Sandwich recipe, 242

autolyze, defined, 265

autolyzing sourdough bread, 35

avocado, Mashed Avocado Spread recipe, 218

B

Babkallah recipe, 160–161

bacon
  Bacon and Cheddar Scones recipe, 208–209
  fat from, 16

bagels
  Sourdough Spelt and Sesame, 86–87
  Wheat, 128–129

baguettes
  French, 134–135
  German Twisted, 136–137
  spelt, 80–81

Baked Dutch Oven Pancakes recipe, 201

baker's schedule, 40

Bakery Sandwich Rolls recipe, 118–119

baking dough, 22–24

baking ingredients, 2, 15–17

baking pans, 235

baking sheets, 43–44

baking techniques, 236

baking tools, 41–44

banneton
  defined, 37, 265
  description of, 14, 44
  example of, 38

Barton Springs Mill, 263

basic breads
  Crusty Overnight Bread recipe, 54–55
  Dark Rye Bread recipe, 68–69
  Farmhouse Bread recipe, 64–65
  Golden Egg Bread recipe, 62–63
  Grandma's White Bread recipe, 56–57
  Hearty Whole-Wheat Bread recipe, 60–61
  Oatmeal Bread recipe, 70–71
  overview, 51–53
  Potato Bread recipe, 66–67
  Wheat Sandwich Bread recipe, 58–59

Beck's Bakery, 263

Beer-Battered Vegetable Tempura recipe, 210

beets, Summer Beet Bread recipe, 108–110

bench scraper, 43

biga. *See* poolish

Blueberry Sourdough Coffeecake recipe, 212–213

Bluebird Grain Farms, 263

Bob's Red Mill, 263

boiling, 23

boule, defined, 265

bread crumbs, 250

bread flour, 12

bread lames, 23, 44, 266

bread making
  dough, 19–24
  food scales for, 9
  recipes for, 54–71
  science of, 7–8
  storing bread, 24
  techniques for, 236
  tips for, 231
  weather affecting, 233–234

Brown Bread recipe, 142–143

Brownies recipe, 211

Bruschetta recipe, 254–255

bulk fermentation, 36–37, 265

bulk rising, tightening dough after, 239

Buns recipe, 116–117

Burned Bread recipe, 240

butter

  baking with, 16

  herbed, 216

  Honey Cardamom Butter recipe, 225

Buttery Dinner Rolls recipe, 112–113

C

cake flour, 12–13

California Club Sandwich recipe, 244

California Fruit and Nut Sourdough Bread recipe, 162–163

Calzones recipe, 184–185

Camas Country Mill, 263

cardamom, Honey Cardamom Butter recipe, 225

Carolina Ground, 263

cast-iron pans

  baking with, 235

  cleaning, 42

Castle Valley Mill, 263

Central Milling Petaluma, 263

Challah Bread recipe, 122–123

cheese

  Bacon and Cheddar Scones recipe, 208–209

  Cheesy Kinder Crackers recipe, 206–207

  Cottage Cheese and Dill Bread recipe, 92–93

  Pepperoni and Cheese Calzones recipe, 184–185

Chia Apricot Jam recipe, 226

Chicken and Pesto Sandwich recipe, 242–243

chocolate

  Chocolate Hazelnut Spread recipe, 227

  Chocolate Swirled Bread recipe, 170–171

  Salted Dark Chocolate Brownies recipe, 211

Ciabatta recipe, 78–79

cilantro, Southwestern Cilantro Bread recipe, 102–103

cinnamon

  Apple Cinnamon Bread recipe, 164–165

  Cinnamon Raisin Bread recipe, 166–167

  Cinnamon Rolls recipe, 174–175

  Salted Pecan Cinnamon Rolls recipe, 174–175

closed crumb, defined, 265

Coffeecake recipe, 212–213

cold proofing

  defined, 265

  description of, 37–38

cold weather, 234

commercial yeast, 15

Community Grains, 263

cooling sourdough bread, 40

Cottage Cheese and Dill Bread recipe, 92–93

Crackers recipe, 206–207

cranberries, Orange Cranberry Bread recipe, 168–169

Croissants recipe, 120–121

cross contamination, in starters, 33

Croutons recipe, 250–251

crumb, defined, 265

crust, lifts in, 240

Crusty Overnight Bread recipe, 54–55

cups, 9

D

Dark Rye Bread recipe, 68–69

dates, 17

DaySpring Farms, 264

degrees. *See* temperatures

dense bread, 239, 240

digestibility, 25

digital scales, 231

digital thermometers, 232

dill, Cottage Cheese and Dill Bread recipe, 92–93

Dinner Rolls recipe, 112–113

dips, 215–227

discard, 29, 199–213

Doubting Thomas Farms, 264

About the Author

Wendy Jo Peterson, MS RDN, is an award-winning author, speaker, culinary nutritionist, proud military wife, and mom. Whether at work or at the table, Wendy Jo believes in savoring life. Check out her other *For Dummies* titles: *Mediterranean Diet Cookbook For Dummies, Air Fryer Cookbook For Dummies,* and *Instant Pot Cookbook For Dummies.* When she's not in her kitchen, you can find Wendy Jo strolling a SoCal beach with her Labradors and daughter or exploring the great outdoors in #OlafTheCampervan. You can catch her on social media at @just_wendyjo or check out her website, www.justwendyjo.com.

Dedication

This book would not have come to fruition had it not been for my time living in Germany, experiencing great breads and the friendships formed around food, so to my Foodie Freunden, Franzi, Marina, Antje, Dunja, Rachel, Christian, Hannes, Rainer, and Helga. To my ever-supportive husband, Brandon, and cherished daughter, Anya, for their continued love, support, and willingness to taste every recipe. I hope you enjoy this book as much as I loved creating the recipes with all of you in mind!

Author's Acknowledgments

Although I wrote this book alone, my village of friends, family, and colleagues helped along the way. Thanks to Franziska Bürker for her endless contributions of cherished German bread recipes; Rachel Bürker for the help of translating Franzi's recipes; Jasmine Hormati, who helped me capture measurements and photos; Geri Grace Goodale for her guidance and help behind the camera; Marina Bauer and her mother-in-law, Helga, for their German contributions; Chef Diana Ausderau for sharing her recipes and culinary guidance while we taught together; Sharon Salomon for her challah recipe and Norene, who inspired this recipe; Hope Damergis for her beloved Greek contributions; Chef Josh Brown for sharing his prized Klobasneks recipe; Mom Nancy, and friends Ann, Jane Gray, and Meghann for testing out recipes; Sydnie Ozanus for digging deep into local millers; my dear friend Heather, who enjoys testing out all my breads and arranging playdates. I could not have hit this deadline without the assistance of each of you. I appreciate the support throughout this project. I'll cherish it forever.

No book is ever achieved without a great team, and I'm blessed to have worked with this team on many books. Thanks to my agent, Matt Wagner, for believing in this project and advocating for me, as the writer. I'm forever grateful for Tracy Boggier, senior acquisitions editor at Wiley, who believed in my love of bread making and allowed me to share it with the world, and for project and copy editor, Elizabeth Kuball, for keeping me on track with deadlines. I thoroughly enjoy the creative process working with each of you. Thank you for your collaboration!

Publisher's Acknowledgments

Senior Acquisitions Editor: Tracy Boggier

Project Editor: Elizabeth Kuball

Copy Editor: Elizabeth Kuball

Production Editor: Mohammed Zafar Ali

Cover Image: Courtesy of Wendy Jo Peterson

Take dummies with you everywhere you go!

Whether you are excited about e-books, want more from the web, must have your mobile apps, or are swept up in social media, dummies makes everything easier.

Find us online!

dummies.com

Leverage the power

Dummies is the global leader in the reference category and one of the most trusted and highly regarded brands in the world. No longer just focused on books, customers now have access to the dummies content they need in the format they want. Together we'll craft a solution that engages your customers, stands out from the competition, and helps you meet your goals.

Advertising & Sponsorships

Connect with an engaged audience on a powerful multimedia site, and position your message alongside expert how-to content. Dummies.com is a one-stop shop for free, online information and know-how curated by a team of experts.

- Targeted ads
- Video
- Email Marketing
- Microsites
- Sweepstakes sponsorship

20 MILLION PAGE VIEWS EVERY SINGLE MONTH

15 MILLION UNIQUE VISITORS PER MONTH

43% OF ALL VISITORS ACCESS THE SITE VIA THEIR MOBILE DEVICES

700,000 NEWSLETTER SUBSCRIPTIONS TO THE INBOXES OF
300,000 UNIQUE INDIVIDUALS EVERY WEEK

# of dummies

Custom Publishing

Reach a global audience in any language by creating a solution that will differentiate you from competitors, amplify your message, and encourage customers to make a buying decision.

- Apps
- Books
- eBooks
- Video
- Audio
- Webinars

Brand Licensing & Content

Leverage the strength of the world's most popular reference brand to reach new audiences and channels of distribution.

For more information, visit dummies.com/biz

PERSONAL ENRICHMENT

9781119187790
USA $26.00
CAN $31.99
UK £19.99

9781119179030
USA $21.99
CAN $25.99
UK £16.99

9781119293354
USA $24.99
CAN $29.99
UK £17.99

9781119293347
USA $22.99
CAN $27.99
UK £16.99

9781119310068
USA $22.99
CAN $27.99
UK £16.99

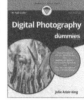
9781119235606
USA $24.99
CAN $29.99
UK £17.99

9781119251163
USA $24.99
CAN $29.99
UK £17.99

9781119235491
USA $26.99
CAN $31.99
UK £19.99

9781119279952
USA $24.99
CAN $29.99
UK £17.99

9781119283133
USA $24.99
CAN $29.99
UK £17.99

9781119287117
USA $24.99
CAN $29.99
UK £16.99

9781119130246
USA $22.99
CAN $27.99
UK £16.99

PROFESSIONAL DEVELOPMENT

9781119311041
USA $24.99
CAN $29.99
UK £17.99

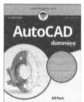
9781119255796
USA $39.99
CAN $47.99
UK £27.99

9781119293439
USA $26.99
CAN $31.99
UK £19.99

9781119281467
USA $26.99
CAN $31.99
UK £19.99

9781119280651
USA $29.99
CAN $35.99
UK £21.99

9781119251132
USA $24.99
CAN $29.99
UK £17.99

9781119310563
USA $34.00
CAN $41.99
UK £24.99

9781119181705
USA $29.99
CAN $35.99
UK £21.99

9781119263593
USA $26.99
CAN $31.99
UK £19.99

9781119257769
USA $29.99
CAN $35.99
UK £21.99

9781119293477
USA $26.99
CAN $31.99
UK £19.99

9781119265313
USA $24.99
CAN $29.99
UK £17.99

9781119239314
USA $29.99
CAN $35.99
UK £21.99

9781119293323
USA $29.99
CAN $35.99
UK £21.99

dummies.com

dummies
A Wiley Brand